Contemporary Action Cinema

[E]very distinct kind of film – maybe every film in its singularity – requires a different kind of response, a particular 'shakedown', a special angle of attack. Action films, of all the cinema's forms, pose this question most acutely.

Adrian Martin (2005: 175)

Contemporary Action Cinema

Lisa Purse

Edinburgh University Press

© Lisa Purse, 2011

Edinburgh University Press Ltd
22 George Square, Edinburgh

www.euppublishing.com

Typeset in 11/13 Ehrhardt
by Servis Filmsetting Ltd, Stockport, Cheshire, and
printed and bound in Great Britain by
CPI Antony Rowe, Chippenham and Eastbourne

A CIP record for this book is available from the British Library

ISBN 978 0 7486 3817 8 (hardback)
ISBN 978 0 7486 3818 5 (paperback)

The right of Lisa Purse
to be identified as author of this work
has been asserted in accordance with
the Copyright, Designs and Patents Act 1988.

Published with the support of the Edinburgh University
Scholarly Publishing Initiatives Fund.

Contents

Illustrations

Acknowledgements

It has been a great pleasure to write about a form of mainstream cinema for which I have an ongoing fondness, and to subject it to the sustained attention that I feel it demands and deserves. Certainly, in the writing of it, this book has helped me answer some of the questions I wanted to ask of this popular form, about how and why it moves me, and about why it takes the shapes that it does. By the same token, I hope that readers will find within these pages answers to some of their own questions, useful tools with which to approach action cinema as a form, and interesting perspectives on a mode whose pleasures and politics are all too often dismissed as obvious and straightforward. I thank Sarah Edwards and the anonymous readers who reviewed the proposal for seeing the potential in the project, and for offering useful and generous comments at the start of the writing process. I also thank Vicki Donald and the rest of the editorial team at Edinburgh University Press for their enthusiasm, assistance and advice as the project took shape.

I owe a debt of gratitude to Jim Hillier, whose intellectual guidance and support I have benefited from and valued greatly over many years. His own approach to cinema has been an inspiration to me, and without his encouragement this project might never have begun. The 'Sewing Circle', an informal film seminar group at the Department of Film, Theatre and Television at the University of Reading, has also provided invaluable intellectual stimulation, and founding members of the circle Doug Pye, Iris Luppa and John Gibbs deserve special mention for their keen observations, support and friendship over the last fifteen years. The Department of Film, Theatre and Television's vibrant culture and collegiate atmosphere have been a great motivator, as have the colleagues I have worked alongside and met along the way. Thanks are also due to the students I have taught on the US Cinema 2 module, who allowed me to share my ideas with them, and in return shared their own responses to the films with me.

I am grateful to the network of friends who have been generous on all fronts with brain food, light relief and moral support, including Kelly Conway, Laura Beggs, Brenda McGonigle, Claire Breeze and the London 'set'. Thanks to Ian Banks, who shared his enthusiasm for cinema and real ale on numerous enjoyable occasions; to Iris Luppa, whose generosity of spirit is as striking as her insights on film; and to E.J. Rodican Jones, an incisive mind but also a true friend. Welcome distractions from the computer were provided by the cats, Rafiki and Hendrix. I am deeply grateful to my family – my parents Sandra and Rodney and siblings Beth and Joe – for their unfailing love, encouragement and humour, which I endeavour to return in equal measure. Finally I want to thank Tamzin Morphy, for her unstinting patience, support and editorial assistance during the writing process, and for being a stimulating and wonderful fellow traveller, through action cinema and through life.

The book is dedicated to the memory of my grandparents: Ernest and Olive Bagwell, who were not here to see it begun, and Ray and Doreen Purse, who are no longer here to see it finished.

To my grandparents.

Introduction: 'Where are we, and how did we get here?'

I stand in the lobby of my local multiplex on a summer evening in 2010. I'm in the queue for *Predators* (2010), but I have the choice to see several other action movies, including action thriller *Inception* (2010), action fantasy *Prince of Persia: The Sands of Time* (2010), the vampire themed action romance *The Twilight Saga: Eclipse* (2010) based on the best-selling Stephenie Meyer *Twilight* books, or the action romantic comedy *Killers* (2010). The summer season has already taken in *Iron Man 2* (2010), *Robin Hood* (2010) and *Clash of the Titans* (2010), with nostalgic fare like *The A-Team* (2010) and *The Expendables* (2010), action fantasy *The Last Airbender* (2010), female action film *Salt* (2010) and comic action thriller *Knight and Day* (2010) still to arrive on multiplex screens before the season's end. Since the start of the millennium the acceleration of new entertainment technologies has turned cinemagoers into gamers, bloggers, video-texters, Twitterers and downloaders of television, movies, video clips and music, but they still see action movies in their droves. This book explores why action movies remain such a popular strand of Hollywood production, and what form action movies take in the first decade of the twenty-first century.

DEFINING ACTION CINEMA

Action cinema's cultural and commercial resilience can be partly explained by its adaptability. As my attempt to classify the films at my local multiplex illustrates, contemporary action cinema is a resolutely hybrid form. As both Steve Neale and Richard Maltby have pointed out, Hollywood genres are not stable categories, because most movies 'use categorical elements in combination' and because critics, audiences, film marketeers and filmmakers often mean different things even when they are using the same genre identifiers

(Maltby 2003: 75; Neale 2000: 51). However, the roster of what Maltby calls 'generic hyphenates' that make up my list of multiplex releases ('action thriller', 'action comedy' and so on) hints at the extent of the action movie's generic adaptability. Action cinema has always incorporated and repurposed tropes from other popular genres, most obviously the western, but also melodrama, romance, science fiction and horror to name the most common (see Neale 2000: 52–60). Action cinema's capacity for generic hybridity prompts José Arroyo to comment that it 'exceeds the boundaries of a genre', even as it 'cannot quite constitute a mode' (Arroyo (ed.) 2000, 'Introduction': iii). This problem of defining what constitutes an action film has exercised a number of writers, and the different terms they use ('action', 'action/spectacle', 'action-adventure') illustrate the difficulty of demarcating action cinema's generic parameters. Nevertheless, as I have already begun to suggest, this is not a new problem (or indeed one unique to the action film). In his genealogy of what he calls 'action-adventure' Steve Neale notes that such films, which 'have been a staple in Hollywood's output since the 1910s', have 'always encompassed an array of genres and sub-types: westerns, swashbucklers, war films, disaster films, space operas, epics, safari films, jungle films, and so on' (Neale 2000: 55). This puts the multi-genericity and generic hybridity of action films of the 2000s into the context of a longer history of generic hybridity, and of action filmmaking. In the light of the categorical challenge posed by the breadth of action cinema's generic permutations, several writers have suggested that the most productive way to define action cinema is through its salient characteristics. Eric Lichtenfeld asserts that the 'foundation for defining the action movie must be that the films showcase scenes of physical action, be they fistfights, gunfights, swordfights, fights against nature, or other derring-do' (Lichtenfeld 2007: 5).[1] Neale's definition moves beyond physical action and 'derring-do' to suggest some specific narrative and visual tropes that an action movie might involve, such as 'a propensity for spectacular physical action, a narrative structure involving fights, chases and explosions, and in addition to the deployment of state-of-the-art special effects, an emphasis in performance on athletic feats and stunts' (Neale 2000: 52).

In my view action cinema is defined by its persistent and detailed attention to the exerting body, a focus which shapes its audio–visual aesthetics as much as its characterisation and narrative design. Richard Dyer enthuses that the action film offers spectacles of extreme sensation 'experienced . . . in the body's contact with the world, its rush, its expansiveness, its physical stress and challenges' (Dyer 2000: 18). In documenting acts of physical exertion, action cinema does so specifically through a spectacular mode of presentation that calls attention to the physiological attributes and corporeal attitudes of the body in action, as well as to the exhilarating, risk-infused environment which that body is moving through, the forces it is subjected to and the counterforces that it directs outwards at that environment. This body is a physically empowered one, strong, agile and resilient, asserting itself in the field of action and risk, and thus acts out fantasies of empowerment that are inherently literalised and physicalised, rather than abstracted. The fantasies of empowerment that action cinema offers are affecting precisely because, through staging and presentation, the work of exertion, of moving towards mastery of the situation, is also foregrounded. That might be through the naturalistic depiction of the physiological effects of exertion, such as sweat or straining muscles, or through a more stylised or fantastical staging. In either case, the action cinema's mode of presentation invites the audience to experience the action body's empowerment in a correspondingly physicalised way. That is to say, the action film addresses the spectator's sensorium as well as his or her rational faculties, encouraging an embodied response to the spectacle of embodied empowerment playing out on the screen. In Chapter 2 I will elaborate on this sensory address, and in Chapter 3 I will take these ideas further in a consideration of the aesthetics of the action sequence and the impulses that lie behind the shape the contemporary action sequence takes. Of course the importance of risk in both my developing account of action cinema's pleasures and Dyer's illustrates that the exhilaration action films generate might have a lot to do with empowerment's opposite: disempowerment. I would suggest that, in an environment fraught with risk and danger, it is the body poised between mastery and loss of control that holds our attention, and in the action film it is the precarious predicament of the action hero mid-action, as well as the hero's eventual overcoming of the presented challenge, that the action film underlines in its staging and presentation. In order to intensify both the impression of physical risk and the expression of the action hero's mastery, violence and destruction are the other key ingredients, perhaps tapping into primal fantasies about dominating others, or being free from social and behavioural constraints. Despite the generic hybridity and heterogeneity of contemporary action cinema, it is these characteristics – a preoccupation not simply with physical acts but with the processes of exertion, a sensory address to the spectator, and an emphasis on the contingency as well as the power of the action body – that can help us define it.

A POPULAR FORM

Not all blockbusters are action movies, and not all action movies become blockbusters. Still, the action picture – as cop drama, fantasy adventure, or science fiction – remains the exemplar of the box-office triumphs of modern Hollywood. (Bordwell 2006: 113)

Today the majority of the key 'tent-pole' releases that underpin studios' block-buster seasons are action or action-adventure movies, and studio executives continue to bankroll such films because of their massive profit potential.[2] As Thomas Schatz observes, 'spectacular CG effects and action sequences . . . are now the sine qua non of blockbuster hit films' (Schatz 2009: 32), and the spectacular qualities of the contemporary action movie – intensified by digital imaging technologies that bring the impossible and the previously prohibi-tively expensive to the screen – are a key attraction to cinemagoers, one that the first three chapters of this book will explore in detail. The action movie's dialogue-light emphasis on spectacle allows it to travel well in both English-speaking and non-English-speaking international markets – which the major studios seek to maximise through their own globally extensive distribution and marketing networks (Scott 2009: 178) – as well as being 'easily reformatted as a video game and cross-marketed by the fast-food and toy industries' (Lewis 2008: 402). This means that, beyond initial box office takings, huge profits can be generated in related revenue streams domestically and globally, through sales of soundtrack music, computer games, toys, other promotional tie-in merchandising and new online and pay-TV delivery routes, alongside the highly lucrative DVD and Blu-Ray markets which have expanded to include multiple edition, box set and directors cut releases (see Schatz 2009). The advanced 'home cinema' technologies now available – HD televisions, Blu-Ray and 'upscaler' DVD players, and sophisticated sound systems – are extremely well-suited to showing off the spectacular nature of the contemporary action blockbuster for home viewing, an experience Barry Langford suggests 'can rival or even surpass that of the multiplex'. Rather than having to substantially alter their primary film product to suit a domestic viewing market, then, the major studios have 'every incentive to continue to concentrate on proven and profitable blockbuster production' (Langford 2010: 206).[3] In these ways the action film in its blockbuster form becomes crucial not just to the studio's desire to maximise profits in primary, secondary and ancillary markets but to their strategy of using such profits to spread their significant financial risk in the face of the spiralling costs of feature film production (Maltby 2003: 211).

My discussion of the exhilarating fantasies of empowerment offered by action cinema, a discussion that will be continued in the first three chap-ters, illustrates one of the key reasons that action cinema remains popular. However, there are other cultural imperatives that continue to motivate our decision to see and take pleasure in these films, some of which we will consider in later chapters, and some of which it is productive to list here. As a number of writers have noted, action cinema resonates with and beyond its domestic audiences in its enactment of the foundational tenets of US national mythol-ogy, a set of ideas celebrating an individualist heroism that can be traced back to classical mythology and equally to a Christian tradition to which 'martyrdom and sacrifice are central' (Tasker 1993: 39; see also Lichtenfeld 2007). Contemporary action cinema invokes this national mythology, this heroic ideal, in a number of ways. The lone hero fights for personal interests or for those of family, community or nation, protecting property, policing boundaries. Moreover, the hero figure must succeed by taking violent action, in an affirmation of the American constitutional right to bear arms, and an enactment of the process of 'regeneration through violence' that Richard Slotkin has identified is at the heart of American frontier mythology (Slotkin 1992: 8). And the notion of the frontier experience itself – that Geoff King points out is still 'alive and well' in contemporary Hollywood cinema – operates as a metaphorical reference concept in the genre (King 2000: 4). Action narratives construct situations and locations that return us to the cluster of meanings the frontier generates in the North American imagination: the site for the policing of otherness as well as more tangible boundaries, and the site of physical renewal, progress and possibility. In Chapter 1 we will look in more detail at the kinds of narrative tropes and trajectories to which this gives rise.

Beyond the specificities of national mythology, the action genre offers a more general function common also to other types of Hollywood movie. It allows deeply felt socio-cultural desires and anxieties to be explored or, equally importantly, disavowed within 'the relative safety of a well-regulated fiction'; that is, within a fantasy framework that reassuringly reaffirms notions of control and empowerment by the movie's end (Maltby 2003: 17). Certain of these desires and anxieties are existential and enduring in nature, such as the place of the individual in society, the powers and vulnerabilities of the human body and so on. But the action cinema's generic structures also permit the exploration of much more historically specific questions, prompted by contemporaneous and recent events, about the basis upon which it is right or necessary to take violent action, about what constitutes heroism, and more generally about what can and cannot be represented on screen in a cinematic fiction at this contemporary juncture. Post-1990s action cinema necessarily speaks to its own historical moment, explicitly, implicitly, emphatically, or by omission. Given that the first decade of the twenty-first century has been a period during which notions of justified action have been problematised and politicised in striking ways, the historical specificity of contemporary action movies' responses to this in their form and content will be explored across the book, but in particular detail in Chapter 8. More generally action cinema also continues to incorporate textual, narrative, visual and aesthetic elements from other cultural forms to keep its own form fresh and marketable: for example the resurgence of the graphic novel as a source for characters, narratives but also a stylised visual aesthetic in films like *Sin City* (2005), *300* (2006), *The Spirit* (2008) and *Watchmen* (2009); direct video game adaptations like *Doom* (2005) and *Max Payne* (2008); films exploring gaming themes, like *Death Race*

(2008), *Surrogates* (2009) and *Gamer* (2009) or borrowing a video game aesthetic, which includes the aforementioned but also films like *Children of Men* (2006); movies that incorporate reference to GPS tracking and surveillance technologies, including the *Bourne* franchise (2002, 2004, 2007), *Eagle Eye* (2008) and *Casino Royale* (2006); and the ecology and conservation themes in *Avatar* (2009). It is this inherent adaptability that has allowed action cinema to respond effectively to shifts in cultural taste and changing audience interests in new developments in culture, media and technology.

'WHERE ARE WE, AND HOW DID WE GET HERE?'

There is extensive scholarship on action films of the 1970s, 1980s and 1990s, but the engagement with post-1990s examples has been more piecemeal, most often discussing specific films, trends or methodological approaches in isolation.[4] As a result, at the end of the first decade of the twenty-first century, it is an opportune moment to explore action cinema's most recent manifestation in a more wide-ranging way. As this form of popular filmmaking continues to evolve, what are its continuities with earlier action cinema, and what are its newer aspects? How has action cinema of the last ten years responded both to the need to 'internationalise' its product, and to other developments like the huge growth in the computer games market, the intensification of conglomeration, and advancements in networked communications technologies? How does it take into account current debates about ethnicity, gender, sexuality and nationhood? The latest phase in a long tradition of action narratives, contemporary action cinema operates within a set of familiar generic co-ordinates, but is also shaped by its own cultural moment. In the pages that follow we will investigate the ways in which the action cinema of the past decade interacts with its historical, cultural, economic and media contexts, what it valorises, references and turns away from, how it repurposes cultural material and what current forms its generic hybridity takes. We will ask what such tendencies can tell us about contemporary US culture and the still-dominant ideological machine that is contemporary Hollywood. The book is not intended as a comprehensive taxonomy of post-1990s action films (which would always be incomplete in some sense or other), and equally does not propose that contemporary action cinema is a homogeneous entity about which we can draw fixed conclusions: as the following paragraphs attest, action cinema continues to be a multifarious mode of Hollywood filmmaking. Instead, the pages that follow propose a flexible critical approach to the action film that draws on a range of pertinent areas of critical discourse (on genre, narrative, the body, aesthetics and social, cultural and political contexts) in order to accommodate the action film's varying traits and characteristics. Eric Lichtenfeld opines that action cinema is a form of filmmaking that 'most critics simply take for granted and therefore approach too imprecisely' (Lichtenfeld 2007: 6); this book will demonstrate how we can take action cinema as a serious object of study, and in doing so will suggest what we might make of action cinema's current manifestations.

In *The Way Hollywood Tells It: Story and Style in Modern Movies* David Bordwell warns that on the whole 'critics have exaggerated the novelty of current developments' (Bordwell 2006: 9) and proposes an approach to contemporary cinema that remains alive to its historical continuities as well as its innovations. Sharing Bordwell's concerns, across the chapters that follow I discuss recent shifts in the formal, thematic, representational and industrial shape of the action film in the light of the longer history of the action movie. Nevertheless, as my discussion of historical specificity above will already have indicated, my strong sense is that the contemporary action film is not constructed in a vacuum, and thus its relationship to the cultural, industrial and artistic 'moment' in which it is produced is a valid and indeed necessary strand of enquiry. As a result, in the remainder of this Introduction, I want to use two films from roughly each end of the decade – *The Matrix* (Andy and Larry Wachowski, 1999) and *Live Free or Die Hard* (Len Wiseman, 2007) to begin to locate post-1990s action more explicitly in its historical, social and artistic contexts, re-posing the question in the Introduction's title: 'Where are we, and how did we get here?'

The return of the *Die Hard* hero John McClane (Bruce Willis) to cinema screens in the summer of 2007 in *Live Free or Die Hard* seemed oddly redundant. The knowing self-referentiality of the original *Die Hard* film (John McTiernan, 1988), manifested most frequently through its star's wise-cracks, humorously deconstructed the 1980s action genre even as it continued to supply the exhilarating, spectacular action sequences for which the genre was popular. But in 2007 the ubiquity of smart, 'knowing' Hollywood movies that refer us explicitly to their own processes and conventions through verbal, visual or narrative punning had removed the novelty of McClane's quipping. Contemporary action cinema displays a self-conscious knowingness that proceeds from the popularisation of irony as a postmodern media practice in the previous decade. Early 1990s disaffection with Reaganism and Bush (Senior)'s conservatism, and a growing awareness of debates in identity politics and related practices of cultural resistance (such as late 1980s/early 1990s queer activism), had resulted in the strategic deployment of irony to deconstruct mainstream culture, and in a resisting or dialectical relationship with traditional moral values and structures. This cultural turn manifested itself across a range of media, including advertisements, comedy shows such as *The Simpsons* (1989–) and *Seinfeld* (1990–8), and as a predominant trend in independent US cinema. Jeffrey Sconce labels its indie sector incarnation 'smart cinema' that 'experiment[ed] with irony and disengaged tone as a means of critiquing mainstream taste and culture' (Sconce 2006: 430). Independent movies such as *Welcome to the Dollhouse* (1995), *Safe* (1995) and *Magnolia* (1998) were marked by an irony that was darkly nihilistic in tone, but in the subsequent decade this irony is assimilated back into mainstream cinema (and action cinema specifically) as a rather a different beast, and for different ends.

In order to explore this, we must first recognise that post-1990s action cinema is a cinema defined in part by its proximity to the passing of the millennium. While it develops and responds to tendencies observable in pre-2000s culture and cinema, it is also indelibly marked by the *fin de siècle* with which it is directly proximate. Through the 1990s certain cultural anxieties gained momentum in Western societies in response to social, political and technological developments, and as aspects of postmodern thought gained a foothold in the public consciousness. As Laura Mulvey notes, the 1980s and 1990s had been 'a period of accelerated political and economic upheaval and crisis' (Mulvey 2006: 23), but other emergent developments were equally concerning: the arrival of the Internet's ability to simultaneously expand the reach of the media, problematise the veracity of information, unpredictably reconfigure social networks, and anonymise communication; digital images' achievement of photorealism and the resulting return to old debates about the 'truth-value' of images; the saturation coverage of the first Iraq War which raised equally pressing questions about the partiality of news media reporting. Paul Virilio's work on technological mediation and Jean Baudrillard's on simulation gained cultural valence as anxieties deepened about the increasing pervasiveness of communications and media technologies and their impact on the Western individual's ability to perceive the world accurately.[5] Following a pattern that was characteristic of previous *fin de siècle* moments in human history, as the millennium approached apocalyptic narratives began to circulate in Western culture (examples in action cinema included *Independence Day* (1996), *Twister* (1996), *Volcano* (1997) and *Armageddon* (1998)). Various 'ends' were mooted, including the end of the world (via war, global warming, social implosion and so on), the end of cinema and television (via new media and delivery technologies, a dearth of artistic creativity or loss of faith in traditional narrative forms), and the end of the traditional family unit, an anxiety (explored in the apocalyptic action films mentioned above) prompted by a resurgence of debates about abortion, divorce and gay rights, and the reassessment of gender roles and challenging of racial hierarchies in 1990s US society. Meanwhile certain postmodern theorists (particularly Jean Baudrillard and Francis Fukuyama) were moved to characterise postmodernity as the end of history.[6] Jonathan Bignell suggests that these end of history theses are gendered, that 'the end of history is simultaneously the end of masculine mastery for a Western male subject' (Bignell 2000: 9). Hollywood ended the decade depicting male protagonists' 'crises of mastery' within uncertain, subjugating universes in films such as *Dark City* (1998), *The Truman Show* (1998), *The Matrix*, *Fight Club* and *eXistenZ* (1999), a challenge to the notions of heroism and empowerment traditionally celebrated in the action film.

While the presence of knowing irony in post-1990s action cinema might be seen as an attempt to reassert a kind of mastery in response to the passing of the millennium, it has a longer history of functioning to master a socio-cultural and media environment that continues to shift troublingly and mutate. The practice of irony – visual, verbal or narrative – becomes a reassuring display of reclaimed power, the power to judge, to remove or assign value. A populist notion of what postmodernism 'is' becomes productively assimilated into mainstream cultural production, as Hollywood claims itself as postmodern – read 'intelligently knowing' – while asking its audiences to take pleasure in their own cultural knowingness, in the play of intertextual references that are signalled and correspondingly understood. This knowingness and the asserted stability of the value judgments that emanate from the texts must be interrogated, not simply in terms of what has been asserted, but in terms of what is disavowed, pointed away from. Equally, what has been absorbed into the realm of knowing performance should also be unpicked. For example, 'positive' space may be given to persons of minority gender, ethnicity or sexuality, but within performance or narrative frameworks that are most frequently depoliticised or at worst characterised by reactionary impulses. Such representational strategies and their relationship to the notions of mastery and control that circulate in the action genre, to questions of film style, and to more general economic and cultural imperatives, are investigated more closely in Chapters 4, 5 and 6.

Contemporary action cinema's historical specificity is of course not just defined by its proximity to the millennium, but to what followed. Laura Mulvey comments,

> It only took a subsequent gestation period of a year and nine months for apocalypse to catch up with the millennium. With the events of September 2001 in New York and Washington, DC, the indistinct sense of foreboding that belonged to the year 2000 found an emblematic embodiment. Politicians, journalists and cultural commentators of all kinds argued that the world had been irrevocably changed. (Mulvey 2006: 23)

For hours on 11 September 2001 live television broadcast images of destruction that had only been seen before in Hollywood action and disaster movies, but were now disconcertingly and horrifyingly relocated to the realm of the real. While the distance of those images from the framing and presentational conventions of Hollywood movie sequences has been usefully pointed out by Geoff King (2005: 45–57), there is no doubt that 9/11 prompted a serious consideration within the movie industry about what kinds of pleasures, spectacles, narratives and fictional worlds were desirable, appropriate or commercially attractive to audiences. In the immediate months that followed, purveyors of action cinema were forced to re-evaluate what could be shown, what kinds of action could be taken and justified, and what kinds of heroism could be celebrated on screen. But the subsequent cultural, social and political 'convulsions' were equally significant in their influence on the form contemporary action cinema has taken since, such as the co-existence of political discourses of war and retribution with those of tolerance and understanding; the development in the media of a more sophisticated perception of Muslim culture and religion alongside damagingly reductive caricatures; responses to the US government's covert interrogation and deportation of suspected terrorists, and incarceration without trial; debates about the mandate for the invasion of Iraq and its attempted reconstruction, and similarly for military action in Afghanistan; consternation at the loss of so many Iraqi civilians' lives and those of an increasing number of US soldiers. I do not wish to suggest that action cinema of the past decade is solely defined by 9/11 and what followed; such an extreme conclusion fails to take account of the wide range of drivers, industrial and cultural, that shape feature film production. But I do want to propose that the traces of these historical events and political developments, and the debates they have generated, can be detected in post-2001 action movies, and have influenced contemporary action cinema's negotiations about how to construct its narratives, its fictional worlds and its heroes.

While this question is the explicit focus of Chapter 8, it is worth illustrating some of the issues already elaborated here by turning back to *Live Free or Die Hard*. On one level the film is (as one would expect of a sequel) a return to a familiar, popular formula, McClane once again fighting terrorists and deploying his trademark humorous quips, prompting gunfights and spectacular explosions. But the changes in the formula's post-1990s articulation are noteworthy. The title's opening instruction to 'live free' is an explicit assertion of the democratic principle the US wishes to protect and promote to non-democratic nations in a post-9/11 world. The phrase's absence when the film was released in European territories (the title became *Die Hard 4.0*, signalling the film's narrative preoccupation with computer technology) surely speaks to the uneasy status of US foreign policy in Europe. Chapters 8 and 9 address precisely the kinds of questions raised by this territory-specific positioning of the film, exploring the aesthetic exchanges between European and US action cinemas in the context of issues of nationhood, globalisation and attendant economic and industrial factors. The terrorists McClane is battling against are not 'foreigners' as they were in previous *Die Hard* films, but mostly US citizens, operating from within the country, using the nation's communications and transport infrastructures against its own people. Their modus operandi, targets and the reach of their powers are unexpected: even specialist government units such as the CIA and FBI cannot stop them. If their 'American-ness' points rather disingenuously away from Hollywood's traditional ethnic stereotyping of its terrorist characters (and the problematic reality of the 9/11 hijackers' ethnicities), the terrorists also embody the 'enemy within' threat mobilised by 9/11, the recognition that terrorist cells were operating in the US, and that US nationals could be radicalised against the state (the chief terrorist character's previous job was in US national security). The simultaneous exploration and disavowal of post-9/11 and 'post'-Iraq and -Afghanistan fears about control and security, that I will argue in Chapter 8 characterises some post-1990s action movies, finds striking expression in the spectacle of the Capitol building's destruction and the subsequent revelation that this was an illusion.

A further difference from McClane's earlier *Die Hard* outings is that Bruce Willis is an older actor now, but this fact becomes more than an excuse for a few jokes. McClane's crisis of confidence – his bemused sense of dislocation from contemporary technologies and fashions, and anxieties about his ageing body's ability to get the job done – echoes the US crisis of mastery that extended beyond the millennium, in response to 9/11 and to the government's subsequent struggles to be effective in its 'war on terror'. Against terrorists using highly sophisticated web- and computer-based digital technologies, McClane's ineptitude with computers and even basic mobile phones is pointedly significant (and rather different from his often ingenious uses of technology in previous films), and he struggles to find the right way to best the terrorists' plans. While more traditional forms of heroic action are gestured towards – he manages to overcome several henchmen with sheer brute force – he can only save his daughter and thwart the terrorists by drawing on the creative IT skills of a young computer 'geek' Matthew Farrell (Justin Long). McClane must collaborate with others and rely on other kinds of skills to succeed. As I explore further in Chapters 5 and 8, here and elsewhere in contemporary action cinema, what constitutes heroic masculinity and appropriate forms of action are being recalibrated.

Live Free or Die Hard also refers to its own place within contemporary action cinema output. Alongside the film's rather heavy-handed narrative references to the everyday omnipresence of the Internet and digital technologies, McClane directs particularly cutting verbal derision towards the physically inept computer-game-playing hackers he is forced to ask for help, and the chief terrorist's girlfriend Mai (Hong Kong action star Maggie Q) a martial arts expert who McClane dubs – in a phrase both sexist and racist – 'the Asian chick who likes to kick people'. Through such references, the film grudgingly acknowledges and at once disparages some of the directions action cinema has taken from the late 1990s onwards, and which post-1990s action cinema has assimilated or responded to in various ways: the increased influence of Hong Kong, Chinese and Japanese martial arts films on contemporary action sequences; shifts in the construction of the male hero's masculinity and physicality; and the proliferation of female action heroes after the 1990s. The modification of the *Die Hard* series' interracial 'buddy' relationship trope (McClane now has two 'buddies', his young techie Matthew and the Native-American FBI deputy director Bowman (Cliff Curtis)) and the racist construction of the female villain Mai are examples of the recalibration of ethnicity that I explore further in Chapter 6. In its diegetic preoccupation with computer hacking and the threat of physically powerful women, and its jibes at martial arts, *Live Free or Die Hard* seems to be in some kind of dialogue with *The Matrix*, the hugely successful action film released on the eve of the millennium in 1999. Given the earlier film's significant cultural impact, this is unsurprising: elements of *The Matrix*'s visual style, music and iconography were subsequently incorporated into a proliferating range of media texts such as music videos, advertisements, television and other films. Certainly many action films that followed showed their debt to *The Matrix*, from direct homages to the film's 'bullet-time' special effect in *Charlie's Angels* (2000) and *Swordfish* (2001) to the action sequences, costume and set design of films including *Equilibrium* (2002) and the *Underworld* movies (2003, 2006, 2009). It would be misleading to conceptualise *The Matrix* as a prototype for a subsequently unchanging post-1990s action movie format. However, it certainly can be seen as a watershed moment in recent action movie production, responding to some of the cultural debates circulating in the 1990s that I have already mentioned, but simultaneously displaying nascent tensions and tendencies – in particular in relation to issues of film style and representations of gender, race and sexuality – that are then addressed, developed, refused or otherwise negotiated in post-1990s action movies. In the final part of the Introduction, I want to illustrate this by taking a closer look at the Wachowskis' influential film.

The Matrix is a film that seems caught between two projects: on the one hand a 'progressive' agenda that incorporates a philosophical enquiry into perception and existence in a technologised society, and attempts to deploy progressive conceptions of ethnic and gender equality; on the other hand a more 'conservative' impulse to try to guarantee large box office returns by providing specific pleasures such as special effects, objectified bodies, violent action, and 'cool' clothing, accoutrements and gadgets. This central tension plays across the film's representational hierarchies, stylistic characteristics and narrative processes in ways that indicate the kinds of negotiations subsequent films would have to enter into in the post-1990s period. Earlier I located *The Matrix* as one of a number of films in which the male protagonist experiences a crisis of mastery. In the film Neo (Keanu Reeves) discovers his mind is being forced unwittingly to participate in an electronic simulation of reality, so that his body along with thousands of others can be used as a power source for malevolent machines. This narrative situation, reflective of a cluster of millennial anxieties in locating its male hero in a state of extreme powerlessness, develops in a manner that seems to destabilise the conventionally gendered hierarchies of power present in the action genre. Conceptions of gender roles and behaviours in cinema and in the wider culture have historically been structured in binary terms (simplistically: male as active, strong, hero; woman as passive, weak, victim), but here it is Neo who is disempowered through a process of feminisation. Dialogue positions him as Alice in *Alice's Adventures in Wonderland* (Carroll, 1960) and Dorothy in *The Wizard of Oz* (Victor Fleming, 1939), and after being 'unplugged' from the matrix for the first time, he emerges from his 'human battery' pod in a hairless, unco-ordinated, baby-like condition incongruous with his adult form, and exhibits behaviours more usually ascribed to women, such as fainting and hysteria. From a literally unconscious (sleeping and hallucinating) start, Neo's passivity, hesitancy and lack of active agency in the first half of the film are radical breaks from earlier formulations of the male action hero.

In an emerging pattern of gender reversals the film juxtaposes its passive male figure with an empowered, active female protagonist. The film's opening moments do not reveal the male hero to us in the customary declaration of his

Neo must become like Trinity in order to fulfil his destiny in *The Matrix*

incipient abilities; instead a kinetic action sequence emphatically establishes the striking capabilities of the female protagonist Trinity (Carrie-Ann Moss). Single-handedly despatching a team of police officers sent to apprehend her, leaping impossible distances between rooftops and escaping seemingly into thin air at the end of the sequence, Trinity is constructed as an extremely potent action body, and continues to display agency, physical strength and skill thereafter. Compared to late 1980s and early 1990s movies featuring action heroines, such as *Aliens* (1986) or *Terminator 2: Judgment Day* (1991), the film is more progressive in its construction of Trinity as an action heroine. Her physical power does not have to be authenticated through the display of visibly 'trained-up' musculature, her agency and power is not seen as unusual in the film world, and her physical aggression is not 'explained' through recourse to heavily gendered motivations, such as an overriding maternal instinct or an avenging impulse triggered by the trauma of rape. The film's destabilisation of conventional gender binaries is consolidated by the ways in which *The Matrix* brings Neo and Trinity together in the visual frame. Fighting together to rescue resistance leader Morpheus (Laurence Fishburne) from capture, the pair's visual correspondences are striking. Neo's slim, non-muscular frame is comparable to Trinity's straight-backed and not particularly curvaceous body, and both characters' angular, expressionless features, matching sunglasses and slicked-back hairstyles foreground their visual resemblance while suppressing obvious markers of gender. As an androgynous pairing, Neo and Trinity's bodies symbolise an erosion of conventional gendered distinctions in a way that is directly relevant to their relative status as action heroes. While Neo must become 'like Trinity' in order to find his own empowered agency in these key action sequences, their similarity in appearance also means Trinity cannot be boxed easily into the role of female sidekick. Where the female sidekick traditionally 'provides a point of differentiation, emphasising the masculine identity of the male hero' (Tasker 1993: 28), here Trinity's composure and active physicality point up Neo's moments of doubt and hesitation.

Despite the film's gender play, the narrative of *The Matrix* is revealed to have a rather traditional trajectory, conferring the privilege of ultimate empowerment on its male protagonist, and making his passage towards that point its focus. In relation to the millennial context within which the film was conceived and produced, Neo's journey from profound disempowerment to a position of mastery over the matrix programme at the end of the film is clearly an attempt to resolve millennial and gendered anxieties about loss of control in a heavily technologised, consumerist and media-saturated world. This impulse to reassure, through a persuasive fantasy of 'becoming-masterful' enacted by the traditional figure of the white male, comes into conflict with the more progressive aspects of the film's treatment of gender and race. Even the specific characteristics of the film's special effects work in the service of this project to reassure and reaffirm white male control. The famous 'bullet-time' special effect is distinctive in the way it places the moving body at the literal centre of its signature dynamic frame.[7] The action is recorded by an array of still cameras timed to take a sequential series of pictures along the path of a notional camera; the still images are later digitally composited with traditional footage to 'animate' the camera movement around the action. This results in striking sequences where the physical action unfolds in variable-speed slow motion while the camera moves at a different pace and along a different spatial trajectory. At each bullet-time moment the visual and spatio-temporal dynamics of the special effect (and the technological expertise that produced it) operate as a metaphor for and narrative declaration of Neo's growing skills in manipulating the physics of the matrix universe. After the film's opening action sequence, it is Neo's body in action that is the focal centre of the effect, that the notional bullet-time camera seeks out and circles around; his heroic progress that is signalled as the camera arc each time marks out a progressively larger space of mastery around his body.[8]

Bullet-time slows the action almost to stillness to allow maximum contemplation of the body's physical movement at its moment of empowered exertion, while its digital technology allows the composited images to achieve an impossibly seamless photorealism. The notional camera trajectory around the space of action gives the illusion that the spectator has broken into the three-dimensional space of the fictional world. In its flaunting of the verisimilitude of the action from 'all angles', then, bullet-time is a declaration of the film's mastery over the visual – its ability to show everything – to meet the spectator's desire for mastery of the visual – to see everything. If *The Matrix* is thematically concerned with millennial anxieties about a loss of control in the context of processes of mediation, commodification and technologisation, then bullet-time functions to reassure the spectator that he or she can still occupy a position of wholeness, of mastery. It is fitting that milestones in Neo's reassuring progression towards full mastery of the spatial and temporal dynamics of the matrix program are expressed through a specific special effect that, for its duration, offers the spectator an omniscient view of the movement of the action, and the body's characteristics in the act of motion. Thus the film invokes a fantasy of omniscience, a reassuring totality of vision, that is as relevant for the spectator as for the film's characters.

The film's refusal to display Trinity's physical feats using 'bullet-time' after the opening sequence are a symptom of a wider logic of exclusion that progressively moves other strong, active characters out of the space of action so that Neo can assume his central position as hero, in a conservative – and reassuring – return to conventionally gendered and raced tropes of male mastery and heterosexual union. This logic of exclusion works to sideline Trinity, preventing her from displaying her potency as an action heroine because she can no longer access the matrix (a broken 'hard line' means Neo is left to fight the Agents alone in the simulation), relegating her to the role of Neo's love interest. But after Agent Smith shoots Neo through the heart, in a final example of the gender reversals that punctuate the film, Trinity plays prince to Neo's sleeping beauty, bringing him back from death with a kiss. Notably Trinity's kiss – on one level the visual consummation of her role as love interest – is the catalyst for life-saving changes that occur not just in the matrix simulation, but in the real world. In contrast Neo only achieves mastery of elements within the matrix itself.[9] Such narrative moves speak to the tensions in the film's exploration of gender and power. The final image of Neo's mastery is emphatic but extremely overdetermined: he declares his intent to overturn the matrix program's subjugation of the human race in a voice-over, a device frequently used to impose dominant meanings on a film text, while his metaphorical ascension to mastery is literalised in a dramatic flight into the air, recalling a familiar trope from superhero iconography. These final moments seem to be trying to compete with the kinetic potency of Trinity's opening action sequence, evidence then of the problem *The Matrix* has created for itself; its reflexive gender play and presentation of a more flexible conception of the gendered action hero (male or female) complicate and undermine any attempt to reinstate dominant gender norms in the narrative resolution. However, this is less the case in the film's treatment of race, where the same logic of exclusion that sidelines Trinity also removes people of colour from the frame to ensure the white male remains in a position of mastery.

The Matrix signals its progressive credentials by self-consciously assembling a resistance group that is inclusively multi-racial, consisting of African Americans and Hispanics as well as Caucasians, with a black character as its leader. Nevertheless, as I point out in Chapter 6, the presentation of a pan-culturally-inclusive group does not necessarily prevent the mobilisation of racialised stereotypes, and this group is organised in rather problematic terms in relation to racial and class boundaries. Morpheus aside, the other group members of colour are foot soldiers or ship mechanics with little personal autonomy, in a long tradition of 'black helpers' (Tasker 1993: 36) who sacrifice themselves for the white male. Other identities are grouped together in this band of 'helpers', who will be killed off with little ceremony to save Neo. The presence and subsequent death of the Hispanic male Apoc (Julian Arahanga) testify to the historical place of Hispanic or Latin American characters in Hollywood's representational hierarchy that I discuss further in Chapter 6. The equally marginal role of the lesbian character Switch (Belinda McClory) speaks to action cinema's more general oscillations between referencing and disavowing homosexuality, which I will explore in Chapter 7. In contrast, Morpheus and the Oracle, played by African Americans Laurence Fishburne and Gloria Foster, occupy positions of explicit power within the storyworld of *The Matrix*, but are both constructed using a rather problematic visual shorthand that draws on the racialised stereotypes from Hollywood's dubious history of African American representation. The Oracle's access to privileged knowledge has a significant influence on events, but her position as the nominal 'good mother' of the resistance movement is visualised in literal 'homely kitchen and home-baked cookies' terms, uneasily reminiscent of the 'comfortable mammy image' presented in films like *Gone With The Wind* (1939) and *Imitation of Life* (1959) (hooks 2000: 515). Morpheus is a potent figure at the film's start, his seemingly omniscient knowledge helping to guide Trinity and Neo in their early attempts to evade the insuperable Agents. He registers as a rather over-determined conflation of guidance figures, some clearly racially focused. Mentor to Neo, 'father' to the resistance group, martial arts master and military commander, he is also an articulate 'preacher-man' figure, erudite philosopher and theologian, a militant resistance leader reminiscent of the Black Power movement's key figures, and he wears a costume that combines the long black leather coat of the blaxploitation hero with the smart suit of mainstream middle-class affluence. The resistance fighters are set in opposition to the all-white Agents who police the oppressive matrix universe. Indeed, during Agent Smith's interrogation of Morpheus, Smith's celebratory assertion of the machines' subjugation of the human race – 'You are a plague, and we are the cure' – is inflected with the rhetoric of ethnic cleansing and white supremacy, while Morpheus' preceding capture and sickening beating by a group of police officers uncomfortably mimics the brutal beating of Rodney King by police in 1991. The very convenience of using these associations to position the Agents as bad is troubling, especially alongside the supposedly unproblematic assumption that the white Neo is the inevitable saviour of humankind. That all the black characters are shown to unquestioningly display this same belief simply confirms the film's reluctance to reflect explicitly on either the politics of its own racialised representational framework, or dominant representations of race in the wider culture. It is not surprising, then, that by the end of the film Morpheus has also been sidelined into a passive supporting role: after his rescue he watches the remaining events unfold from outside the matrix. Formerly the apparent gatekeeper of the matrix, offering Neo the red pill that will unplug him from the simulation, Morpheus' evangelical belief in Neo divests him of agency, placing him in the 'established tradition of representation in which the black man is suffused with a passive, Christian imagery' (Tasker 1993: 40). Morpheus' last words are a wondering declaration of Neo's supremacy ('He is the One') uttered prior to Neo and Trinity's kiss and Neo's triumphant flight up into the air. In these final two scenes Morpheus is not just passive but invisible: absent from the cinematic frame, his marginalisation is complete.

The narrative and representational tensions evident in *The Matrix* betray its attempts to reflect the millennial zeitgeist and respond to 1990s debates about society, philosophy, technology and culture while simultaneously supplying an attractive commercial product and an aesthetically creative action movie to its audiences. But *The Matrix* also poses a set of questions to the decade of action cinema that will follow, about the ways in which the action spectacle, film style and special effects will develop, the shape of narrative structure and the apportioning of narrative power, the shifting of representational hierarchies and their relationship to wider ideological and cultural sea-changes, the genre's interactions with a proliferating media landscape, and the commercial strategies adopted by filmmakers, film producers and the studios that finance them.

This book tracks how post-1990s action cinema answers these 'questions'. Each chapter addresses a particular issue in the context of wider relevant critical debates, but focuses its discussion around detailed analysis of case study films. The first three chapters explore the key structural and stylistic elements of 2000s action films and the spectatorial processes that result. Chapter 1 assesses the narrative processes of the contemporary action movie, considering structural tendencies that characterise a period in which narratives travel across sequels and other media. The chapter suggests that the action body enacts a 'narrative of becoming' in the very action sequences that have been traditionally seen as providing spectacle rather than narrative information. Chapter 2 develops this point further, arguing for the centrality of the action body to the production of meaning in the action movie, and suggesting new ways to account more fully for the experience the action movie offers and the meanings it generates. Chapter 3 examines the aesthetics of the contemporary action sequence, analysing how stylistic elements generate connotations about the heroic body and its relationship to the spaces and processes of the contemporary world. The second section of the book builds on the first section by considering questions of representation in the context of action cinema's aesthetics, exploring how different representational decisions intersect with each other and with stylistic choices to produce complex meanings and tensions. Each chapter addresses a different area of representation, but draws into the discussion detailed reference to other areas of consideration in an integrated approach. Chapter 4 considers the representation of femininity in the action film, Chapter 5 masculinity, Chapter 6 different ethnicities, Chapter 7 homosexuality and Chapter 8 analyses the construction of heroism in the post-9/11 cultural environment. The final chapter of the book addresses the complexities of aesthetic 'exchange' between US action cinema and its European counterparts. Several books already deal with US action cinema's relationship to the martial arts cinemas of Hong Kong, Japan and China, so I do not duplicate the existing writing here. Instead, in a period in which European action movies are increasingly visible in the US market, Chapter 9 investigates the interrelationships between European and US action cinemas, how they influence each other in their representations, narratives and film style.

I want to end this Introduction by directing the reader to the epigraph which opens this book. Adrian Martin suggests that the task of analysis requires attention to the specificities of the object of analysis, and that this is 'most acutely' the case with action films (Martin 2005: 175). This book will explore various areas of aesthetics and representation in the contemporary action film in turn, but its project is not to advocate keeping each of these areas separate for the purposes of analysis. Instead it seeks to encourage – and provide the tools to achieve – an integrated approach that considers these different areas at their most meaningful, complicated and culturally resonant intersections, including the moment of action itself. At the same time the illustrative analyses are designed to demonstrate the value of staying alert to the specificities of each film, and in turn to reject once and for all the tendency towards dismissive generalisation that has occasionally blighted the discussion of action cinema. The pages that follow combine enthusiasm for action cinema's pleasures and the serious analysis it demands as a popular cultural form. I hope you enjoy the ride.

NOTES

1. Lichtenfeld worries that such a definition is so broad as to be meaningless, and goes on in the rest of the book to argue for a definition much more closely aligned to the characteristics of the 1980s action film. His account of the way in which this particular manifestation of the action film emerged out of the genre revisionism of the 1970s is enjoyable and persuasive, but in the later chapters on 1990s and 2000s action films the question of what constitutes action cinema in its more recent forms seems less clearly drawn.
2. For more on the contemporary blockbuster, see King 2002: 49–84, Maltby 2003: 189–225 and Wyatt 1994. For a historicised perspective, see Hall 2002 and 2006.
3. King suggests that contemporary action films combine more traditional forms of large-scale spectacle with rapid montages which emphasise impacts and action close up (what he calls the 'impact aesthetic'), and that the latter have the benefit of registering as spectacular on domestic screens, as well as in movie theatres (King 2006: 341). Bordwell acknowledges the trend towards rapid cutting but is unsure of its effectiveness, arguing that extreme instances 'don't read well on the big screen' (Bordwell 2006: 123). We will return to this issue in Chapter 3.
4. See Tasker 1993 and 1998, Lehman 1993, Jeffords 1994, Willis 1997, Arroyo (ed.) 2000, Holmlund 2002, Tasker 2004 and Lichtenfeld 2007.
5. See Virilio 1991, Baudrillard 1993 and [1981] 1994.
6. See Fukuyama 1989 and 1992; and Baudrillard [1992] 1994.
7. The 'bullet-time' effect entered public consciousness as a result of its dynamic deployment in *The Matrix*. See Rehak 2007 for an interesting discussion of how this special effect subsequently 'migrated' across a variety of media forms and contexts.

8. For a more detailed discussion of physical movement, space and power in the *Matrix* franchise see Purse 2009.
9. In a similar vein G. Christopher Williams argues that Trinity is the real hero of the film (Williams 2003: 5). In the film's sequels, *The Matrix Reloaded* (2003) and *The Matrix Revolutions* (2003), Neo is gradually able to extend his powers across both the matrix simulation and the real world; significantly, after *The Matrix*, Trinity is never again depicted as possessing powers that extend beyond the bounds of the simulation.

CHAPTER 1

Narrative and the action film

So tired is Avatar's tale that you hardly notice it. The film is mere spectacle, about as emotionally engaging as the associated videogame. Perhaps
the importance attached to this game tells us what Fox's bosses were up
to. Maybe they reckoned that the digital-native audience has moved on
from concern with motive, thought and feeling ... thinking like this
seems pretty pervasive in Hollywood. (Cox 2009: paragraphs 4–5)

Action cinema has a reputation for narrative paucity, for giving spectators all
action and no plot, a reputation that seems to have gained further traction with
the increasingly ubiquitous and frequently exhibitionist use of digital effects
in action sequences. The action fantasy *Avatar* (directed by James Cameron)
was released at the end of 2009 to great fanfare, promising a spectacular display
of ground-breaking digital 3D and motion capture technologies. However,
those same qualities made it vulnerable to the criticism of 'too much' spectacle
in certain quarters of the media. David Cox's on-line article for the British
newspaper *The Guardian*, published three days after the film's UK theatrical
release, is unrelentingly dismissive of the film. Calling it 'mere spectacle', the
journalist blames *Avatar*'s spectacular nature for what he sees as its lack of
narrative engagement. For Cox, the narrative is not just outdated but almost
completely absent, a situation he suggests is caused by an assumption by
studio executives and filmmakers that audiences are no longer interested in
the subtleties of characterisation and narrative motivation ('motive, thought
and feeling'). In this way Cox makes a link between narrative paucity and the
industrial imperative to create textual elements that can 'travel' easily into
ancillary markets like computer games. Cox suggests that this is not simply a
weakness in *Avatar*'s artistic project but a larger cinematic trend – spectacle
over narrative – that is itself a symptom of the commercial structures and
pressures that frame all contemporary Hollywood production.

Given the vehemence with which such allegations are made in the popular press, one would be forgiven for thinking that this is an incontrovertible recent development in Hollywood filmmaking. Indeed, some film writers also make a similar case, voicing their own concerns about narrative being subsumed by spectacle, and often characterising this as a facet of 'New' Hollywood as opposed to 'Old' or classical Hollywood.[1] And yet the regularity with which press stories on this topic appear should give us pause. Newspaper articles with titles like 'Should all CGI be banned?' (Child 2007) and '*Inception*, effects-fest and the big-budget unreality curse' (Leigh 2010) may spring up at the release of each new digital effects-laden action blockbuster, but the anxieties and cinematic characteristics they discuss can be found throughout cinema's history (often being heralded as a 'new' development). William Eaton could have been complaining about any number of contemporary blockbusters when he wrote, 'The eye and the mind are both bewildered by the too sudden and too frequent shifts of scene. There is a terrible sense of rush and hurry and flying about, which is intensified by the twitching film and generally whang-bang music.' But Eaton's article, titled 'A New Epoch in the Movies', was published in *American Magazine* in 1914 (cited in Shone 2004: 61). The German writer Clare Goll's 1920 essay on American cinema was much more celebratory, but identified the same spectacular mode of filmmaking that had caused Eaton such dismay six years earlier:

> What is happening or rather racing by on the screen can no longer be called plot. It is a new dynamic, a breathless rhythm, action in an unliterary sense . . . The American cinema has already accustomed its public to much. Tanks ride into houses, three cars race into one another or into the sea; 2,000 metres up, a man performs acrobatics from one airplane to another and comes down on a parachute over the ocean and New York without knowing whether and where he will land. (Goll [1920] 2004: 50, 52)

Popular cinema 'is and has long been a spectacular, indeed sensational tradition', as scholars including Tom Gunning, Geoff King, Steve Neale and Yvonne Tasker have noted (Tasker 2004: 2).[2] Goll's description makes strikingly apparent the continuities in the types of exhilarating, risk- and destruction-filled action spectacle Hollywood has offered its audiences over more than a century: each of the stunts she glosses would sit equally well in a contemporary action movie. Such continuities put pressure on the oppositions between 'Old' and 'New' Hollywood or between 'Hollywood Renaissance' and contemporary blockbuster that underpin many negative accounts of the predominance of spectacle in contemporary cinema. Those oppositions seem to rely on nostalgic (mis)conceptions of a classical or 'renaissance' cinema in which narrative is dominant, conceptions that are flawed because they are based only on a limited number of canonical texts. As Richard Maltby has argued, spectacular blockbusters may presently be seen as 'more aberrant in the *longue durée* than they should be, not because of their own properties but because of what is excluded from accounts of earlier periods' (Maltby 1998: 40).

The most damaging aspect of derogatory responses such as the one that began this chapter is that they have the potential to close down useful avenues of reflection and analysis, on the part of viewers certainly, but perhaps also on the part of some scholars and film critics. The implicit suggestion is that one should avert one's eyes and critical faculties, that the films are unworthy of further intellectual consideration, that their aesthetic qualities and processes can be taken for granted, to use Lichtenfeld's phrase. The fact that narrative is so often dismissed as an absence or weakness in these films makes it even more pertinent to subject this area to further consideration. As a result, this chapter will investigate the status of narrative in the contemporary action movie, and will attempt to move beyond assertions of narrative paucity and counter-assertions of narrative plenitude (see for example King 2000, 2002 and Bordwell 2006), to offer an account of how narrative operates in this most 'popcorn', but most successful, of Hollywood products.

THE PRESENCE OF NARRATIVE

Avatar opens with a visual spectacle: we seem to be speeding through the air over a vast, mist-strewn, forested landscape that extends further than the eye can see. The image is accompanied by a voice-over from an unseen male character: 'When I was lying there in the VA hospital, with a big hole blown through my life, I started having these dreams of flying. I was *free*. Sooner or later, though, you always have to wake up.' The cinematic convention of the first-person voice-over ('I was', 'I started') designates the speaker as the central protagonist, and is also used to introduce certain facts and possibilities about him. But it is not the only purveyor of information in these first shots of the film. Sound and image tracks work together to supply information, pose questions and establish expectations for the narrative which will follow. In the voice-over the narrator's stint in the 'VA hospital' signals he is a soldier or ex-soldier, which means he is likely to bring particular skill sets (combat, reconnaissance and field skills) and character traits (resilience, determination, assertiveness) to the narrative situation. But he also has an injury debilitating enough for him to feel like 'a big hole' has been 'blown through my life'. Thus the voice-over establishes the protagonist's strong sense of lack, and introduces the possibility that the narrative development will address that lack in some way. More specifically, his dreams indicate that his physical incapacity is creating in him a yearning for a form of physical freedom he can no longer attain. The juxtaposition of this yearning with an image of a vast landscape being penetrated at speed, an image whose temporal relationship to the voice-over is unclear, connotes both an experience that the protagonist feels he can no longer access and an experience that this landscape may yet provide in the future. Over the image of the forested landscape the protagonist's wistful delivery of the phrase 'I was free' is accompanied by surging drums on the soundtrack which intensify our sense of the dynamism of the 'freedom' being imagined. But sudden darkness and silence foregrounds a new flatness in the narrator's vocal delivery as he declares, 'Sooner or later, though, you always have to wake up.' The sudden shift in visual and auditory tone abruptly reintroduces the constraining nature of a mundane reality, and a cut to a claustrophobic extreme close-up of an eye opening (on the words 'wake up') completes this sense of a present life defined by unwanted enclosure.

In its first thirty-three seconds the film has already communicated key narrative details such as its protagonist's motivations and desires, and the tension between physical freedom and constraint that will define the narrator's progress through the film. The rest of the opening sequence gives a few more details to set up the circumstances of the protagonist's arrival on the planet. The figure we will soon know as Jake is first shown waking from an extended sleep in a 'cryo chamber'; when he exits the pod-like individual container he is in a larger vault in which hundreds more cryo chambers are visible. Given the weightlessness exhibited by Jake and those around him, and the numbers of fellow travellers exiting from their chambers, it appears this is a space station of some sort. Exterior shots confirm the space station where Jake is being temporarily housed and the planet Pandora the station is orbiting. A flashback follows that combines voice-over and brief dialogue scenes to fill in more of Jake's backstory. Jake's twin brother Tommy has been killed during an armed robbery just before he was supposed to set off for a scientific mission to Pandora, and even as Jake watches his brother being cremated, his brother's employers urge him to step in as Tommy's replacement. Jake's voice-over has already made clear his reluctance ('Tommy was the scientist, I'm just another dumb grunt going someplace he's going to regret') but the company men emphasise his genetic compatibility for the role, the big money he could earn (with the implication that, as an injured veteran, this is money he keenly needs) and the 'fresh start, on a new world' the job represents. The transition back to the present cuts between the brother's cremation and the space carrier taking Jake to Pandora's surface. The edit matches the roaring cremation flames circling the coffin in the flashback to the roar of the jet engines on the space carrier in the present. As Jake embarks from the carrier with a group of company-hired Marines, his injury is revealed as paralysis of the lower body, and he leaves the carrier in a wheelchair, jibes from the waiting armed forces ringing in his ears.

In this way this part of the opening sequence gives additional direct narrative information, but in its presentation it also develops the thematic opposition between the freedom and restriction of physical movement that was introduced in the first seconds of the film. Jake's initial acute enclosure, strapped into the small cryo chamber and framed in extreme close-ups, is contrasted with the literal and metaphorical release into the spacious receiving deck; unstrapped and in the weightlessness of space Jake is free (using his arms) to move his body nimbly around the deck, raising the possibility that in this new place and role Jake's injury will not be as physically debilitating as it has been. In the flashback the company men posit Pandora as the solution to the constraints Jake is labouring under, constraints that are not simply physical: his veteran's benefits won't pay for a spinal operation that could cure him, but the money being promised by the company could. The transition from the flashback to the present is a striking audio-visual expression of Jake's ambivalence about the company job, and at the same time of Pandora's (and the narrative's) possibilities, which complicates the simple opposition between constraint and freedom the film had started with. The coffin, confined to a cremation oven rapidly filling with flames, serves as a resonant metaphor for Jake's economic and physical confinement, but also evokes colloquialisms like 'baptism of fire' and 'from the frying pan into the fire' that point to the risks posed by the unknown future Jake is barrelling towards. The second image in the transition captures the space carrier in long shot, which makes it seem like a tiny, confining structure compared to the planetary reach and beauty of Pandora visible behind it. Here the container has a dual connotation, both potential coffin for its inhabitants and a claustrophobic precursor to a more hopeful and expansive future. The cut between the two images thus prompts questions. Is Jake exchanging one form of containment for another (the space carrier may simply be the first of many company vehicles he is restricted to; Jake may not achieve the physical cure he is working towards)? Or will this be the 'fresh start' his employers promise and Jake himself is fervently hoping for (do the expansive images of Pandora already hint at a freedom Jake has not yet imagined)?

In under six minutes *Avatar* quickly and deftly establishes the narrative setting and situation and some key facts about the main protagonist that will be central to his narrative trajectory (he is injured but wants to be physically 'free'; he is an ex-soldier determined to achieve despite his injury, but a reluctant employee; he hopes to start a new life). As we have seen, it also establishes certain narrative themes and oppositions that will be developed further as the film progresses: the prospect of a fresh start or new life; the competing interests of science (mission), commerce (the company), the personal (Jake's desires) and nature (Pandora); physical constraint versus physical freedom; the tension between economic necessity and gut feelings. Indeed these themes become central to the narrative as well as the action sequences, as a brief summary of subsequent events will illustrate. In order to explore the lives of Pandora's indigenous people, the Na'vi, the scientific mission connects Jake's brain to a cloned Na'vi body which he can control as if it were his own. Operating a body free from spinal injury, Jake revels in his new freedoms and gets close to a local Na'vi tribe; the prospect of a new life as a member of the tribe is raised. But the economic hierarchies which forced Jake to take the job in the first place now exert a different kind of pressure: the company and the military they have co-opted want to move the tribe off the land so that they can mine for precious minerals, and Jake is instructed to exploit his closeness to the Na'vi to gain insider information that might help. Jake is forced to decide between loyalty to the company (which will pay for his spinal operation) and loyalty to the tribe (which could offer a different kind of 'fresh start'). The key moments of spectacular action show Jake exploring and enhancing his newfound physical abilities, on foot and on the backs of galloping and flying animals; the dynamic penetration of the landscape promised by the first image of the film is fulfilled in these sequences. The exhilaration Jake – and we – experience at such moments provides narrative motivation for his desire to save and fight alongside the Na'vi people to protect their land, and the later battle sequences demonstrate the resulting fervour with which Jake fights. Sketching some of the subsequent narrative developments and moments of spectacle thus illustrates how the thematic tensions set up in the earliest moments of the film energise both the narrative progression and the action sequences in which Jake first explores and then defends his Na'vi life.

Avatar's first minutes carefully elaborate its narrative set-up and areas of thematic interest, establishing a fictional universe that operates on legible principles, and is peopled with characters with credible motivations. These cumulatively function to situate both plot developments and the spectacular sequences that will follow. We cannot watch Jake and his human and Na'vi compatriots and antagonists in action without being conscious of what is at stake for them in both 'unspectacular' and spectacular moments, and this sense of what is at stake flows from the narrative framework, which as we have seen is being mapped out right from the start of the film. On this evidence, assertions that the film fails to accommodate an audience concerned with 'motive, thought and feeling' appear insupportable. If Cox's real gripe with *Avatar* is that its narrative is lacking in originality, he conflates this subjective judgment with a separate and much less tenable charge that the narrative is almost absent. King warns against conflations of this nature, pointing out that while a film narrative 'might not be rated very highly in terms of quality or originality', that is 'not the same as [it] lacking significant dimensions of coherent narrative at all' (2002: 222). A further conflation is evident in Cox's account, one that merits highlighting because it is frequently an element of negative responses to action films that are particularly spectacular: the presence of weak narrative design within a spectacular film is taken to be indicative of narrative being replaced by spectacle, as if they were binary opposites. Interestingly we also find this binary opposition in Clare Goll's much more positive account of 1920s American cinema ('What is happening or rather racing by on the screen can no longer be called plot . . .'). Once again, this is a rhetorical move that appears difficult to sustain under scrutiny, for the same reasons we have already set out. The narrative information *Avatar* puts in place prior to its first significant moment of spectacular action would seem to suggest a desire that viewers then take that narrative information with them through the subsequent spectacle. Indeed, it seems perfectly reasonable to suggest that the viewer will draw on any narrative information provided to aid understanding of what is at stake in the exertions that are displayed in action sequences. *Avatar*'s subsequent narrative developments seem designed to engage directly with the situational and thematic tensions, questions and expectations the film's opening mobilises. *Avatar* thus seems to correspond with Geoff King's description of the contemporary blockbuster, which

> display[s] carefully honed narrative structures designed not just unceremoniously to unload a series of great dollops of action-spectacle but to engage viewers and to increase the impact of the action and spectacle by locating it in relation to character and plot. (King 2002: 202)

King suggests that spectacular sequences, rather than being 'the antithesis of narrative' (Darley 2000: 104), could work in conjunction with the narrative, embedding the action in the fictional world the narrative sustains, and possessing the capacity to 'help to move the plot significantly forward' (King 2000: 5). In the next section, I want to explore this idea further and in doing so propose ways in which spectacular action sequences might in themselves be narratively communicative.

NARRATIVE WITHIN THE ACTION SPECTACLE

As we saw in the Introduction, audio-visual spectacle is a commercially effective element in the action blockbuster that has the potential to increase a film's competitiveness in the global marketplace and travel well into ancillary product markets. Economic as well as artistic imperatives thus drive filmmakers' desire to generate a powerful 'wow' factor with their action sequences, to see off the competition and exceed previous films' audio-visual spectacle in novel, unexpected and usually also technologically impressive ways. It is this commercial imperative that prompts accusations of 'spectacle for spectacle's sake', but whatever the quality of some action blockbusters' audio-visual realisation or narrative design, such accusations fail to move forward our understanding of the action spectacle's potential for narrative communicativeness. Instead it is worth pausing for a moment to consider what we mean when we use the terms 'spectacular' and 'spectacle', in the context of popular cinema more generally and action cinema in particular. The words denote something presented to view, a displayed object or event that is in some way unusual, something beyond the realm of everyday experience. The words can also refer to the mode of presentation. A sense of spectacle can often be intensified by specific presentational strategies designed to produce emphasis through differentiation: for example a slowing or quickening of editing pace, or of movement within the frame; a significant change of scale or of the spatial relations between objects; the explicit display of special effects that register as out of the ordinary. In both what is shown and how it is shown, then, spectacle's novelty is relational, depending for its impact on marking itself out from its context. These differentiating strategies contribute to spectacle's capacity to trigger a range of intense responses, from shock and surprise to wonder and exhilaration. The prospect of experiencing such responses has the potential to draw audiences into movie theatres, a knowledge that has long inspired filmmakers to find forms of film spectacle that could generate the desired 'novelty effect' in cinema goers. This search for novelty does not preclude the continuities in Hollywood spectacle we have already observed; a novelty effect can be created through even quite small shifts in aesthetic presentation, elements of staging, narrative framing or context, which can single out a spectacle either cursorily or more emphatically from its predecessors.

Clare Goll's enthusiastic response to 1920s American cinema that I quoted earlier is useful not just because it demonstrates that spectacular action in Hollywood has a long history. Goll's words also give a clue as to what might be compelling or pleasurable about such spectacles even in action cinema of the present day. When she describes tanks riding into buildings or the parachutist not 'knowing whether and where he will land', what is palpable is not just the excitement that comes from witnessing events that are outside the bounds of quotidian experience, but the exhilarating effect of the presence of forces that explicitly put the human body at physical risk: speed, gravity, forceful impacts and so on. As we saw in the Introduction, Dyer has argued that much more recent action cinema provides similar thrills. It persistently returns to the spectacle of the human body operating at – and frequently exceeding – the limits of what is humanly possible, but it is the physical stakes for the body, and the body's responses to these, that is the focus and usually generates the narrative force within such sequences.

In *I, Robot* (Alex Proyas, 2004) Detective Del Spooner (Will Smith) is investigating the sudden death of acquaintance and robotics scientist Dr Alfred Lanning (James Cromwell) when he becomes trapped in a particularly hostile risk-filled environment. It is the year 2035 and sentient robots supplied by corporate giant US Robotics occupy the majority of service roles in city areas, their behaviour controlled by three rules hardwired into their brains that prevent them from harming humans. Despite this Spooner has a long-standing suspicion of robots, born of a car accident where a rescue robot prioritised the detective's life over that of a young girl deemed less likely to survive. This traumatic memory drives him to suspect that Lanning's apparent suicide might be foul play perpetrated by a robot, a theory dismissed out of hand by those around him. On an investigative evening visit to Lanning's property he comes across a US Robotics demolition robot sitting dormant outside, due to demolish the house at 8 o'clock the next morning. But while Spooner is inside the building, the robot is remotely reprogrammed to begin the demolition immediately. Just after the detective has rejected the attentions of Lanning's cat on the upstairs landing, the demolition robot's huge claws smash through the adjacent window and walls. Spooner grabs the cat and runs downstairs, but is thrown to the floor as sections of ceiling and bannister collapse on top of him. The cat runs off just before a claw swings above him to take out the walls of the stairwell. Spooner scrabbles back up to the landing, sprinting away from the robot while dodging debris and the robot's jabbing,

Detective Spooner sprints away from the robot that is demolishing the corridor in *I, Robot*

swinging claw. Ceiling and floor collapse simultaneously, throwing a yelling Spooner down into the ground level of the house. The demolition robot is now powering right through the centre of the building, and Spooner runs full pelt along the ground-level hallway, tumbling building fragments gathering into a thundering mass behind him. On the run he shoots the fastenings off the front door, and in a continuous movement with the cat back under his arm, kicks it outwards and uses the now horizontal door panel to ride the tide of debris to a soft landing in the swimming pool next to the house.

The sequence is spectacular for a number of reasons. Firstly, it is beyond our everyday experience – very few us will have experienced (or desired to experience) being on the inside of a domestic house as it is demolished, given the physical risks to the human body. Secondly, it is an opportunity for the exhibitionist display of digital imaging technologies that lend verisimilitude to a vision of the logically impossible, as digital compositing brings together real-world elements like Spooner, the cat and parts of the set with computer-generated wreckage, fragments of floor, ceiling and walls, and the robot's lights, claws and chassis.[3] But thirdly the sequence also emphatically foregrounds the physical feats Spooner must achieve to stay ahead of the wreckage and avoid being hit, crushed or pulled under, feats we find pleasurable not just because they are impressive in themselves, but because they ensure the continued survival of this sympathetic hero. Even though we are not yet sure whether his robot murder theory is accurate, the film has already aligned us with Spooner in other ways; we have had access to his apartment, his ablutions, his pride in his vintage shoes, his visit to his grandmother (Adrian Ricard), his traumatic flashback to the car accident which returns repeatedly to haunt him in his dreams. These moments provide information about Spooner's physical and psychological wounds: there are hints that his divorce may have been precipitated by the crash, and he has a stiffness in his left shoulder which seems to be connected to the accident (he touches it and winces after each bad dream). But positive qualities have also been communicated. He is a police officer who is both observant and energetic: his investigative questions are penetrating and deductive; he has already been highly effective in two chases by the time he enters Lanning's house; and he is happy to challenge his superiors in the pursuit of knowledge. He may work alone but he is also able to relate to people, prone to lively banter with those he cares about such as his grandmother and a rambunctious street youth Farber (Shia LeBeouf) he has taken under his wing (which also suggests a tolerant and liberal mind). Such access thus builds a picture of a psychologically coherent figure, marked by a past trauma physically as well as mentally, but with other more positive characteristics that, taken together, make him a sympathetic protagonist. Whether Spooner is correct about the robots is a question that will not be clarified until he is close to solving the narrative's key enigma, but importantly he is firmly located in the traditional detective role familiar from the police procedural, detective film, crime thriller and film noir. It is clear that Spooner is the only person willing to press forward with the investigation, and without him, Lanning's death will be deemed a suicide. As a result, during spectacular action sequences like the demolition of Lanning's house, investment in Spooner's survival is driven both by a desire for a narrative resolution only Spooner's presence can guarantee, and the more general alignment with the protagonist that the film has encouraged in a range of ways. Pleasure in the spectacle flows partly from witnessing those skills Spooner demonstrates that will ensure his survival and, by extension, will ensure the solution of the narrative enigma.

This spectacular sequence moves the narrative forward in three different but related ways. Firstly, it visualises a pertinent plot development: Spooner's search of Lanning's house for clues is thwarted by a demolition robot that the film shows is being activated remotely. The only explanation for this kind of premeditated obstruction of Spooner's investigation that seems likely is that Lanning's murderer is trying to cover their tracks, so the sequence's internal mystery of who remotely activated the robot becomes a reposing of the central narrative enigma: who (if anyone) killed Lanning? Secondly, the sequence progresses a significant narrative theme of the film: the potential impact of the ubiquitous presence of robots on the human population. Lanning's death fall seemed to indicate a local, limited impact, an individual malfunctioning robot killing an individual human. But the presence of robots in every aspect of life and every area of the city begins to introduce the possibility of a threat on a much larger scale, one of which Spooner is all too aware. The demolition of Lanning's house matches that scale in the spectacle it offers, functioning as a metaphorical foreshadowing of the realisation of that threat. In place of damage to individuals, here domestic space, a central feature of almost all human habitation, is razed utterly to the ground, its destruction made even more striking by the impression of solidity the house's high ceilings, wood panelling, stocky furniture and stone pillars had given prior to the robot's actions. Thus the sequence recalibrates our sense of human vulnerability in this technologised Chicago, and of the potential reach and scale of the robot threat. In turn the import of this sequence will later serve to intensify our response to the revelation that both Spooner's grandmother and the US Robotics associate assisting with the investigation, Dr Susan Calvin (Bridget Moynahan), have robots occupying their homes as domestic assistants, a decision which puts them both in mortal danger.

But the demolition sequence also moves the narrative forward in a third way, by consolidating and progressing our sense of Spooner's heroism and the capacities that will in due course allow him to reveal and defeat Lanning's murderer and eradicate the threat of the rogue robots. The sequence reiterates the skills that have been established in earlier action sequences. In the first action sequence of the film, where Spooner chases a suspected robot purse-snatcher through the streets, he demonstrates his running speed and agile ability to leap between different levels – from staircase to walkway, walkway to street level – as well as his quick responses, bursting into action within seconds of thinking that a theft has taken place. In the second action sequence Spooner attempts to stop Lanning's robot Sonny (voiced by Alan Tudyk) from escaping his dead creator's laboratory, and those quick response times are combined with sharp-shooting skill; as Sonny unexpectedly leaps from the lab window Spooner manages to shoot the fast-moving robot in the leg. The demolition sequence puts these skills to a more robust test in a new, more hostile environment. The entire structure of the house is collapsing in on Spooner, forcing him to deploy his agility, speed and rapid responses to negotiate the shifting surfaces of the disintegrating house, and his accuracy with a gun to shoot down the door on the move, allowing him and the cat to escape being crushed under the rubble. The relentlessness of the assault leaves Spooner shouting to motivate himself to match the speed of the destruction with his own movement. In this way his psychological resilience and determination (and compassion as he rescues the cat as well as himself), already observed in the earlier chase sequences, are also reconfirmed in this more dangerous new context. Such capabilities will be crucial in the further tests the film sets for Spooner, in which he must fight directly against swarms of hostile robots: the attack while speeding through an underground motorway tunnel and subsequent hand-to-hand combat with a persistent robot after his vehicle has crashed; his rescue of Farber and Dr Calvin from a street attack by robot forces trying to subdue the urban human population; and the film's final action sequence, in which Spooner, Dr Calvin and Sonny work together to repel scores of hostile robots while they try to deactivate V.I.K.I., the supercomputer that has turned against the humans and is controlling the entire city's robot population.

NARRATIVES OF BECOMING

An essential function of the spectacular sequence in the action film is, then, to display the extraordinary capacities of the action hero. But it does so in a way that is inextricably linked with narrative process. In the example from *I, Robot* we have seen how the demolition sequence both reconfirms Spooner's exist-ing physical and mental agility and demonstrates a new level of flexibility in the deployment of that agility, as Spooner manages to overcome proliferating obstacles in this new, dangerous context. But by examining the relationship of the demolition sequence to the action sequences that precede and follow it, we can also see that the action sequences have a developmental purpose, progressively increasing our sense of the hero's capacities as he or she moves towards the final showdown or confrontation that will precipitate the narrative resolution. We need to believe that the hero is, or will become, capable of overcoming the ultimate obstacle the narrative puts in place, and the action sequences are the primary method by which an action film convinces us of this.[4] Action sequences are not, then, a series of stand-alone tests of the hero's endurance, stamina, strength and ingenuity. Instead they operate developmentally across the action film to construct the hero's 'becoming-powerful', what I would like to call a 'narrative of becoming' that articulates the protagonist's physical and emotional trajectory towards achieving full occupation of the heroic action body. This narrative of becoming is an integral part of the main narrative thrust that moves the film towards its resolution. Like *Avatar*, some films thematise this narrative of becoming explicitly, in that part of the plot will involve the training of the hero figure in essential new skills. We might think of *Batman Begins* (2005), in which Bruce Wayne (Christian Bale) must develop his crime-fighting abilities from scratch, teaching himself or being taught a range of skills from street brawling to martial arts to technologically-assisted tricks of perception that allow him to outwit his foes. Or *S.W.A.T.* (2003), which follows a crack team of Special Weapons and Tactics police trainees as they develop their new skills, displayed (in an extended action sequence) in a plane hijacking response exercise before they are put to the real test apprehending an escaped convict and two renegade SWAT officers.

The trigger that prompts the protagonist onto the path towards a heroic physicality can occur within the timespan of the events with which the film is directly concerned, or it can occur further back in the protagonist's past. Either way this trigger often takes the form of a physical or psychological trauma, the memory of which lends vehemence to the hero's motivations and actions in the present. In *I, Robot*, Spooner's memory of his traumatic car accident is inscribed on his mind (the recurring nightmares) as well as across his body (the stiff prosthetic arm), and motivates a hatred of robots that makes him a more persistent detective in the face of others' incredulity (given how safe robots are supposed to be). By the end of the film that hatred is shown at one level to have been misplaced prejudice; Lanning's robot Sonny, who Spooner suspects of murder, was in fact instructed by Lanning himself to assist him in suicide. This was the only chance Lanning had to alert Spooner to the real threat: V.I.K.I., the super-computer controlling all other newly built robots, had decided to ensure humanity's survival by planning to institute a particularly brutal form of martial law, but had been keeping Lanning prisoner in his lab so that he could not communicate his suspicions. At another level Spooner's deep distrust of robots is precisely what drives his investigative journey towards the truth and lends fervour to his actions. The narrative even offers Spooner the opportunity to cathartically re-enact his traumatic memory and transform its outcome second time around. When he is attacked in the motorway tunnel by robots secretly being controlled by V.I.K.I., the attack is initiated by a robot smashing his car window and reaching in to grab Spooner, just like the rescue robot in his flashback. His failed attempt to elude the rescue robot's grasp in the original crash in order to force it to rescue the dying twelve-year-old girl instead is re-enacted, but this time Spooner successfully avoids the scores of malevolent robots as they try to wrench him from his car. The cathartic possibility of a different outcome is encapsulated in Spooner's exchange with the first robot to breach his windscreen. The robot, who is trying to force Spooner to crash at high speeds, reaches in and declares with some irony, 'You are experiencing a car accident.' Spooner's response – 'The *hell* I am' – is an emphatic refusal of the robot's assessment of the situation, this time successfully followed through as Spooner fends off the robot attack. In this way, the trigger for the narrative of becoming I have described is itself narratively relevant; to our sense of the protagonist as a fully psychologised character, and to our sense of his or her motivations, which in turn allow us to understand the ways the hero chooses to move through the causal chain of events in general and through the action sequences in particular.

This is equally true of Jake in *Avatar*, but Jake's case also illustrates the ways in which the narrative of becoming can occupy a complicated trajectory. As I pointed out in the first part of this chapter, Jake's battle injury, which landed him in VA hospital and left him paralysed from the waist down, is the initial trauma that drives him forward, landing him on the planet and spurring his enthusiasm for his Na'vi body and Na'vi life in the Pandoran jungles. This precipitates the first phase of his narrative of becoming, as he learns how to navigate the forest, how to use Na'vi weapons, how to fly and ride Pandoran animals and escape from Pandoran predators, in a series of spectacular action sequences. All these skills seem to be moving him towards being accepted into the Na'vi tribe, the chance to keep his Na'vi body and walk among them permanently. But the skills are also preparing him for the massive battle that climaxes the narrative, when he must put all his newfound skills together with his pre-existing military training, determination and ingenuity in a bid to defend the Na'vi from the human corporation's final military onslaught. The company has discovered that the largest deposit of the precious minerals they are mining for lies beneath the Na'vi tribe's settlement, and after destroying the settlement the company and its military decide to eradicate the Na'vi, who have become obstacles in the path of their commercial mining ambitions. The destruction of the Na'vi settlement, which is firebombed into the ground killing scores of Na'vi including the father of Neytiri (Zoe Saldana), the Na'vi woman with whom Jake is romantically involved, represents a further traumatic trigger. Occurring within the film's timeframe, it intensifies his fervour and his motivation for the final phase of his narrative of becoming.

He witnesses the devastation wreaked by the firebombing firsthand, knowing throughout that it is his intelligence that has made the attack so effective, and afterwards he is rejected by Neytiri and her people. But we know that Jake has amassed a range of skills, both human and Na'vi, that offer the possibility that he can rise above this failed defence of their indigenous tribal home and progress towards a longer-lasting protection of the Na'vis' existence. Jake discovers the humans' plan for an all-out attack intended to exterminate the Na'vi. He works with the Na'vi to orchestrate and lead a surprise ambush of the military's ground and air attack, raining Na'vi and human firepower (arrows, rocks, bullets and Pandoran predators) down onto the humans. The final phase of Jake's narrative of becoming thus shows him not only bringing together his knowledge of military strategy and his newly acquired Na'vi fighting skills, but executing his own cathartic re-enactment of his second traumatic trigger – the firebombing of the Na'vi settlement – this time to defend the Na'vi. This example shows the dynamic relationship between trauma, empowerment and redemptive violence possible in the hero's narrative of becoming, how this is communicated through the action sequences themselves, and how this is integral to our understanding of the hero's psychology, motivations, capacities and actions.

As with other types of popular mainstream Hollywood product, action films embed their spectacular elements in narrative frameworks which, as Dyer puts it, 'situate the thrills' for us (Dyer 2000: 18). While we can debate the relative quality and originality of such narratives, their presence and their often complex operations cannot be denied. Moreover, we have seen that spectacular action sequences also have the capacity to be narratively communicative. Action sequences can function to depict key plot developments, develop and explore the film's themes, and progress our sense of the hero's growing powers and capacity to bring the drama to its resolution. Indeed action sequences are central to our engagement with the hero, tracing a narrative of becoming that is integral to the larger progression of the plot. Presumptions about narrative paucity can result in a lack of reflection and analysis, not just of the narrative itself but the way in which it helps to shape the representation of people in the action film, an issue we will return to in the later chapters. In Chapter 2 we will explore in more detail the heroic action body and the ways in which the audience engages with and invests in its progress, while Chapter 3 will return to the action sequence, investigating its aesthetic characteristics in its contemporary form. Murray Smith's wry observation that 'Reports of the death of narrative in Hollywood filmmaking . . . are surely much exaggerated' (Smith 1998: 13) may continue to fall on deaf ears in some quarters of the press, but this chapter has suggested that despite persistent rumours to the contrary, narrative is 'alive and well' in the contemporary action film and, crucially, in its spectacular action sequences.

NOTES

1. For example, see Schatz 1993, Wyatt 1994, Gross 2000, Dixon 2001 and Sobchack 2006.
2. See Geoff King, who argues that claims about spectacle replacing narrative are 'often based on an exaggerated assumption of the extent to which Hollywood movies were ever *dominated* by a commitment to classical narrative norms' (italics in original) (King 2002: 180). See also Gunning 2000 and Neale 2000.
3. The cat's presence in the scene is interesting. Even a trained cat could not perform (or indeed stay still) in the midst of a building collapse achieved with practical effects (given the fright-inducingly loud explosions and falling objects that that would involve), so the cat's apparent interaction with other scenic elements is clearly constructed in post-production. Aside from introducing a comic element and perhaps also emphasising the fragility of animate forms when faced with the onslaught of debris from the disintegrating house, then, the cat's purpose seems to be to point reflexively to the presence and skill of the digital compositing in the sequence.
4. Sarah Street ascribes a similar function to spectacular costuming in *The Matrix*, in that the 'spectacular garments convince us that the characters are capable of undermining the Matrix' (Street 2001: 99).

CHAPTER 2

The action body

A man chases another man through a construction site and onto a steel building frame. The pursued climbs a ladder to reach the top of the frame and jumps to an adjacent batch of industrial tubing that is suspended mid-air by a large tower crane. His pursuer takes a more direct route, using speed and grip to scale a vertical steel girder, but misses his target by seconds, leaping onto the tubing while his quarry is already climbing up to the horizontal crane jib.[1] Seeing the opportunity to make up some distance the pursuer disconnects the tubing from the crane hook (whereupon the load smashes into the steel construction frame below) causing the hydraulic pulley system to pull the hook block on which he is standing up to the horizontal jib. The two men climb through the metal frame of the jib hundreds of feet above the ground, before the pursued man seizes his chance and leaps to another stationary crane's jib and then onto a nearby partially constructed building shell. The other man, still on the first crane, pauses: he almost missed a lesser jump earlier in the chase, and is unsure if he can make it across the distance between the two cranes. But if he breaks off the pursuit he won't reach his quarry. He steels himself, leaps and misses his footing, dangling precariously from the jib of the second crane before regaining his feet. The jump to the top of the concrete building shell is similarly scrappy – he covers the distance but hits the structure's roof too fast, going into a roll that sends him over the roof edge and crashing into the top of a small out-house before hitting the floor. He shakes his head as if to clear it, and continues the chase.

These three minutes of frenetic action form part of an extended, nine-minute action sequence early in *Casino Royale* (Martin Campbell), the first James Bond film to feature Daniel Craig as agent '007'. Bond is chasing bomb-maker Mollaka (Sébastien Foucan) in order to take him in for questioning. The men sprint, scrabble and jump across the terrain at speed, Bond eager to catch his target, Mollaka equally keen to evade capture. Every stage in the chase involves each man performing risky, stretching physical feats. The presentation matches the frenetic quality of the action with fast cutting between a wide variety of camera positions and angles, and dramatic shifts between close-ups, medium shots and extreme long shots, many of which are in motion. Each of these filmmaking choices draws our gaze to the body in action. For example, an extreme long shot shows Mollaka on the crane's load while Bond, close by at the top of the steel frame, moves off-screen to get sufficient run-up to make the jump to Mollaka's location. The shot distance from the action conveys the scale of the space and its physical risks and challenges: hundreds of feet above the ground, the men must contend with the potentially lethal effects (at this height) of wind and gravity. In addition the shot is not static; it is a creeping zoom that focuses our attention on Mollaka's tenacity and strength as he pulls his entire body up the crane wires in a bid to reach the hook block. To press the point, this shot is bookended by closer shots of construction workers on the ground looking up in amazement at the same sight. A few seconds later in the sequence, as Bond inches closer to Mollaka on the jib, this moment of the pursuit is captured by no fewer than three extreme long shots in quick succession, each sweepingly mobile, each attending to these two bodies in action. First a high angle shot that begins at a distant position left of the two adjacent cranes: it initially frames the jibs of both cranes at once, but swoops into a much closer two shot of the men. Next, as the men move frame right hundreds of metres up, a low angle shot from within the cross-hatched girders of the steel frame sweeps left, rotating to keep the men in view. The final extreme long shot begins from yet another vantage point, a high angle to the right of both cranes and the steel building frame: it swoops round the action from a distance, always keeping the men in the centre section of the frame. These shots also have a further function: to keep the action momentarily at arm's length in order to generate anticipation for the subsequent close-up of Mollaka's determined physical effort to stay ahead of Bond. In both these examples the stylistic choices work to focus attention on and to foreground the work of the body, keeping it constantly in view.

These filmmaking strategies are the key elements of the 'intensified continuity' system that David Bordwell identifies as the 'dominant style of American mass-audience films today': that is, 'rapid editing, bipolar extremes of lens lengths, reliance on close shots, and wide-ranging camera movements' (Bordwell 2006: 120–1). Bordwell explains that '[v]irtually every contemporary mainstream American film will exhibit at least some of them' at some point or other (ibid.: 137). What we can notice immediately from the action sequence in *Casino Royale* is that all four of these strategies are in evidence in the same sequence; moreover, that they are interacting with each other towards the same goal. While any film deploying these strategies (on their own

Bond prepares to make the jump from one crane to the next in *Casino Royale*

or in combination) will use them to focus on what is of narrative interest, most often character action, in the *Casino Royale* sequence the strategies are used to produce a sustained, unambiguous focus specifically on the physically rigorous aspects (exertions, impacts, risks, consequences) of the character action. Close-ups and medium shots pick out the sweating, grimacing faces of the two men as each struggles to best the other, and the crunching thumps as their bodies come in combative contact on the jib. Extreme long shots punctuate the sequence, their distance from the action underscoring the vulnerability of these bodies, who look small in the face of the situation's substantial risks: of losing balance, yielding to gravity from a great height, and suffering a deadening impact on hard surfaces below. The swooping, mobile nature of these long shots intensifies the sense of physical risk by emphasising the drop to the ground from above or below. Rapid cuts between these different lens lengths and camera positions work with a dramatic, percussive musical score to lend the sequence a breathless pace and rhythm that matches the varying rhythms of the men's movements (bursts of activity interspersed with pauses to collect body and mind). Here, then, the different filmmaking strategies Bordwell identifies are not simply all evident in the same sequence, but work together in an emphatic, insistent way for a particular purpose: to focus our attention on the spectacle of the body in action, its exertions and achievements, its persistence and agility, and the environmental risks and challenges it faces at each moment. Other strategies not yet mentioned are also deployed for the same ends, such as slow motion and louder soundtrack elements, elements I will be discussing further in Chapter 3. Overall the mode of presentation conforms to the strategies of emphasis I described in the previous chapter as also defining spectacle: that is, framing and foregrounding striking feats of physical achievement through formal means that attempt to achieve an intensification in the spectator's engagement with the body. In this way, the body itself is constructed as spectacle.

This rather emphatic mode of presenting the body in action is a staple of contemporary action cinema, observable in a range of films including the *Lord of the Rings* trilogy (2001, 2002, 2003), the *Transformers* movies (2007, 2009, 2011), the *Matrix* sequels (2003), the *Pirates of the Caribbean* franchise (2003, 2006, 2007), and the *Transporter* films (2002, 2005, 2008). This is not to suggest that such a presentational mode is unique to contemporary action films; Bordwell argues that contemporary mainstream film style is, for the most part, simply an intensified version of classical filmmaking practices, what Bordwell calls 'Hollywood's judicious balance of continuity and innovation' (ibid.: 27). Instead, in this chapter I want to use the body-focused nature of these filmmaking practices – as they are deployed in contemporary action cinema, and as demonstrated by the *Casino Royale* sequence – as a jumping-off point to explore more fully the importance of the body in the action film. I argued in Chapter 1 that the physical experiences of the hero are central to the action film's narrative, mapped out and developed in significant part in action sequences that articulate the hero's physical narrative of becoming. As the example from *Casino Royale* illustrates, this 'body-centredness' also extends unequivocally to the audio–visual presentation of the action sequences. Both narrative and aesthetic design thus appeal explicitly to our sense of the hero's physicality. At the same time, writers, commentators and film critics regularly describe action movies and the effects of watching them in bodily terms. For example, Richard Corliss at *rogerbert.com* praises a vehicular action sequence in *Live Free or Die Hard* that 'lets crazy-gifted stunt drivers bend the laws of physics, geometry and adrenaline to create a moviegoer's contact high' (Corliss 2007: paragraph 3); for A.O. Scott in *The New York Times* the *The Hurt Locker* (2008) is 'a viscerally exciting, adrenaline-soaked tour de force of suspense and surprise' from which spectators will emerge 'shaken, exhilarated and drained' (Scott 2009: paragraph 2). Scholarly responses include Arroyo's assertion about *Mission: Impossible* (1996) that it 'assaults the senses' (Arroyo 2000 'Mission': 22), and Barry Langford's suggestion that more recent spectacular action sequences are 'designed to hammer the audience into a state of dazed battle fatigue' (Langford 2010: 255). How might we more precisely account for the viewer's experience of action cinema, and specifically his or her engagement with on-screen action bodies? And how do on-screen bodies generate meaning in the overtly body-centred action film?

THE CHALLENGE OF 'LANGUAGING' EXPERIENCE[2]

I want to begin by addressing the viewer's experience of action cinema, which as we have seen is so often characterised in sensory terms. Indeed, the 'sense-ational' qualities of the contemporary action film are often taken for granted, without a clear picture emerging of exactly how such films exhilarate their audiences. Amongst scholars sympathetic to action cinema's mode of address there has been a tentativeness about how to describe or account for the mechanics of the relationship between the spectator and the action film. Richard Dyer has proposed that action films promote

> an active engagement with the world, going out into it, doing to the environment; yet enjoyment of them means allowing them to come to you, take you over, do you . . . we may identify with [the action heroes], imagine the rush of excitement as we brace ourselves against, and master, the world; but we're also letting ourselves be carried along, going with the flow of the movie, ecstatically manipulated. (Dyer 2000: 21)[3]

Dyer's account highlights the contrast between what he characterises as the spectator's submission to the images, and the films' own thematic emphasis on active, physical interactions with the film world. But there is also an interesting contradiction here between this allegedly passive or disempowered viewing position ('take you over, do you'), and Dyer's simultaneous description of the spectator's experience in terms of a lively interplay of emotional and experiential responses, as we 'imagine the rush of excitement' and 'brace ourselves' in response to the heroic action we are witnessing. Tasker's definition of action is equally alert to action cinema's capacity for dynamic affect, but harbours its own contradictions. She suggests that 'specific qualities of action are, it seems, to do with pace, excitement, exhilaration: a visceral, even sensual, evocation of movement and violence' (Tasker 2004: 5). While some of the terms Tasker uses relate either to action cinema's mode of depiction ('pace', 'evocation of movement and violence') or to its effect on the spectator ('excitement', 'exhilaration'), some words revealingly oscillate between the two: 'visceral' and 'sensual' seem, in my view appropriately, to refer to both the presentation of and viewing of cinematic action.

The press and academic accounts of viewing action cinema quoted above clearly suggest that the spectator's engagement with the action film should be understood as an *experience* that manifests itself physically as well as mentally and emotionally. But as Tasker's and Dyer's attempts illustrate, it is precisely this vivid experience of viewing the action film's preoccupation with spectacles of active bodies that writers have found difficult to articulate. Tasker's sound assertion that 'the cinema as sensuous experience is too often neglected' was prefaced by her acknowledgment that a complete account of action cinema's sensuous pleasures was 'rather difficult to render in academic prose' (Tasker 1993: 6). For his part Dyer was happy to assert cinema's 'celebration of sensational movement' but more tentative about its effects, suggesting that we respond to these celebrations 'in some still unclear sense "as if real"' (Dyer [1994] 2000: 18). As Vivian Sobchack observes, 'although Dyer acknowledges the importance of the spectator's direct bodily experience of cinema, he is at a loss to explain its very existence' (Sobchack 2004: 58). In the years since, several scholars including Sobchack have extended the study of the phenomenology of aesthetics to address film directly, proposing phenomenological accounts of the spectator's embodied relationship to film images. As the next two sections of this chapter will seek to argue, this approach makes possible an explanation of the embodied nature of the spectator's engagement with the action body and with action film's modes of presentation, which Dyer et al. so vividly gesture towards.

EXPERIENCING THE ACTION BODY

As Laura U. Marks declares in *The Skin of the Film: Intercultural Cinema, Embodiment, and the Senses*, '[f]ilm is grasped not solely by an intellectual act but by the complex perception of the body as a whole' (Marks 2000: 145). Phenomenological film theory proceeds from the basic principle that our perception of the world, like our material existence in the world, is always already embodied. In his influential study *Phenomenology of Perception* Maurice Merleau-Ponty declares:

> Our own body is in the world as the heart is in the organism: it keeps the visible spectacle constantly alive, it breathes life into it and sustains it inwardly . . . My body is the fabric into which all objects are woven, and it is, at least in relation to the perceived world, the general instrument of my 'comprehension'. (Merleau-Ponty 2006: 235, 273)

This idea that we understand the world through our bodies has been taken up and applied to the cinematic viewing experience by a number of writers. Vivian Sobchack explains that as ' "lived bodies" ' our visual perception of the world 'is always already "fleshed out" ' so that when we watch a film our vision

> is 'in-formed' and given meaning by our other sensory means of access to the world: our capacity not only to hear, but also to touch, to smell, to taste, and always to proprioceptively feel our dimension and movement in the world. In sum, the film experience is meaningful *not to the*

side of our bodies but because of our bodies. (Sobchack 2004: 60, emphasis in original)

This certainly moves us away from the idea that filmgoers are passive receptacles for cinematic information. Instead, filmgoing is a lively encounter in which the spectator has an embodied response to onscreen stimuli. Described by Sobchack as a process of 'reciprocation', the spectator's body 'fills in the gap in its sensual grasp of the figural world onscreen by turning back on itself to reciprocally (albeit not sufficiently) "flesh it out" into literal physicalised sense' (ibid.: 82). When we are watching *Casino Royale*'s energetic Madagascar crane sequence our senses respond to the images, sounds and rhythms of the physical acts displayed. As the men force their bodies up the steel building frame, fight against gravity while scrabbling to gain their footing on the crane's wires and structure, and punch and kick each other, the viewer's senses reciprocate, fleshing out the perception of each exerting stretch of the active body, each impact with another body or object, each swing, jump and fall. Sobchack's ideas also seem to explain those moments when our bodies react in outwardly obvious ways to what is unfolding onscreen: recoiling from the sudden unexpected appearance of an attacker, tensing our bodies during scenes of suspense, shifting in our seats or ducking to dodge an object flying straight at the camera, as well as less obvious reactions – the hairs pricking at the back of the neck, the momentarily held breath, the knotted stomach. We know rationally that we do not occupy the fictional world in which these objects or situations would have purchase, but our bodies fill in the gap, fleshing out some of what that 'being in the film world' might feel like.

This fleshing out helps to account for our engagement with characters' bodies onscreen and is particularly pertinent to certain modes of Hollywood filmmaking which, through their subject-matter and style of presentation, repeatedly foreground the body's active physicality. In her article 'Film Bodies: Gender, Genre, and Excess', Linda Williams calls horror, melodrama and pornography 'body genres' because they provide 'the spectacle of a body caught in the grip of intense sensation or emotion' (Williams 1991: 4).[4] Williams suggests that these films are marked as excessive, and acquire low cultural status, because of a 'perception that the body of the spectator is caught up in an almost involuntary mimicry of the emotion or sensation of the body on the screen', evidence of 'an apparent lack of proper esthetic [sic] distance, a sense of over-involvement in sensation and emotion' (ibid.: 4, 5). Notwithstanding the fact that the viewing of any film involves an embodied, sensory experience, I would want to extend Williams' category of body genres to include action cinema, which depicts the body 'in the grip of intense sensation' because it is operating at physical extremes, and which has the potential to prompt involuntary physical responses in the spectator. Indeed it is notable that the low cultural status accorded to pornography and horror has also been bestowed on action cinema at certain points in its history.[5] David MacDougall points out that the type of involuntary mimicry when looking at another body that Williams describes is observable from 'earliest infancy, when babies imitate their mothers' facial expressions and cry upon hearing others cry' (MacDougall 2006: 23). Drawing on psychologist Martin Hoffman's account of this phenomenon, MacDougall's explanation is worth quoting at length. He notes that involuntary mimicry consists of:

> two phases, the first a motor response, the second an emotional response, although the two occur in close succession. In the first, the spectator involuntarily and unconsciously imitates the expressions and postures of the other person and tends to move in synchrony with them. In the second, there is feedback from these expressions and posture to the emotions, creating feelings appropriate to them. (ibid.: 23)

This account underlines the fact that we make sense of images of other bodies on a corporeal level before we make intellectual sense of them. However, I want to add a little more definition to our developing account of the spectator's sensory engagement with the action body.

While involuntary mimicry has an outward-facing, communicative function (people often subconsciously mirror each others' expressions and postures if they are trying to put each other at ease, for example), my sense is that the spectator's corporeal recognition/reciprocation extends beyond signs of mimicry that are outwardly visible to responses that are internal and less obvious. In the mid-1990s a group of Italian neuroscientists discovered what they call 'mirror neurons' in the part of the brain responsible for controlling movement, the premotor cortex. These 'mirror neurons' respond in the same way whether a person is watching an action or performing it, introducing the possibility of mental rehearsal of an action without the body having to move itself (see Rizzolatti et al. 1996; Cisek and Kalaska 2004). This discovery does not counter the existence of involuntary mimicry, but introduces the possibility that the brain's capacity to process and corporeally 'flesh out' viewed actions extends beyond literal, physically enacted mimicry. This makes sense if we think of the phenomenon of synaesthesia, whereby sense impressions are created in one of the bodily senses (taste, hearing, sight, smell, touch) but experienced in another. Marks notes that cinema's sensory effects are often 'intersensory' in this way: 'sounds may evoke textures, sights may evoke smells (rising steam or smoke evokes smells of fire, incense, or cooking)' (Marks 2000: 213). In fact as Marks points out, cinema is by definition a synaesthetic medium, appealing 'to the integration and commutation of sensory experience within the body' through its basic, ever-repeating act of 'appealing to one sense in order to represent the experience of another' (ibid.: 222). The way in which the action body addresses the spectator is a complicated reciprocal process, difficult to 'grasp' in the act of intellectual analysis undertaken 'after the fact' of immediate but transient corporeal response. Just as the operations of synaesthesia are fluid over time, the relationship between the film and the viewer is, in Jennifer Barker's words, 'immediate, tangible, and yet tenuous; the possibility of tension, slippage, and resistance inheres' (Barker 2009: 15). And yet, armed with an awareness of the body's capacity to 'flesh out' in different ways the physical acts it witnesses, we have the tools to understand or at the very least suggest how particular moments in action cinema communicate 'through the body', to make sense of why the hero's physicalised narrative of becoming is of central importance to the action film's narrative, and why these films might appeal in the first place.

Action films trade in spectacles of physical mastery, in fantasies of empowerment. Their appeal rests at base on the nature of everyday human existence. We lead complicated lives, in which our own sense of empowerment can shift moment by moment, subject to social, economic, natural and psychological forces over which we can have only partial (if any) control. Moreover the urban existence that is common for many people brings its own shifting dynamics, its own uncertainties and spatial constraints. As Tasker has pointed out, 'images of physical power' can function 'as a counterpoint to an experience of the world defined by restrictive limits' (Tasker 1993: 127). Action bodies, with their capacity to escape physical constraints, to subject environments, people, and more abstract entities like institutions and unruly criminal organisations to their physical mastery, offer fantasies of empowerment that allow us to rehearse our own dreamed-of escapes, our own becoming-masterful, in a fantasy context, allow us to 'feel' this mastery for ourselves through our sensorial connection with the body of the hero. Of course, this mastery is often achieved after momentary losses in the hero's control of the situation, so that we also 'feel' the loss before mastery is regained. Obvious examples in *Casino Royale* include Bond being mistaken for a bomber at an airport and being pressed into the ground, his hands pulled behind his back, all his bodily potential constrained by over-enthusiastic police officers; and the torture scene, in which arch-villain Le Chiffre (Mads Mikkelsen) beats Bond's genitalia repeatedly while he is bound to a chair, hoping the excruciating pain will force him to reveal the code to a bank account containing money Bond won from him in a poker game. Such temporary losses of control make the body's subsequent return to mastery register with even more force. These fantasies are grounded in physical movement, and while we may not have ever leapt from a car onto a moving train, or used mixed martial arts to fell several opponents, we are familiar with the sensory experience of human comportment and physical exertion, and this informs our embodied engagement with the spectacle of the body's mastery. Whether in the gym, running for a bus, or racing with friends in childhood, even the most sedentary of human beings have become conscious of their physical limits at some point, when exertion became unpleasant, when the body strained to complete the task at hand. It is at the fictional equivalent of this real-world borderline between the physically possible and impossible that the action body demonstrates its tenacity, skill and strength, and thus supplies us our fantasies of empowerment.[6]

The 'rules' of the fictional universe in which these bodies move are often carefully designed to preserve a viscerally felt sense of physical effort. A relationship to real-world physics and physiology, to real-world physical correspondences of weight, momentum, force and the materiality of bodies and objects, is retained. This permits a sensorial recognition on the part of the spectator of physical principles that seem to approximate to our own real-world universe. These correspondences may of course be more strained in some strands of action film than others: beyond the generic conventions of the action hero's pronounced physical resilience and unusual amount of luck, each action film establishes its own rules for its physical universe, a process dependent in part on the particularity of the generic mix. In each action film the limits of the onscreen body's capacities are established, usually in the first action sequences, to be reiterated in later sequences. These limits make reference to real-world correspondences, and set the boundaries for what physical acts will be effortful, risk-filled, easy or impossible.[7] For example, the opening of *Rollerball* (John McTiernan, 2002) features the hero Jonathan Cross (Chris Klein) engaged in an illegal downhill street luge race in San Francisco: we see his body absorb significant impact as the luge repeatedly catapults into the air and slams back down to earth, and his strength and precision as he takes knocks from vehicles and from his antagonistic opponent while directing his luge through the tightest of spaces and the shifting landscape of San Francisco traffic. Cross also strives to avoid impacts that would kill him in the real world. As a result the opening establishes both the physical capacities that will make him an excellent player in rollerball (which is his destiny in the film) and the physical limits to those capacities. Such rules might be subtly or more extensively different in scale from our own experience of 'being-in-the-world', and can help to intensify our sensing of the body's work. The *Casino Royale* crane sequence works hard to remind us of the rules that apply to its protagonists' bodies, in part by the way in which the business of the chase acts on the environment and people of the construction site. When Mollaka and Bond are both traversing the structure of steel girders, Mollaka finds his way blocked by a construction worker, and sends him tumbling to the ground. The man's prone body speaks of the fatal force of the impact from that height. Later Bond disconnects the load of industrial tubing from the crane and the metal tubes respond to realistic-looking levels of gravity and physical resistance, bouncing down through the gaps in the structure of steel girders to the ground (rather than, say, mysteriously passing through the girders, bending their surfaces, or hovering in mid-air, as might be the case in a stridently fantastical science fiction or fantasy film where the physical rules of the diegetic world could be quite different). Thus we are reminded that gravity operates in a familiar way, and witness close to realistic notions of weight, momentum, movement and the force of impact, all of which emphasise the risks and challenges the chased and chasing bodies are encountering. The men's own physical limits are also established: Mollaka's fluid running and jumping contrasts sharply with Bond's less agile movements, making 007's mastery of the environment seem tenuous rather than certain. The contrast between the two men's physical capacities comes to a head as Bond mismanages both the jump from one crane to the next and the jump from the second crane to the building shell, risking serious injury in the resulting uncontrolled fall.

Here we are witness to that moment where Bond comes up against what he (and we, based on the earlier mis-jump) perceives to be his physical limit, but it is also the moment that we see him use mental determination and physical control to press against this limit and move slightly beyond it, jumping further and surviving. When the action film establishes the physics of its world and the human body's limits within it, then the prospect is also offered that, if the heroic body pushes itself hard enough, it might reach or indeed even cross the borderline of physically achievable action. What is at stake in the action film and in the fantasies of empowerment it provides is thus not simply the fact of the hero's physical capacities as we see them, but his or her physical potential: we often thrill at the possibilities of what the action hero might do next, as well as what he or she is doing now. Dancer and theorist Erin Manning suggests that our bodies are always vibrating with physical potential: '[o]ur bodies,' she proposes, 'are vectors of emergence that generate virtual embodiments in a future anterior we can only reach towards' (Manning 2007: 120). The action body vibrates with the future possibilities of its own becoming, generating a corporeal anticipation on the part of the spectator (in addition to the intellectual anticipation he or she might also experience). Manning's concept can help us to see that action sequences (and moments within action sequences) are periods of duration across which the potential of the action body is enacted. That is, the action body expresses its potential over time, across particular gestures or actions, as well as across the film as a whole. These 'vectors of emergence', intended in an abstract sense in Manning's formulation, become literalised in the action body's corporeal trajectory towards mastery across the narrative, and in its physical trajectories through space in each action sequence. We will subject the orchestration of bodies and elements in the contemporary action sequence to further scrutiny in the next chapter. But as the moment at which Bond renegotiates his own limits illustrates, the action body is in a continual state of 'becoming', perpetually renegotiating limits as his or her mastery develops and as the film seeks to escalate the spectator's sensory engagement with and exhilaration at that body's achievements. So to qualify the assertion made earlier in this chapter, the action film does not trade in fantasies of empowerment where empowerment is a fixed and stable state, but in fantasies of becoming-powerful, that transitional state where the possibilities of the body are both in the process of being revealed and still full of potential; where the body's power is not 'fixed' in place but open to the imagination's speculations and aspirations, to fears of loss of power and aspirations to becoming-powerful. Where action narratives come and go, end and begin again, the fantasy of overcoming that the spectator rehearses through the action body can exist in perpetuity rather than being brought back down to earth, always present in action cinema's fictional universe, waiting to be accessed and experienced once more. In this way the popularity of action films, their expansion into myriad generic hybrids, and their status as the primary form of blockbuster product, seem a product of the desire to return again and again to a state of embodied exhilaration, to the fantasies of becoming-powerful that have the capacity to resonate corporeally in the most arresting ways.

FLESHING OUT MEANING

Having established the spectator's embodied connection with the action body in the context of the film's mapping of that body's skills, limits and potential, I want to offer a brief illustration of how these processes might inform the production of meaning by looking again at *Casino Royale*. The film's physical universe and its hero's own capacities seem much closer to real-world equivalents than in some other action films (witness the hero of *Transporter 2* (2005), Frank Martin (Jason Statham), being impervious to hails of bullets from two semi-automatic weapons pointed directly at his body, for example), or indeed than in earlier James Bond films. The filmmakers had made a conscious decision to revivify the franchise by delivering a 'new, grittier Bond',[8] and by taking us back to the beginning of Bond's tenure as a 'licensed to kill' spy. The film opens with a sequence that gives a sense – in both senses of that word – that Bond's capacities are nascent and thus unproven. It shows the two kills that Bond must undertake in order to achieve promotion to 'oo' status, making clear he is at the beginning of his 007 career. Shot in black and white and filmed quite differently from the more common strategies employed in the crane sequence, it establishes the almost fully realistic physical and physiological rules of the film's universe, and demonstrates some of Bond's physical capacities. But it also works through the bodies of spectator and character to pose questions about the inexperienced agent's uncertain potential.

In a starkly monochrome low-angle shot, a car quietly rolls up outside an imposing but expensive-looking office block. A title reveals we are somewhere in Prague; it is night, and the snow-covered street is deserted. In a series of low-angle shots the driver exits the car and makes his way to his office. Safe inside, he realises with a start that there is someone sitting in the shadows. It's Bond, here to stop section chief Dryden (Malcolm Sinclair) selling further national secrets. Dryden explains his confidence that Bond hasn't been sent to kill him, because there are no kills on his file and to become an 'oo' takes two. As Bond finishes his sentence for him, the scene's stillness is ruptured by a cut to the middle of a frantic fight in a men's toilet. Bond kicks his unidentified opponent through the door of a toilet stall, punching him twice before the man pushes the stall door shut behind Bond while trying to get purchase. Bond responds by slamming him through the stalls sideways until they meet a brick wall, whereupon his opponent counters Bond's punch, elbow chop and door face-slam by pulling them both bodily through the final stall's door. Bond is on his feet before the other man, kicking him in the face and blocking a thrown waste bin with his foot. An equally sudden cut throws us back into the present: Dryden is now pointing a gun straight at Bond. But it is not loaded, the ammunition removed before Dryden's arrival. Realising he is Bond's second kill, the section chief asks how his contact (the man in the bathroom) died. 'Not well' Bond replies, prompting a second abrupt cut back to the end of the earlier fight. A massive punch sends the contact crashing into the sinks and onto the floor. Bond grabs the man and starts pressing into his windpipe, dragging him by the neck to a full sink, in which he proceeds to drown him. Afterwards we cut back to the present once again, and after a short exchange of words Bond shoots Dryden dead.

This description just of the action itself in the flashback and present-day sequences (rather than, say, how it was shot and performed) illustrates already that the scene seeks not just to establish Bond's physical capabilities but to characterise them as divided – even contradictory – in nature. Silent and stealthy when he needs to be, he is also able to use speed, strength and a brawling fighting style to best his opponent in the men's room sequences. This might have indicated an all-rounder, but such an extreme difference in the manner of the two kills makes it instead seem almost as if there are two Bonds, one more 'civilised', organised and quietly effective from a distance (he shoots Dryden from his seat across the room, with a gun fitted with a silencer), the other more uneven, scrappier and unpredictable in approach. In addition, he allows himself to get into the close-quarters brawl with his armed target in the men's room, which puts him at more risk of injury, of being unbalanced, of the advantage shifting to his opponent. Bond wins the fight, but it seems more through brute force than fighting skill, and it looks untidy and contingent. This contrast between killing 'styles' is intensified still further by the style of presentation, and the physical performances of the actors in each part of the scene. The Prague sections are marked by chiaroscuro lighting reminiscent of *film noir* as well as a menacing stillness that is expressed by static compositions and a fairly slow editing pace but also by the men's poses, both of whom openly perform relaxed, seated postures while remaining poised for action. In comparison to the stillness and spaciousness of the Dryden office, the men's room fight takes place in much smaller spaces including the toilet stalls themselves, and the handheld camerawork and the editing communicate the two men's scramble for dominance. The camera is quite mobile, adjusting often to reframe the shifting axis of physical advantage. While this gives an impression that the camera is trying to keep up with an unpredictable fight unfolding 'live', these pans and tilts also emphasise the force of particular actions: the kicking of the contact through the door of the first stall, the crash of both men through the final stall door and onto the floor, Bond dragging the contact up bodily by his neck. The men's performances foreground the extreme exertions demanded of them in what is at base a brutal and desperate fight for survival: grimaces in both pain and exertion are accompanied by effortful grunts, yelps of pain and, later, the drowning man's gurgles and Bond's snatched, heavy breaths. Cutting is faster and more dynamic than in the Dryden sequences, combining shots from a diverse range of angles in quick succession, and including a striking jump cut early in the first sequence which emphasises the dazing impact of one of Bond's punches. The pace of the editing slows in the second bathroom sequence for the purpose of emphasising physical action and advantage: the longer takes underline the sustained physical force Bond is having to apply to keep his target's head underwater long enough to drown him: a hands-on, exhausting and very different kill from the 'clean', at-arm's-length shooting of Dryden.

In this way the opening sets in play a narrative theme that will focus on the fact that, newly promoted to 'oo' status, Bond's capacity to be 'up to the job' is still in question. Bond is unpredictable not just physically (because his spying and killing skills are unproven) but in his attitude. Early in the film Bond sparks a diplomatic row by killing Mollaka in full view of surveillance cameras inside an embassy, despite the fact that, as dialogue at the start of the Madagascar scene reveals, he has been instructed to take Mollaka alive. His superior 'M' (Judi Dench) is livid, accusing him of letting his arrogance affect his professionalism, and opining that she cannot trust him: 'I knew it was too early to promote you.' For his part Bond feels his job is inherently conflicted, responding to M's dressing-down with the question, 'So you want me to be half monk, half hit-man?' This Bond may be expressionless, but his divided state and his (and others') uncertainty about his judgment and abilities make sense to us not simply because of our intellectual assimilation of the opening's key narrative details and its dramatic action, but because our bodies have 'made sense' of the beginning sequences too. Through the staging and presentation, and thus 'through their body', the spectator experiences the divided Bond in the dichotomous nature of the two hits, the apparent stability conveyed in the Dryden killing compared with the free-wheeling, tenuous control Bond displays in the bathroom brawl. The unknown extent and nature of Bond's capacities is 'felt' through the juxtaposition between the two Bond kills, and reiterated in an embodied way in later scenes: when he misjudges the jumps in the Madagascar crane sequence; gets caught out by poison at the card game; and gets caught out once again by the bound body of Vesper (Eva Green) lying on a road – in swerving to avoid her he rolls his car and is snatched by Le Chiffre's men, incarcerated and tortured, only to be rescued by an unidentified man. In a film world where who one can trust and the extent of criminal machinations is difficult if not impossible to discern, the action body here is an unsettling site of uncertainty rather than of unproblematic and stable mastery.

The sensory impressions left by these sequences contribute to both our intellectual and corporeal responses to Bond's later attempts to negotiate the narrative's obstacles and bring narrative resolution. The final action sequence, in which Bond battles to get a briefcase of cash back from criminals amidst the crumbling structure of a Venetian house that is sinking into the canal, provides a perfect opportunity to enact the culmination of his narrative of becoming-powerful. Bond is shown bringing together the opposing styles he first displayed at the film's start, as he combines smooth marksmanship with hand to hand combat to dispatch the members of the criminal gang. Yet the sequence does not permit Bond full mastery of the situation: one of the criminals escapes with the case while Bond is trying to save his love interest, Vesper, from drowning. The dynamic, shifting rhythms of the action in the main section of the sequence are replaced by the sombre rhythm of Bond giving chest compressions in vain to the motionless Vesper, a rhythm that soon falters into stillness as he accepts she is dead. This feels like the culmination of our embodied uncertainty about Bond, instead of the triumph of his capacities as hero. The film ends with a brief scene in which Bond finds the man who set in motion the events that led to Vesper's death. Bond stands above the man in a static pose, gun in hand, back in the franchise's trademark black suit. He declares, perhaps for the first time in his career, 'The name's Bond – James Bond,' and while we might thrill momentarily at the impression that he is no longer a divided figure, encouraged by the brassy blare of the James Bond theme exploding onto the soundtrack, our bodies have experienced the contingency of that confident self-assertion in all the action sequences that preceded it. Offering a divided hero, then, the film works through the body to express that contingency, lending force to the verbalised uncertainties of those around Bond and to our anticipatory apprehension as each action sequence unfolded. What reads on paper as a straightforward inversion of key elements of the traditional James Bond universe (including Bond's usual self-assurance and competence, and – excluding exceptions that prove the rule – the uncomplicated overcoming of clearly identified antagonists) compels because it resonates and is communicated through the body. In Sobchack's words, the film 'provoke[s] in us the "carnal thoughts" that ground and inform more conscious analysis' (Sobchack 2004: 60). By keeping in mind the ways in which the spectator fleshes out their engagement with the action body as we analyse how the action body addresses its spectator, we see how this embodied experience also has the capacity to 'flesh out' our narrative comprehension.

EXPERIENCING THE ACTION FILM

I want to end this chapter by thinking beyond the action body, to suggest that action film itself – not just the action body – seeks to engage the body of the spectator. A running theme in these first two chapters – which will be continued into the next chapter and throughout the book – is the importance of aesthetics: how action is shown, how the action body is presented to us and foregrounded for us, how force, impact and exertion are conveyed through the different strategies at filmmakers' disposal. As we explored the spectator's embodied engagement with the action body, it was impossible not to mention these elements of presentation, the audio–visual strategies that point us to bodies and encourage us to experience them and sensorially respond to them in particular ways. A further point has been implicit in my discussion so far, and is worth now making plain: that the context the film provides for the action body is, as much as the work of the body itself, experienced by the spectator. In the *I, Robot* demolition sequence we considered in Chapter 1 for example, I spoke of the risk-filled environment that contextualised our sensory appreciation of Spooner's exertions and physical achievements; and in the *Casino Royale* crane sequence I noted the ways that the extreme long shots forced us to experience the scale of the space Bond and Mollaka were suspended above, and thus the physical stakes of their actions. So part of this context for the body is how the film itself seems to be stylistically 'in sympathy' with the action body's predicament, inviting the spectator's sensory recognition of the situation by using means that extend beyond the body. To take account of this we need to broaden our understanding of the spectator's embodied engagement with the action film, taking it beyond a direct connection with the action body to the film as a whole.

In her discussion of Linda Williams' essay on 'body genres', Jennifer Barker argues that the concept of mimicry needs to be expanded in order to account fully for how the film addresses the viewer:

mimicry is too complex to be only character-centered. That is, viewers' bodily responses to films might be mimicry in another sense: not mimicry of characters, but of the film itself. Perhaps viewers respond to whole cinematic structures – textural, spatial, or temporal structures, for example – that somehow resonate with their own textual, spatial, and temporal structures. (Barker 2009: 74)

Drawing on Sobchack's seminal formulation of the 'film body' set out in *The Address of the Eye: A Phenomenology of Film Experience* (1992), Barker suggests a film body that is informed by human 'bodily behaviors' (Barker 2009: 81), for whom human movement is the constant point of reference. Conceptualising a film body that is more than the sum of its literal parts, Barker argues that this body's different technological and artistic aspects combine either to mimic or transcend the limits of human movement and embodied cognition. 'The film adopts our proprioception,' Barker argues, 'the sense we have of our bodies in space; it may confirm it or thwart it by its own movements, but always it is indebted to it' (ibid.: 81–2). In *Casino Royale*, when the film joins Bond and Dryden's contact in the claustrophobic space of the toilet stall, the camera swish-pans and reframes urgently, performing the movements of an observer caught reluctantly in the space of the fight and trying to keep up with it. Here in some respects there is a literalisation of the notional observer's human comportment in the camera's own movements. At the same time the cutting to different camera angles communicates on a more abstract level the tenuous nature of Bond's 'hold' on or position in the fight. In other sequences, the difference between human comportment and capacities and the film body's movements are much more marked. When the camera swoops around the battling bodies of Mollaka and Bond atop the crane, it is enacting a mastery of space which the men aspire to but cannot achieve, and extending this exhilarating experience also to the spectator, so that we feel this gap between what the men aspire to and their actual physical limits. Elsewhere a film's transcendence of the limits of human movement can map directly onto and intensify the fantasies of becoming-powerful being enacted by the action body. For example, the web-slinging sequences in each of the *Spider-Man* films (Sam Raimi, 2002, 2004, 2007) depict the titular hero swinging between the buildings and skyscrapers of New York, while the camera tracks Spider-Man and mimics his exhilarating, impossible movements with its own swooping aerial manoeuvres. Thus the gap between human and film bodies generates meaning as efficiently as the film's mimicking of the human body. Barker eloquently sums up the film body's address in the following way:

> We are invited and encouraged to commit ourselves to the film's space as well as our own, caught up 'there' and 'here' at the same time. We hitch

ourselves to the film's body because we can, because it seems so easy, because the film's body moves in ways similar to ours. The empathy between the film's and viewer's bodies goes so deeply that we can feel the film's body, live vicariously through it, and experience its movements to such an extent that we ourselves become momentarily as graceful or powerful as the film's body, and we leave the theater feeling invigorated or exhausted, though we ourselves have hardly moved a muscle. (ibid.: 83)

Here Barker's words allow us to bring together the film's, and the action body's, address to the spectator, and the spectator's reciprocal fleshing out. If the action cinema is 'body-centred', so too is its subject-matter and its pre-occupations, its spectacles and modes of presentation. What we haven't yet considered is the different kinds of bodies that are permitted, celebrated and denigrated in action cinema, an enquiry that will be central to the chapters on representation that follow later in the book. In the next chapter, we place the action body in the 'landscape' of the action sequence, as we consider the aesthetics and impulses of this most spectacular element of the action film.

NOTES

1. On a tower crane, the horizontal section of the structure that carries the load is called the 'jib'. The crane load is suspended from a 'hook block' by metal wires and the height of the load is dictated by a hydraulic winch positioned on a 'counter-jib' on the opposite end of the crane's horizontal section. The winch controls the wires that connect the load to the hook block.
2. This phrase is a reference to phenomenologist Maxine Sheets-Johnstone's essay 'On the Challenge of Languaging Experience' in which she addresses the problem that '[B]odily feelings are not easily or readily describable, especially when it comes to affectivity and movement,' problems that scholars and commentators also encounter in their attempts to describe the lively sensory effects mobilised by the action film (Maxine Sheets-Johnstone 2009: 363).
3. Dyer's essay is also worth consulting for its provocative reflection on how action cinema positions the spectator in gendered terms.
4. The phrase 'body genre' was first used by Carol Clover in a 1987 article (Clover 1987: 189) that would become part of Clover's seminal contribution to scholarly writing on the horror film, *Men, Women and Chain Saws* (1992).
5. For example, the low cultural status afforded the later manifestations of the 1970s urban vigilante cycle (such as the *Death Wish* series (1974, 1982, 1985, 1987, 1994)) and the 1980s action B-movies that proved so popular in the home video market (such as *Forced Vengeance* (1982), *Bloodsport* (1988), *Above the Law* (1988), *Kickboxer* (1989) and so on). We can see traces of this kind of value judgment in the tendency to dismiss big budget action films as devoid of narrative interest or quality.
6. This does raise the question of whether the level or nature of sensory engagement would be

different for individuals who have not had access to this kind of sensory experience in their own lives – perhaps through being drastically less able-bodied from birth or having suffered some kind of brain damage at birth, for example. Such a question, although outside the immediate scope of this book, demands further research.

7. Here I am drawing on Stephen Prince's theory of correspondences, which he applied in relation to the perceived veracity of digital imaging (2002: 116).

8. A quote from *James Bond: For Real*, featurette on the *Casino Royale* 2-disc 'Collectors Edition', released by Sony Pictures Home Entertainment UK, 2007.

CHAPTER 3

The action sequence

The action sequence is one of the defining elements of action cinema, displaying dramatic physical action with a dynamism and intensity that marks it out from other sequences. It is perceived by scholars and industry executives alike to be a crucial ingredient in the blockbuster format, and can provide exhilarating and riveting spectacles for audiences. Geoff King (2006) and David Bordwell (2006) have both offered useful accounts of the visual strategies that characterise the modern action sequence, and we will be touching upon some of their ideas in this chapter. However, rather than providing another summary – or indeed an exhaustive taxonomy – of action sequence characteristics, the main project of this chapter is twofold: to suggest productive areas of enquiry when analysing any action sequence (and its place in the wider film), and to build on the discussion in Chapters 1 and 2 by elucidating the pleasures that action cinema offers as a form of cinematic entertainment.

THE SPEEDS OF ACTION

Fast and Furious (Justin Lin, 2009) opens in emphatic motion on an open road, cracked asphalt whipping underneath the camera at speed. The frame tilts up to bring a lorry cab into view. It is powering towards the camera, which is tracking backwards to keep it in shot; when the lorry cab passes the camera it becomes clear it is carrying six tanks of petroleum gas, the giant wheels of each tank whistling past the camera in turn. As the last tank exits the frame a car and two pickup trucks appear on the road, gunning their engines. A cut to a close-up reveals the male and female occupants of the lead car, Dom (Vin Diesel) and his girlfriend Letty (Michelle Rodriguez). After a brief dialogue exchange Letty clambers out of the passenger window and onto the hood of the car, and a wider shot from the tail-end of the car shows her nonchalantly holding position on the hood despite the fact that the car is accelerating towards the back tanker. Dom radios back to the other two cars ('Everyone in position?'), before a long shot frames the three-car convoy preparing to begin their operation. The team plan to disengage two tanks at a time and tow them away on the pickups while the lorry is still in motion. Dom distracts the driver by driving erratically in front of the lorry cab, while Letty's role is to climb up onto the tanks and disengage each pair by shattering the connector with nitrogen spray and a hammer. The first hook-up goes smoothly: the pickup truck spins into reverse with precision and the end tank is hooked up without fuss. The second pickup truck whirls round and into position with relative ease, and its passenger climbs into the back to launch the hook onto the tank's towbar while Letty makes her way across the roof of the tanks to disengage them. The pickup truck passenger hesitates – is he in the right position? will he time it correctly? – but he gets it right, and cheers the successful hook-up with relief. However, just at this moment, the lorry driver spots Letty on the tank roof in the rear view mirror and in an attempt to dislodge her and retain his load he swerves back and forth, making both Letty and the passenger of the still-connected pickup truck lose their footing. Now on a slope, the whole convoy is accelerating. Letty sprays nitrogen on the connector to release the next two tanks and in the absence of the hammer (dropped when she lost her footing), Dom smashes his car into the side of the tank to snap the connector. The second pickup tows its load away, and Letty – still with the remaining two tanks – prepares to jump onto Dom's car so that they can make their getaway. But now there is a new problem, which both Dom and the lorry driver have spotted: they are about to run out of road. The lorry driver slams on his breaks and bails out of the cab, leaving the cab and tanks careering dangerously across the road. Letty jumps to Dom's car just in time; the two tanks separate, one running ahead down the hill and overturning at the end of the road, the other overturning further up the hill, catching fire and careening down the hill towards Dom and Letty's car. Dom turns to face the approaching tank, gunning the engine. The tank gets closer and closer and just as it reaches them Dom powers the car forward and sideways so that it slips through the gap created by the tank's bounce. The tank crashes into the rest of the jack-knifed lorry, generating a huge fireball, as Dom and Letty leave the scene with a squeal of tyres and a roar of the engine.

The film thus pitches the spectator immediately and directly into a high speed chase, the camera tracking as fast as and sometimes faster than the vehicles in the scene in order to keep the team's various death-defying actions in view. The nature of this opening is not surprising given that this is the fourth instalment of a franchise that centres on the high-speed driving skills of a community of street racers: it is fast and furious in terms of the rush of diegetic events and in its style of presentation. Vehicular chases and races are an integral ingredient of contemporary action cinema (to illustrate, the following are only a tiny proportion of the recent action films featuring chases and races: *Charlie's Angels* (2000, 2003), *Fast and Furious* (2001, 2003, 2006, 2009), *Transporter*, *Transformers* and *Bourne* films, *Wanted* (2008), *Death Race*, *Live Free or Die Hard*, *The Expendables*). But in fact chases and races have been popular since cinema's inception. Think of the post-studio films like *Bonnie and Clyde* (1967), *Bullitt* (1968), *The French Connection* (1971), *Vanishing Point* (1971), *Duel* (1971), *Death Race 2000* (1975), and *The Cannonball Run* (1981), or the vehicle-related stunts of Buster Keaton, or Edwin Porter's *The Great Train Robbery* (1903), a large proportion of which takes place on a speeding train, or indeed D.W. Griffith's *An Unseen Enemy* (1912), which features a brother in his car racing against time to get to his two sisters, who are being menaced at their home some distance away by two armed criminals. The Futurists had celebrated speed as one of the central experiences of modernity, declaring in celebratory fashion in 1909 that 'the glory of the world has been enriched by a new beauty: the beauty of speed' (Filippo T. Marinetti, in Martin 2006: 7). In a US context, an obsession with speed takes its primary form in the national fascination with the automobile, expressed in Indy and NASCAR racing (the first speedway circuit opened in Indianapolis coincidentally also in 1909), the US 'muscle car' trend and a long tradition of films or film sequences focused on cars and other vehicles moving at speed, all of which have found their way onto the screen at some point or other. Indeed Eric Mottram has noted the way in which US film 'reflects America as a nearly century-old car culture of remarkable tenacity' (Mottram 2002: 106). In a moment I want to speculate as to why this obsession with speed exists, and what speed as an element might mean in the action sequence, but first it is worth noting that the action sequence's fast speeds do not just pertain to propulsive vehicles but to propulsive bodies, to the quickening of the sequence of events in any particular scene, and also to aspects of audio-visual presentation.

In his work on intensified continuity Bordwell suggests that speed is a defining principle of contemporary editing, now that cutting has become inexpensive. He comments that '[t]oday films are on average cut more rapidly than at any other time in US studio filmmaking. Some films flirt with shot lengths reminiscent of late 1920s Soviet silent montage' (Bordwell 2006: 122). The *Fast and Furious* sequence illustrates this rapid cutting, particularly at moments when the action is intensifying: for example, when the lorry driver spots Letty on the top of the tank and begins to swerve violently, resulting in members of the team being thrown around on the moving vehicles, and when Dom has to take evasive action as he is fired at by the lorry driver, the shots accelerate to between only one and two seconds in length. Bordwell also points out that other strategies are combined with fast cutting to intensify the impression of increased editing speed:

As if fast cutting weren't enough, filmmakers can create a percussive burst of images in other ways. Vehicles whiz through the foreground, breaking our line of sight. Whiplash pans and jerky re-framings present two glimpses linked by a blur. Rack focusing [. . .] can shift a shot's composition as crisply as a cut can. Directors not only cut on bursts of light, like flashbulbs or headlights; pulsations within a shot, yielded by disco strobes or cracks of lightning, can seem to boost the editing rate as well. (ibid.: 123)

The moment at which Letty is spotted is a point of view shot that shows what the lorry driver can see in the rear view mirror: at first he is concentrating on using the mirror to check the road behind him, but then there is a sudden reframing as his attention is caught by Letty's presence on the top of the tank. Multiple reframings follow: after the angry lorry driver has already slammed into the back of Dom's car once, a shot that frames both vehicles frontally tilts downward to capture the moment that the cab speeds up to slam into the car a second time; a whiplash pan initially shows a dislodged Letty hanging precariously off the back of one of the tanks before refocusing on the lorry cab at the other end of the tank; and later another whiplash pan moves from Letty, struggling to hold on, to Dom approaching to help her. In this sequence, then, the reframings function to create a sense that the pace of events is accelerating, but it is notable that they also help communicate and sustain the sequence's dramatic intensity by foregrounding moments in the sequence when control over an aspect of the situation shifts. For example, the shot of the rear view mirror initiates the first shift in the power dynamic, as the lorry driver's response to seeing Letty catches the team off guard; later when Letty is only hanging onto the tank very precariously, the whiplash pans draw our attention to who is 'driving' the scene, in the first instance the lorry driver, who is maintaining an increased speed and swerving the lorry on purpose, and in the second instance Dom, who has arrived to help Letty get off the tank safely.

Geoff King notices the same stylistic tendencies as Bordwell, and argues that they work with some other aesthetic strategies to produce a filmmaking mode he calls the 'impact aesthetic'. According to King this impact aesthetic offers 'a vicarious assault on the position of the viewer through strategies such as rapid editing, unstable camerawork and, in some cases, the propulsion of objects out towards the screen' (King 2006: 340). Once again the sequence from *Fast and Furious* can offer an indicative illustration. The camerawork is persistently unstable, particularly in the second half after the lorry driver takes action, juddering and shifting as if knocked about in the rough and tumble of developing events. Throughout, vehicles (and gunshots, tank connector hooks and in one instance Letty's hammer) are projected towards or past the camera. Take for example the culmination of the sequence. Two long shots establish the fact that Letty and Dom are trapped between two jack-knifed tanks, one overturned but at rest at the bottom of the hill, the other on fire and barrelling down the incline towards them at speed. After a medium shot of Dom turning the car to face the oncoming tank, and a cut in to a close-up of the car occupants that documents their concerned expressions, a closer medium shot shows the tank slamming into the ground before its next bounce, the camera shuddering to convey the vibrations caused by the impact. A further close-up of Letty and Dom is followed by an even closer shot of the tank on its next bounce, dropping into frame from above as if it has landed at the spectator's feet, thick black smoke and flames issuing out of the tank and obscuring the landscape beyond it. More milliseconds tick by as the tank gets closer and Dom waits for the right moment to take evasive action. When the car finally hurtles forward it does so right 'over' the camera in a frontal, low angle framing. In the instant of evasion, as the car skids under the tank mid-bounce with millimetres to spare, the moment is framed from the side so that the nearest end of the tank pushes out towards the camera, the near-side connector hook falling into frame even closer to us as the tank spirals over the car. In this way the sequence asks us also to experience the risk of impact first-hand as the tank bounces towards us as well as towards the fictional characters. Thus the sequence emphasises impacts in the fictional world, but also shapes itself in this and other ways in order to be impact*ful*. It is worth noting that King separates out the impact aesthetic from another tendency he finds in contemporary action cinema; that of the large-scale vista, 'often viewed from on high, either statically, or, more characteristically in contemporary Hollywood, via expansive wheeling, arcing or panning motions of the camera' (King 2006: 340). His opposition here between high/distant and ground-level/close is compelling, but I also want to propose that both modes might well be motivated by the same impulses.

THE THRILL OF ACTION AND THE 'NEED FOR SPEED'

When we watch an affecting action sequence, we are asked not to think of speed in an abstract way but to experience it with the protagonists and for ourselves. The strategies King describes – vehicles and objects travelling outwards towards or past the camera, camera judders and whiplash pans mimicking the effects of contacts happening in the fictional world – work to locate the spectator notionally within the three-dimensional space of the film world, 'in the thick of it', as it were. And as we saw in Chapter 2, the spatial co-ordinates and movements offered are 'fleshed' out by the audience, intensifying their vicarious experience of the pressures the bodies onscreen are experiencing, but also their experience of the camera's own journeys through fictional space and time. So far so good, but observing that certain filmmaking tendencies and preoccupations are present in action cinema only gets us a small way in the attempt to understand better the experiential and thematic dimensions of the contemporary action sequence. We also need to ask what is at stake in this human fascination with speed and in the ways of engaging with the world around us that the presentation style of such sequences might speak to. Peter Wollen reminds us that psychoanalyst Michael Balint breaks down the real-world thrill of speed into three basic, interconnected elements: a fear of or awareness of danger; the voluntary exposing of oneself to that danger and fear for pleasure; and the confidence that the fear and thus the danger will be mastered (Balint 1959, cited in Wollen 2002, 'Speed': 105). Let us apply this to watching an action movie: here scenarios of 'risk-at-speed' are rehearsed for our viewing pleasure; we can vicariously experience the thrill of danger while simultaneously being aware, reassuringly, that we are actually sitting in a movie theatre, separate from the situation onscreen. Moreover, our confidence that the danger will be mastered is underwritten by our knowledge of the conventions of narrative film and action cinema. In a traditional causal narrative structure each scene will resolve in one way or another, rather than being left 'hanging' or open-ended, and we can expect the hero to triumph eventually; and in action films specifically, we know that the action hero will be more physically robust, and that small 'triumphs' will occur in each (or the majority) of a movie's action sequences to demonstrate the action hero's growing mastery. Thus we are experiencing the thrill of high speed and its attendant risks vicariously, from the safety of our knowledge of generic convention as well as the safety of our cinema seats. The *Fast and Furious* sequence is fundamentally about risk: bodies unmoored except by gravity, being thrust through the air on or in speeding vehicles, the soft contours and surfaces of human corporeality persistently contrasted with the rigid, hard surfaces of the road and metal automobile bodywork in a way that confirms the team's physical vulnerability.[1] But our fear and confidence is already being managed by the sequence before the intensity of the risks involved increase. The first phase of the *Fast and Furious* sequence demonstrates the skills that give the team a chance of surviving if things begin not to go to plan – physical balance and confidence, fast cars and responsive, skilled driving styles – so that when the lorry driver starts to fight back we are poised to witness the team's narrative of becoming across the sequence. As the occupants of the tow vehicles move off with their tank loads and an unbalanced Letty finds herself thrust into the role of 'maiden in distress', the dramatic tension in the second half of the sequence centres on the battle of wills and speeds between Dom and the lorry driver, their control over their vehicles and their creativity in the developing circumstances, key qualities that will define the outcome of the confrontation. This is not unusual: it is customary for the occurrence of speed in the action sequence to be 'closely connected to various forms of struggle or contest, ranging from races and, more threateningly, chases, up to its decisive role in combat, where greater speed gives a clear advantage over an opponent' (Wollen 2002, 'Speed': 106). Mastery of the situation by one or other party is usually the outcome of scenes in which the protagonists try to compete with each others' speeds. The 'money shot', in which Dom sidesteps the barrelling tank in slow motion, is the successful culmination of his attempt to use speed to master the situation and the space of action; in contrast the lorry driver has already abandoned the cab and jumped clear, rolling to a halt. This thrill of speed and its culmination in the act of overcoming is central to the resolution and pleasure of both individual action sequences and the action narrative as a whole. It is worth pausing for a moment to consider the way that access to the act of overcoming is allocated to Dom rather than Letty. At the beginning of the sequence, when she is preparing to jump from the hood of Dom's car to the tank, Letty's physical assurance, enthusiasm and balance are an emphatic declaration of her potential as a physically heroic body. Yet by the end of the sequence the same speeds of action that she brushed off at the start have transformed her corporeal attitude into one of fear and disempowerment, and she must be talked through her rescue by Dom. The relocation of Letty into a position of relative passivity indicates a vulnerability that is perhaps intended to foreshadow her death, but it also bears an uncomfortable relation to the traditional gender binary that vests agency in the male and passivity in the woman. As this brief example illustrates, the representational dimension of the staging of risk and mastery is important to keep in mind when looking at any action sequence, and we will be returning to this issue again in this and the later chapters.

Dom and Letty risking impact in *Fast and Furious*

The components of the thrill experience that Balint describes also extend to speed's consequences, that is, where it 'moves' us to. Wollen notes that speed 'enables us to enter exposed and unfamiliar situations, far removed from the zones of safety and normality – to travel into space, for instance, beyond the frontiers of the known' (Wollen 2002, 'Speed': 106). Jennifer Barker correspondingly identifies the tendency in action film towards scenes in which the depiction of speeds and the manner of presentation move us beyond human limits, and suggests that these strategies can produce a significant sense of spatial disorientation in the spectator. Noting the chase film convention of 'alternating shots taken from *inside* vehicles with those taken from cameras mounted *on* them', for example, she suggests that the car-mounted cameras 'force us into movements that aren't meant for humans, only for machines . . . The film throws us out and gives us nothing to hang onto' (Barker 2009: 113). Later she discusses digital camera movements and Steadicam shots that 'base themselves on human movement', and suggests that disorientation occurs through the use of these technologies when the film body

> takes human movement to illogical, impossible extremes. These shots over-perfect our movements or make them too fast, exaggerating the humanlike tendencies of the film to the point that the movement is no longer remotely human: we can't keep up, we feel out of sorts and dizzy and we can barely hang on. (ibid.: 115)

Although I agree that these moments seek to exhilarate by presenting sequences that are sometimes disorienting in their pace or spatial trajectories, I am not sure the body feels quite as unmoored as Barker suggests in the face of more-than-human speed and motion, whether diegetic or stylistic. Balint notes that confidence in the probability of a positive outcome is an integral component of the thrill response – and I have already suggested that the reassurance of the narrative of becoming in the action film as well as the literal 'mooring' of the cinema seat might further bolster such confidence – so that this mitigates the 'unsafe' feeling Barker proposes. In fact in my view these speed sequences provide their own compensatory aspects: 'being in danger' is experienced in the context of the anticipation of mastery; the thrill of risk is followed by the thrill of mastery. This thrill of mastery is not simply experienced through the action hero's body and the feats it acts out, but through the access to the fictional world the film body provides. A return to King's two action aesthetics offers pertinent illustration. During moments that adopt the impact aesthetic, through the camera's instability the spectator experiences a simulation of physical risk but also the resilience of the camera, its ability to continue to show things despite the vibrations and jolts the diegetic situation seems to cause, and to power through the spaces of action. Similar pleasures are to be found in those moments when the camera exceeds the realities of human comportment: the spectator vicariously experiences a spatialised mastery, the fantasy of expansive spatial penetration, of force, forward momentum and progress. In the opening scene of *Fast and Furious* for example, the 'orienting' long shots that punctuate the sequence (Bordwell 2006: 133) are high angle mobile shots that soar through space and take in the extended landscape as well as the battling vehicles. Just before the dangerous downhill section, which the lorry driver spots and accelerates towards to try to throw off his attackers, the camera pushes upwards, the slope falling away below us while the majestic swathe of mountains beyond it extend into the far distance. Thus this is a landscape that the camera is not simply subjecting to its panoramic gaze but is penetrating expansively through its physical motion. The shot is bookended by close-up shots of each of the two warring drivers: the lorry-driver first, and then Dom afterwards, gunning his engine determinedly to match the lorry driver's new speed. Thus the shot has narrative motivation, not just to clarify the space and treacherously sloped surface over which the next phase of the race will take place, but as a visual metaphor for the mastery over the situation (which will only be achieved through controlled penetration of space) that both men desire.

MOVEMENT, MASTERY AND URBAN SPACE

Scott Bukatman has argued that '[i]n spectacular visual media, movement has become more than a tool of bodily knowledge; it has become an end in itself, and it is often accompanied by a utopian sense of possibility'. He suggests that movement 'has become a passage across borders, and it holds the promise of a resistance to external control' (Bukatman [1998] 2003: 125). Such ideas are crucial in understanding the appeal of speed sequences (whether they adhere to the impact aesthetic or the soaring bird's-eye view approach). In allowing us sensorially to experience these promises of resistance and possibility that Bukatman describes, such sequences can be exhilarating in ways that connect directly to our contemporary cultural context. They allow us to rehearse the possibility of rising out of the twenty-first century's urban congestion, the strictures of clogged traffic systems and overpriced housing, the unruly territorialisation of urban space, the intensities of urban social inequality and crime, and the visible and invisible regulatory frameworks imposed in response to terrorist threats. In place of these constraining realities cinematic speed offers a fantasy of overcoming, of powering through or of rising above to transcend the quotidian. This is acknowledged particularly explicitly in a conversation between the hero and his mentor in *The Fast and the Furious: Tokyo Drift* (Justin Lin, 2006). Looking down on the hundreds of people moving through

Tokyo's urban sprawl Han (Sung Kang) says to upcoming driver Sean (Lucas Black) that those other people 'follow the rules' because they are ruled by fear, while street drivers like himself free themselves from such constraints. Having acknowledged the cultural drivers behind the popularity of certain kinds of action spectacle, we can place the contemporary action cinema's preoccupation with speed and transcendence not only in relation to the cinema's long-standing fascination with speed, but in relation to responses in visual culture to 'anxieties regarding urban growth, technological development, and social change' (Bukatman [1995] 2003: 81) at early historical periods. For example, Bukatman notes the turn towards highly visual spectacular entertainments such as phantasmagoria and the panorama in the eighteenth and nineteenth centuries, which he and others have theorised as a response to the disorienting experience of increasingly technologised, industrialised and impersonal urban centres. He suggests that 'the sense of displacement or disorientation produced by the environment of the industrial city gave rise to new entertainments that produced a cognitive and corporeal mapping of the subject into a previously overwhelming and intolerable space' (ibid.: 88). Similarly the speed sequence offers the fantasy of mapping – and sometimes destroying – urban space through assertive, self-directed movement, of pushing through the city's barriers, of rising out of its strictures. Impact is here reconstituted not as a full stop but as a penetration, a moving through.

In *Live Free or Die Hard* this kind of penetration of the city is initially constituted as a problem that John McClane has to solve, but it also quickly becomes the badge of his mastery. McClane has to get his charge FBI suspect Matt Farrell across a gridlocked Washington DC without drawing the attention of terrorists who have hijacked the city's transport control and monitoring systems and have deployed helicopters to search for and kill Farrell. At first it is the terrorists who are associated with both a mastering gaze and a mastering of space: they are using computer technologies to attack the US infrastructure, and thus have access to real-time maps, information and surveillance systems to help them steer their different attack phases past potential obstacles. In addition the camera's bird's-eye views of the city are associated directly with the terrorists' helicopter, while McClane and Farrell are constrained to the ground level, easily exposed to the watchful gazes of the terrorists' monitoring technologies. An extended chase sequence traces McClane and Farrell's progress as they commandeer a police patrol car and are chased by said helicopter, whose occupants are spewing bullets at them from a distance. McClane runs over a water hydrant, projecting a huge volume of water vertically into the sky at the helicopter and sending one of the gunmen tumbling out. Here McClane shows his propensity for using elements of the ground-level urban environment in unconventional ways to breach the distance between himself and his attackers. McClane and Farrell take refuge in a multiple-lane tunnel, but the terrorists redirect traffic through it from both directions to trap them inside. Just as it looks as if they will be cornered, and after avoiding some crashes and careening vehicles in the centre of the tunnel, the aftermath of cars hurtling in different directions smashing into each other, McClane asserts himself once again. He drives the battered patrol car directly out of the tunnel and towards the helicopter's position at high speed. While he jumps out of the vehicle at the last moment, the car's momentum carries it up the sloped side of a toll booth at the tunnel entrance, catapulting it straight into and through the terrorist helicopter. McClane's ability to power through and master structured urban space in unexpected ways is here emphatically declared, and reverses the power dynamic with which the chase began. His rejection of conventional modes of circulation around the city – which characterises the vast majority of action heroes – culminates in him smashing into rows of parked and moving cars while pursuing the terrorists in an articulated lorry. The terrorists redirect an F-35 fighter plane against McClane and in the face-off between the two powerful vehicles the concrete fly-over on which the lorry is travelling is destroyed. Some debris drops into the F-35's engine forcing it to crash. After the ensuing explosion, McClane emerges through a landscape of rubble, twisted metal and wrecked road. Here mastery is characterised by powering on rather than rising above, a fantasy of empowerment deeply tied to a second fantasy common to the action film: of urban destruction.

POSTURES AND GESTURES OF MASTERY

As we saw in the previous chapter, the body of the action hero is a crucial term in these fantasies, enacting a corporeal trajectory towards mastery, subjected to and asserting the speeds of action. Action sequences stage the body of the action hero and his or her antagonists in particular ways that are worth mapping in more detail, not least because advances in digital imaging technologies have intensified aspects of this staging in recent years. Action heroes have always had an empowered stance, what we might call a 'posture of mastery', that they adopt prior to intense moments of confrontation. It usually involves posing with weapon cocked towards the viewer and body poised for action, is accompanied by a determined expression, and can be found in the earliest one-reelers (such as the Edison Manufacturing Company's 1894 film *Souvenir Strip of the Edison Kinetoscope* which featured declarative postures of physical mastery struck by strongman Eugen Sandow), swashbucklers like *The Mark of Zorro* (1920) and *The Flame and the Arrow* (1950), and the spaghetti westerns of Sergio Leone (such as *A Fistful of Dollars* (1964), *A Few Dollars More* (1965), *The Good, the Bad and the Ugly* (1966)) and various other strands of action cinema, like the detective thriller, the combat film and the martial arts film. It is usually these postures that are recreated for publicity images – take for example the poster images for *Wanted* (2008), *Kill Bill Vol. 1* (2003) or for *Rambo: First Blood Part II* (1985). The posture declares the potential of the action body, its capacity for action and for mastery, freezing the body at the moment it is about to unleash its forceful powers. The effect is of course to increase anticipation for the moment at which it will demonstrate these powers; once they are unleashed in motion, what was a posture of mastery defined by its relative stillness becomes a 'gesture of mastery' (or series of gestures of mastery) defined as a flow of action, which expresses the body's narrative of becoming in physical terms. While these postures and gestures of mastery are familiar components of the action film, digital imaging has recently transformed their relationship to each other within the action sequence.

A couple of examples will help us to investigate this further. In *G.I. Joe: The Rise of Cobra* (Stephen Sommers, 2009) a military special forces team with access to an array of high-tech gadgets sends two 'GI Joe' operatives wearing super-powered combat suits to chase down a terrorist group who are planning to unleash a nano-technology bomb on the Eiffel Tower in Paris. The terrorists smash through the Parisian traffic in a modified and 'weaponised' humvee catapulting parked and moving vehicles into the air, while the two GI Joes give chase, running, hurdling stationary cars and dodging those that have been hurled upwards. At various points this vehicle dodging is presented in slow motion to underscore the physical acrobatics the operatives have to display in order to stay alive. When the humvee launches several small rockets towards the GI Joes, the camera tracks speedily towards the men, following the weapons' smoke trails. After a reaction shot a mobile long take documents the men's evasive manoeuvres, beginning just behind them as they throw themselves into the air, then moving alongside them as their bodies somersault to avoid the rockets that are swooshing past with centimetres to spare, then arcing in front of them as the two men hit the ground running while the rockets blow up vehicles behind them. The long take quickly slows down to show the men's evasion acrobatics in detailed slow motion, then when they have successfully cleared the rockets the shot shifts to a much faster speed to emphasise their super-powered nimbleness. In *Charlie's Angels: Full Throttle* (McG, 2003) this presentational mode is also in evidence. In the middle of a shipyard battle between Irish gangsters the O'Gradys and Charlie's Angels, Angel Natalie (Cameron Diaz) uses her martial arts expertise to neutralise her attackers. At one moment she launches herself into the air while spinning to dodge a man coming at her with an axe, then completes the spin as a kick that floors two men who had been getting ready to join the attack. The shot begins briefly in real time then shifts quickly to a slower speed to capture Natalie's jump, spin and kick, before returning to real time to underscore the force of the kick's impact. Later in the fight Natalie is being attacked from both left and right of frame, and fells one of the men before turning quickly to kick the other assailant. This shot (which is interrupted by a short cutaway to an overhead shot, presumably to maintain the impression of pace) starts in slow motion so we have time to register that Natalie is dealing with oncoming threats from both directions, before speeding up to real time to show her prompt reposi-tioning of her body to deal with attacker number two. As she delivers the kick, the speed of the images slows to capture the assertive combat gesture in detail.

These sequences and the many more like them in 2000s action cinema use a process called 'speed ramping', whereby the speed of motion is altered within a shot. Speed ramping became popular following its use in the massively successful *The Matrix*, but it has also proliferated because it is much easier and cheaper to achieve than it was before – and possible to apply to footage retrospectively – due to the digital imaging technologies now used during the edit and post-production.[2] As in the examples above, the most common use for speed ramping is to enable an intensified focus on the body in motion, foregrounding the gestures of mastery the action body adopts during the flow of action by slowing them down radically until they almost register instead as static postures of mastery. Both the GI Joes and Natalie display a projec-tion of force that is captured in this way, their corporeal attitudes conveying their determination, control and physical skill. Perhaps counter-intuitively, slowing gestures down in this way functions to draw sustained attention to the intense speed at which the heroic body is having to operate. Vivian Sobchack has noted this fetishising aspect of slow motion, and speculates on its current popularity by suggesting that, 'against the increasing accelerations of cin-ematic and social life, the operations and effects of [digitally enhanced] slow motion visibly and sensually interrogate those accelerations in what seems a "revelation" – not of immobility or stillness, but of the "essential" *movement of movement* itself' (Sobchack 2006: 342, emphasis in original). Rather than adopting a posture-then-gesture model, speed-ramping complicates the rela-tion between these two points in the action sequence; in emphasising speed and gesture, these slowed moments tend to arrive in the middle of a sequence rather than at the beginning or end (although the second segment of Natalie's fight referred to earlier proves this is not always the case). Speed-ramping and slow motion more generally also have the power to provide a snapshot of the power relations in a particular sequence, important in the action cinema, where overt forms of physical mastery are constantly being sought, fought over and achieved by the lucky few. I have written elsewhere about how this works in a film like *X-Men: The Last Stand* (2006) in which it is not simply the gestures of the bodies involved that give a sense of the power dynamic, but the staging of the bodies in spatial relation to one another (see Purse 2009: 226–8), but it is pertinent to summarise briefly that argument here. The face-off between two mutant telepaths with telekinetic powers – the kind-hearted wheelchair-bound telepath Xavier (Patrick Stewart) and the increasingly powerful but out of control Jean Grey (Famke Janssen) – is a battle of wills in which the spatial arrangement of the characters is of particular significance. Xavier has taken the metaphorical 'higher ground' by trying to convince Jean Grey not to continue to use her powers for destruction, but is mocked in this project as Grey uses her telekinetic powers to lift him up against his will, out of his wheelchair. The traditional association of a raised position with empowerment is unsettlingly reversed here as Xavier hangs helplessly high in the air while Grey looks on malevolently from below. Grey stretches out her arms to signal that she is escalating her attack and attempting to master the space, a signature move also evident in the bullet-time sequences of the *Matrix* films (1999, 2003). At the instant Xavier's powers fail him and he is pulverised, the speed of motion slows right down in order to freeze for a moment the power relations between them in a three-dimensional tableau. Here digital compositing and speed ramping enable the confrontation to be dramatised in a nuanced narratively communicative way, by allowing the spectator access to the detail of gestural and facial performance as well as to the more obvious spatial mastery Grey is ripping from Xavier's grasp.

What we have been looking at in this chapter is a number of aesthetic tendencies evident in the construction of the contemporary action sequence, exploring what might be at stake in their inclusion and popularity, and how they are narratively expressive as well as spectacular. There is one other, neglected, area of action sequence aesthetics that I want to turn to in the final section of this chapter, and which I suggest merits further attention from those of us studying this area of Hollywood cinema. As in the rest of the chapter, we must not simply identify the aesthetic practice, but must explore what might be at stake in its use.

THE SOUNDS OF ACTION

The most obvious function of the action sequence soundtrack, after helping to ensure the verisimilitude of the image track, is to reflect or enhance the affective quality of the action sequence's most intense moments. Aside from the explosions and gunshots that punctuate the action sequence, the musical score is also crucially important. In the sequence from *Fast and Furious* that we discussed earlier, for example, the soundtrack reflects the pacing of the image track in various ways. Diegetic sounds of roaring engines and the swish of the passing road surface expand the spectator's perception of the physical risk involved in the team's operation, and later vehicular impacts and gun shots convey (through their own impactful force and volume) the team's shock and the vehemence of the lorry driver's fight-back. The musical score is fast-paced throughout but its rhythm and tone modulate as each phase of the sequence unfolds. At the beginning when the optimism and confidence of the team is at its highest, a bass guitar marks out a lively rhythm with small flares of cymbals to heighten our anticipation; as Letty climbs out onto the car hood a lead guitar picks out a simple folk-influenced melody. The guitar distortion and volume increases as the first difficult job is attempted (the precision task of getting the first tow truck hooked up to the tank) and a martial drum beat begins as the operation continues, conveying the developing stakes as the team put their bodies and vehicles in harm's way. The successful separation of two tanks from the convoy – and the momentum that achievement implies – inaugurates the next musical phase in which a dance-based synthesised rhythm section and a distorted guitar refrain strike a more robust melody. When the second tow truck team have difficulty lining up their connector with the tank's tow bar a rhythmic violin phrase begins to build on the soundtrack, culminating in the moment the lorry driver spots Letty in the rear view mirror, which is accompanied by a higher pitched blare of violins. At this instant the tempo of the music increases, faster and more dramatic in tone, to match the shift in the tempo of the action onscreen.

The practice of dubbing the sound of larger guns onto images of smaller guns is now commonplace in action cinema, and speaks to the inherent constructedness of the contemporary soundtrack. The drive to reward fictional gun owners with the sound of even bigger guns, and the bizarre principle of one-upmanship it seems to reveal is worth noting, but a different kind of discrepancy between sound and image is what I want to focus on here. In *Aliens* (1986) the sounds ascribed to Ripley (Sigourney Weaver) as she struggled to control her fear, physically assert herself and survive the alien-infested colony were relatively naturalistic. The spectator experienced her exertions in part – and in a very direct way – through the sounds her body made: grunts, gasps, ragged breathing and angry shouts. These were not tidy, polite, controlled sounds, or indeed the normative Hollywood version of what women are 'supposed' to sound like in particular types of film (more of this later), but instead seemed to reflect accurately the noises a body might well make when operating at the edges of its capacity. In the following paragraphs I want to suggest that today's sound mixing of vocal performance and the sounds of the body may be striving for a less naturalistic mode of presentation. Let us first sketch some pragmatic realities of sound capture and editing in action sequences. A general and basic aim of all sound recording – either on location or a sound stage, or in post-production – is for principle dialogue to be as clean and audible as possible. Many action films are shot on large, echoing sound stages, or are filmed on location shoots that involve noisy practical effects, such as wind machines, rainmaking rigs and a range of pyrotechnical technologies. This means that any bodily sounds you hear in an action sequence, from dialogue to punches to breathing, have almost always been added in post-production. For those with a working knowledge of mainstream film production, this will not come as a surprise. But it does mean that bodily noises and utterances in a scene have to be actively designed in, to use Sean Cubitt's phrase (Cubitt 2004: 251). Cubitt was talking about the constructedness of digitally generated film worlds; in invoking him here I hope to encourage us to stay alert to the constructedness of the action body's sounds, alongside its often digitally enhanced visualised movements. This constructedness immediately begs the question: what has been included and what has been omitted from the action sequence's sound track and why?

Let us look first of all at the role of sound in constructing the depiction of the white male action hero, not least because, in the films themselves and in mainstream media discourse, any other gendered or raced permutation of the action hero still seems to need to be negotiated in relation to the white male archetype, an issue I will return to in Chapters 4, 5 and 6. I have picked a typical sequence from the US/France co-production *Transporter 2* (Louis Leterrier, 2005) which stars Jason Statham as Frank, an erstwhile driver for the criminal fraternity who in this film is now working to prevent a chemical weapon from being deployed by a local drug lord. Frank infiltrates a drug smuggler's operation but is discovered by an African henchman who attacks him and pushes him off an office balcony into a warehouse space below. As Frank lands the henchman jumps after him, kicking him so hard that Frank flies some way through the air, and then dragging him bodily along a trestle table. Some oil from the table coats Frank's arm, so that when the henchman moves to grab him he loses his grip and falls backwards. Frank uses this time to jam his hands in coconuts, using them to box the henchman round the ears. The henchman responds by throwing Frank against the side of a dry-docked boat and trying to crush him between it and a smaller motorboat. Frank clambers up the boat's hull and drops inside. There follows a close-quarters fight in which Frank kicks the henchman between the legs and then jams him through a porthole. As the boat unbalances it rolls so that the henchman, trapped in the porthole, is crushed to death. Given that this is an action film it is perhaps not surprising that punches, thumps and slaps register very loudly on the sound track, communicating the force and frequency of destructive impact between these two fighting bodies. While we hear significant contacts we do not hear the sounds generated by intermediate movements (such as cloth sounds as an arms pulls back to deliver a blow, or the scuffle of shoes as a body repositions itself for the next attack), an aural patterning that emphasises the end result rather than progress towards it. Vocal utterances are similarly deployed to highlight moments of particularly damaging contact, and to mark out the rhythms of the sequence's choreographed to-ing and fro-ing, but the nature of these vocal performances is worth analysing a little further.

The hero issues short shouts and grunts whose brevity and force signal his attempts to assert control over the fight. The flat timbre and low pitch of these utterances do not simply convey the character's determination; they also perpetuate normative conceptions of masculine vocalisation – low not high, rational not emotional and so on. Thus a space is opened up for such sequences to draw a distinction between the hero's bodily sounds and those of his villain-ous opponents. In *Transporter 2* as in many other action films, aural markers of difference take on gendered or racial aspects. The opponent starts off with a couple of drawn out roars designed to assert dominance and strike fear into Frank. But the growling and guttural nature of the henchman's subsequent utterances instead suggest physical strain, the economy of Frank's grunts and shouts seeming controlled in comparison. Those straining sounds also take us further away from normative sound etiquette, towards the kinds of bodily noise usually avoided or hidden in polite company, and towards associations with animal utterances. As the scene progresses and Frank gains the upper hand, the opponent also suffers the indignity of being reduced to uttering high pitched noises – first a whimpering gurgle as he is symbolically castrated by a kick to the genitals, and then an almost operatically high extended cry as he is about to be crushed to death by the falling boat. So here the sound track's project to differentiate the fighting pair results in sound design that locates the opponent's body as feminised and animal-like, this in combination with an image track that positions him problematically in racial terms as a dreadlocked black man who is clumsy, grimacing and overweight.

What we do not hear, rather incredibly given the intense physical action that is taking place, is hardly any inhalations or expellations of air to and from the hero's body. From a pragmatic perspective the inclusion of constant breath sounds would weaken the sound track's systematic foregrounding of significant impacts. But I would also suggest that the choice not to reinsert breath sounds is also motivated by a desire to construct the white male hero in a particular way. The implication is that this is a stoical, inscrutable body, whose physical power is conveyed by its silences as well as its sounds. In short, this is a body so controlled, so powerful, that it does not seem to *need* to breathe. The excep-tions to this rule are situations in which the labour of the body is narratively significant, such as injury, or a seemingly insurmountable physical challenge (this in films where most physical feats are achievable, but physical problems have been set for the hero to prove his or her heroism through endurance). For example, *The Bourne Ultimatum* opens with an injured Jason Bourne attempt-ing to evade Moscow police, his ragged breathing audible in every shot as his bullet wound hampers his escape. In the sequence from *Transporter 2* we only hear the hero breathe (and then barely audibly) at the point when he has to work slightly harder than normal to pick up the villain and jam him into the window of the boat, and here it is likely to have been intended to help underpin the sequence's crass running gag about the opponent's obesity (in contrast to the 'norm' of the slimmer, muscular white body). John Belton observed in 1985 that

> [w]hat the sound track seeks to duplicate is the sound of an image, not that of the world. The evolution of sound technology and, again, that of studio recording, editing, and mixing practice illustrate, to some degree, the quest for a sound track that captures an idealized reality, a world carefully filtered to eliminate sounds that fall outside of understanding or significance; every sound must signify. (Belton 1992: 326)

His words would seem to be equally pertinent in relation to today's action cinema. The soundtrack of the contemporary action sequence is not invested in offering us aural impressions of real bodies; it has instead a representational function, and in particular is invested in constructing an idealised heroic body.

It is interesting to compare *Transporter 2*'s approach to sound with that which applies when the action hero is a woman. In *Resident Evil* (Paul W. S. Anderson, 2002), Alice (Milla Jovovich) is an amnesiac trapped in a facility full of zombies. In the sequence I want to discuss Alice has been accosted by zombie dogs and has shut herself in a room for protection. She turns away from the door only to be attacked by an African American security guard zombie, whom she pushes away and high-kicks into a glass cabinet, rendering him immobile. Her previously undiscovered ability to deliver such deadly force gives her pause, and brings on a flashback in which she learns she is a 'security operative'. As she pulls the security guard's gun from his jacket a zombie dog smashes through a glass window in the wall of the room, breaching Alice's momentary safe haven. Alice runs out of the room and shuts the dog in behind her, but this time when she turns to face the new space she is in, she is confronted with no fewer than seven snarling undead dogs. As they launch at her simultaneously she recalls more of her training, instinctively shooting each one in the head with pinpoint accuracy. A final dog appears beside her; she runs up a wall, spins in the air and kicks in its head. The conventions I noted in *Transporter 2* are still here: breathing is not continuously audible, and moments of significant impact are emphasised through loud thumps and vocal utterances, constructing the heroine's body as powerful while also conforming to the horror film convention of loud shock sounds used sparsely to increase tension. As in *Transporter 2* the lack of audible breath sounds confers a stoical, trained physicality on Alice. This is most true after the flashback, when Alice remembers she is a highly trained operative, and must then kill the dogs: she makes no sound as she swiftly despatches each of them before they can launch an attack. There are some telling differences from the conventions evident in *Transporter 2*, though. Jovovich's vocal utterances are different from Mr

Statham's, and not simply because they have different performance styles or are of different sexes. Alice's are extended, longer shouts, relatively high-pitched and tremulous at times, and as such coincide with normative conceptions of female vocal delivery under stress, even as her throaty, ragged voice locates her as unable to conform fully to stereotypical female traits of vocal softness and smoothness. The shout as Alice kicks the dog rises in pitch across its delivery, implying an assertion of hope rather than certainty, a moment of assertive force rather than a continuous assault. This reflects the rhythm of the action sequence as a whole – pauses between thumps or shouts are extended, isolating action in short bursts rather than as a continuum, a flow of action. The implication seems to be that this is an action body that cannot extend itself for too long, a surprising fact given that Alice is supposed to be at military fitness level.

In contrast to the regulated sounds and silences of the male body, this is a body that cannot control itself in the same way. In these subtle changes to the conventional aural presentation of the action body, the sound track helps to naturalise the containment of Alice's capacities. If her fitness levels are not in doubt (given her training as a security operative), then the only explanation for the film's choice to impose this kind of containment on Alice is her gender. Further proof of this underlying gendering of the action body's aural profile can be found if we analyse the presence or absence of breath sounds in the sequence (keeping in mind the *Transporter 2* scene). The sequence's main action is framed by Alice's breath sounds – an audible intake of breath as she reacts with shock to the situation, an audible exhale of relief at the end of the sequence. This framing or bookending is quite common across the four *Resident Evil* films (2002, 2004, 2007, 2010), and while it should be expected that an action horror hybrid might wish to orchestrate regular oscillations between shock and relief across its running time, this framing also has the effect of imposing limits on Alice's physical aggression: it has a defined beginning and end in a way that Frank's actions did not. The female action body is also prone to audible gasps or sharp inhalations in the middle of an action sequence, as if unable to sustain an attack or evasion without the body forcing its physiological need for oxygen to be directly confronted, again quite different from the conditions of Frank's sustained attack in *Transporter 2*. Hearing more breathing sounds emanating from the female heroine, louder and less controlled than in equivalent scenes featuring a male hero, contributes to a sense that the heroine's body is reactive rather than proactive, weaker rather than stronger. At the same time, the persistent aural emphasis on the 'breathiness' of the female body also refers us to conventional cinematic representations of female sexual abandon, the sound track eroticising the display of female physical agency. A good test of this particular aspect of sound design is to listen to an action sequence featuring a female action hero and then imagine the same breathing patterns, phrasings and framing being performed by a male actor: the effect would be quite different. When we remind ourselves that such breath sounds must be actively designed in, it is clear that sound design in the contemporary action film is still shaped by some quite traditional conceptions of gender.

This brings us back to the ideas that have shaped both the chapter and this final section: that rather than assuming that the action sequence's aesthetics are somehow obvious, we should analyse each sequence with an open mind, eye and ear; and that understanding the impulses behind the content and presentation of the action sequence is important, as is an alertness to the often surprisingly nuanced ways in which such sequences can be communicative in narrative and representational terms. In the following four chapters, the focus of the book turns explicitly to the question of representation. We will be asking what kinds of people are permitted to be heroes and villains in the contemporary action film, and how they are constructed. In the process, we will also be addressing ideas about gender, race, sexuality, nationhood and heroism that circulate in Western culture and thus provide contexts and drivers for these representations.

NOTES

1. This is partly the product of the reputation of the car: as Wollen has pointed out, '[i]nevitably, cars are associated with death, not simply because of crashes but, in more general terms, because of the possibility of crashes, the possibility of loss of control and even loss of life' (Wollen 2002, *Autopia*: 17).
2. Prior to the advent of digital technologies this kind of effect was only possible by manually manipulating the speed at which film ran through the camera.

CHAPTER 4

Action women

M edia responses to female heroes occasionally reveal a discomfort about the presence of these powerful women within action cinema. Choosing their words carefully, they describe the female action hero in hesitant terms that betray an underlying conviction that these women are moving in on a territory that should remain male. As I was finishing this study, much was made in the UK and US press of Angelina Jolie taking on a role that was originally to have been played by Tom Cruise, in Phillip Noyce's action thriller *Salt* (2010). Despite her previous action roles (the *Lara Croft: Tomb Raider* films (2001, 2003), *Mr and Mrs Smith* (2005) and *Wanted* (2008)), this casting 'gender switch' divided opinions about whether Jolie convinces in the film's scenes of physical action. While Kenneth Turan of the *Los Angeles Times* approvingly noted that Jolie 'continues to prove she can handle guns, grenades and the bad guys' (Turan 2010: review tagline) Todd McCarthy of *IndieWire* complained that the film 'glosses over how a lone woman, no matter how lethal a weapon, can repeatedly take out a dozen or more armed men' (McCarthy 2010: paragraph 1). If we stop to think about McCarthy's statement, its dubious basis quickly becomes apparent. Male-fronted action cinema regularly posits situations in which the hero achieves the impossible feat of repeatedly taking out 'a dozen or more armed men', and as we have seen in Chapters 2 and 3, such situations are staged in a film world whose correspondences to real-world physics and physiology can be quite stretched. Such complaints are not contemplated in relation to equivalent scenes featuring a man, because the male action hero's surprising ability to carry off this kind of impossible feat has been utterly naturalised. McCarthy's objection to a woman enacting this common action cinema trope reveals a wilful blindness to this cinema's most basic conventions, which seems driven by an explicitly gendered double standard according to which women can only ever be interlopers-in-action. So what kinds of female representation do we see in this supposedly macho world of action? And what kinds of cultural discourse drives these representations and the responses to them?

MUSCLING IN

It's worth remembering, as Neale reminds us, that female action heroes have been with us at least as far back as the 'serial queens' of such adventure serials as *The Perils of Pauline* (Eclectic Film Co., 1914) and *The Hazards of Helen* (Kalem Company, 1914–17) (Neale 2000: 57). Nevertheless it was the 'warrior women' of the 1980s and 1990s action cinema who foregrounded their bodily exertions and their physically capable bodies in ways not witnessed previously in Hollywood. The heroines of films like *Red Sonja* (1985), *Aliens*, *China O'Brien* (1990), and *Terminator 2: Judgment Day* (1991) displayed physical aggression, anger and a pronounced musculature – what Tasker calls 'musculinity' (Tasker 1993: 149). In doing so, they deconstructed the notion of masculinity and femininity as 'natural' categories: their bodies declared that these traditional markers of masculinity were not the exclusive preserve of men, that musculature 'is not in truth natural at all, but is rather achieved' (Dyer 1982: 71). They also explicitly destabilised the binary logic of dominant, normative notions of gendered behaviour. While their biological sex designated them as female and thus set up expectations of traditionally 'feminine' modes of behaviour, dress and appearance, their 'strength and determination and, most particularly, [their] labour and the body that enacts it, mark [them] out as "unfeminine"' (Tasker 1998: 69). The visibility of their labour, the work that goes into the body-in-action, was laid bare on an extra-textual level in the awareness of the training necessary to produce these built-up bodies, a regime that had previously been the preserve of men, and on a diegetic level in the depiction of straining muscles, sweat and the sounds and grimaces of exertion. In the light of these representations' capacity to destabilise conceptions of gender that were long established in Western culture, they exhilarated some while radically disturbing others (see Tasker 1993: 139, Holmlund 1994: 127–51 and Hills 1999: 38–50). The accusation levelled at the time that they were simply 'men in drag' (Tasker 1993: 149) returns us to this idea that women are somehow out of place in action cinema, outside of binary constructions of gendered behaviour, able to proceed only under special conditions. In the light of this it is perhaps not a surprise that the films themselves attempted to 'explain away' their stars' physical aggression, why it was exceptional rather than the norm, why they would be 'driven to do it'.[1] Explanatory devices usually characterised the heroine as in some way less rational; for example, under the sway of an instinctive, irrepressible maternal drive or the hysteria of a mentally strained mind. Extra reassurance that the women's independence was containable was provided by narrative resolutions that often relocated them in a heterosexual union or family unit.

THE ADVENT OF THE 'ACTION BABE'[2]

As the 1990s developed, movie executives seemed to respond to both the popularity of these strong women and the accusations of masculinisation they generated, so that more conventionally feminine-looking, less muscular, but no less serious, action women began to appear in films like *The River Wild* (1994), *Courage under Fire* (1996) and *The Long Kiss Goodnight* (1996). This meant that by the time *G.I. Jane* (Ridley Scott) hit theatres in 1997, the highly muscular body-in-training and strikingly shaved head presented by Demi Moore was out of step with the backlash against the more muscular heroines, prompting the British *Time Out Film Guide* to declare that 'the picture's an irrelevance before it's even begun' (Charity 1997: paragraph 1). Television's response to the popularity of and controversy around figures like the *Alien* films' Ripley (Sigourney Weaver) and *Terminator 2*'s Sarah Connor (Linda Hamilton) was a number of series that, in contrast to the muscular big screen heroines of the 1980s and early 1990s, permitted a female action hero who was not figured as damaged, pathological or 'inappropriate' in gendered terms (although her frequent independence and 'action duties' are sometimes figured as problematic by friends and family). Action heroines such as Xena (Lucy Lawless) in *Xena: Warrior Princess* (1995–2001) and Buffy Summers (Sarah Michelle Gellar) in *Buffy the Vampire Slayer* (1997–2003) were visibly highly feminine women who were also physically super-powered. The open-endedness of television serialisation permitted an action heroine who would succeed again and again, and problematised the application of traditional containment strategies,[3] in that negative explanations of female violence such as prolonged instability, irrationality, hysteria or pathological leanings would damage viewers' ability to align themselves with the series' heroine, and in that containing strategies of narrative closure were more difficult, since the serial nature of the medium meant that narrative closures were either contingent or constantly deferred. Nevertheless, one strategy for framing female action remained. Both Xena and Buffy, and the myriad female action heroes that continue to emerge in their wake in television series like *Alias* (2001–2006), *La Femme Nikita* (1997–2001), *Cleopatra 2525* (2000–2001), *Dark Angel* (2000–2002), *Witchblade* (2001–2002), and *Hex* (2004–2005), have their origins in the TV series of the 1960s and 1970s, such as *The Avengers* (1961–1969), *Wonder Woman* (1976–1979) and *Charlie's Angels* (1976–1981), that constructed a physically-empowered action heroine 'drawn from a stylised cartoon or comic-strip tradition' (Tasker 1993: 19). Such influences shaped a female action hero that is overtly sexualised, a tendency evident in tight fitting or revealing costumes, such as secret agent Sydney Bristow (Jennifer Garner)'s figure hugging 'disguises' in *Alias*. In their 'exaggerated statement[s] of sexuality' these women's representations fit into the tradition of the 'fetishistic figure of fantasy derived from comic books and soft pornography', that Tasker identifies (Tasker 1998: 69). As Tasker argues, these are 'images of women that seem to need to compensate' for the physical potency and agency of the female protagonist (Tasker 1993: 19) by recontaining the active heroine within the terms of heteronormative sexualised display. The television series' huge popularity demonstrated the growing market for female action heroes, and a series of films followed through the 2000s, with action heroines taking roles in franchises like *The Mummy* (1999, 2001, 2008), *X-Men* (2000, 2003, 2006), *Lara Croft: Tomb Raider, Charlie's Angels, Underworld* (2001, 2003, 2006, 2009), *Fantastic Four* (2005, 2007), *Pirates of the Caribbean* and *Resident Evil* (2002, 2004, 2007), and films like *Blade: Trinity* (2004), *Aeon Flux* (2005), *Elektra* (2005), *Sin City, Ultraviolet* (2006), *Wanted, Watchmen* and *Salt*. Like their television counterparts, all these action heroines are displayed in ways that eroticise their gendered form – often precisely at the same moments they are demonstrating their active, capable physicality – and cannot help but evoke the scantily-clad, hyperfeminine, gun-toting women of 1970s exploitation flicks like *Caged Heat* (1974) and *Big Bad Mama* (1974).[4] At the time these exploitation films presented 'serious problems' for second wave feminists because while they provided a space for women who possessed and displayed physical agency, they popularised 'an overtly coded, fetishised image of woman as sexual object' that Pam Cook argued counteracted their status as active subjects (Cook 1976: 123). In investigating the prevalence and apparent homogeneity of the current cycle of female action heroes, one of the questions that will be asked in the course of this chapter is whether such reservations are still applicable in the context of contemporary cultural debates about postfeminism.

CONTAINMENT STRATEGIES

In the action film the relationship of the hero's feats to real-world laws of physics and physiology runs along a continuum between highly naturalistic and radically non-naturalistic: what we might call a credibility continuum, that I illustrated in Chapter 2 by comparing the relatively realistic physical rules of *Casino Royale* with the world of *Transporter 2*, in which Frank is a slightly-more-than-humanly agile, strong and impervious protagonist. What is interesting about many of the films I have listed above (certainly in the context of the press comments about *Salt*), is not just that they are much more likely to occupy a position at the non-naturalistic end of this continuum, but that the films often depict their female heroes' physical achievements in ways that emphasise their non-realist character. In the opening scene of *Charlie's Angels: Full Throttle* (McG, 2003) the Angels (Lucy Liu, Drew Barrymore and Cameron Diaz) infiltrate a criminal gang's beer hall in Northern Mongolia in a bid to extract the US Marshall (Robert Patrick) being held hostage there. The first shot is a convoluted and clearly digitally constructed long take around the beer hall, down through the bowels of the building and back up again, which pinpoints the location of the two Angels already in position for the mission, establishes the narratively important spaces of the scene (the room where the US Marshall is being tortured, the beer hall through which they must escape), as well as developing some deeply racist caricatures of the Mongolian thugs along the way. The long take's obvious constructedness establishes an artificiality that will pervade the scene as a whole: when the third Angel (Diaz) arrives, she feigns a clunky Swedish accent and, rather than asking her who she is and why she is there, the men respond to her blonde pigtails and wide smile with stunned, lustful silence. She spots a bucking bronco sitting improbably in the corner and rides it with whooping abandon to distract the men from the other Angels' rescue attempt: her turn on the bronco is accompanied by Tone Loc's 1989 funk rap 'Wild Thing', an extremely unlikely choice for a jukebox in the northern extremities of Mongolia. When the men discover the rescue, the Angels throw their bodies forward into attack formation, in the process displaying a disdain for real-world notions of gravity, weight and momentum usually reserved for superhero movies. The film is careful to foreground the radical non-naturalism of these movements, presenting them in extreme slow motion to highlight their artifice.

In addition the whole sequence is played for laughs, its anachronisms, performances and excessive, stylised artifice designed to generate comedy alongside the visual jokes about straight men's susceptibility to a beautiful blonde, the knowing references to normative differences between men and women in terms of weight, alcohol consumption and strength, and the racist construction of Mongolians as swarthy, belching, leering figures. Comedy traditionally constructs situations that are 'simultaneously plausible and implausible', in what Jerry Palmer has called the 'logic of the absurd' (Palmer 1987: 56). Placing the female action hero within a comic frame allows the film and the viewer the freedom to position her acts as implausible elements. Using comedy as a containment strategy is particularly pronounced in films like *Fantastic Four* and *My Super Ex-Girlfriend* (2006), where the display of female super-powers is contained within situations that also manage to subject the action heroine to varying levels of humiliation.[5] In *Charlie's Angels: Full Throttle* the heavily accented artifice and comic frame work together to encourage us to be unconcerned about whether these women are actually capable of these amazing feats.

What drives this and other films' positioning of powerful women in an explicitly comical and/or fantastical setting is a desire to set the potentially culturally disturbing possibility of female agency and physical power at a distance from our everyday contemporary reality. Both science fiction and the superhero film can also function in this way, providing a space in which female physical power is permitted, but in a fantastical setting that (with or without comedy) underlines its real-world impossibility. Perhaps this is really what drives McCarthy's objection to *Salt*: that Jolie performs her powerful physicality in a relatively real-seeming rendering of New York; that is, in a fictional universe that looks uncomfortably close to the real world. The strategies we have noted, such as depicting female physicality within comic or fantastical settings, or explicitly underlining the artificial nature of the physical action being displayed – are clearly 'containment strategies' which work to contain the threat embodied by the presence of the physically powerful woman. In this context, it is also important that these films fail to add credence to the stretching nature of these bodily feats. As we have said, in all action cinema the terms of what will be effortful and what will be too much for the body do not always have a very direct correspondence to everyday reality, but a film will establish its rules and the physical limits so that we understand some moments of physical exertion as being more difficult than others. Male fronted action films routinely add cues to cement this understanding; the male body will sweat, become bloodied, will grunt, will contort his face in the moment of exertion, veins popping, face red. Witness Frank in the non-naturalistic world of *The Transporter* (Louis Leterrier and Corey Yuen, 2002): unflappable, but permitted to sweat, strain and be bloodied as he engages in combat. But in contrast in many recent female action films, alongside choreography and presentation that refuses reference to real-world consequences of bodily momentum, weight and impact, there is a persistent tendency to downplay significantly the physical consequences of action, such as pain and injury. By the end of the Mongolia sequence in *Charlie's Angels: Full Throttle* the Angels have been shot at, smashed through plate glass windows, rolled down a rocky, dusty slope, and jumped from a falling truck into a falling Apache helicopter, a series of events that would at the very least have dirtied their faces a little, and more likely would have resulted in their bodies and faces displaying cuts, bruises, dust, profuse perspiration and other signs of extreme exertion (heightened colour, laboured breathing). But they end the sequence looking relaxed, with none of these signs of physical exertion and the bodily consequences of violence visible.

This extreme reluctance on the part of filmmakers to dirty or bloody the faces of their female action heroes bears an interesting relation to these women's dual status as both active subjects and sexualised objects. The avoidance of appearance-warping injuries such as swellings or broken bones combines with an insistence on the cyclical return to the perfectly made-up face.

Here the investment seems to be in preserving the woman's status as sexual object in spite of the action, so that she can retain her erotic appeal. But it seems to me that these principles are also shaped by the traditionally binary conceptions of gendered behaviour that I mentioned earlier. These dictate that a woman should be feminine within certain prescribed parameters, foregoing any activities that might give rise to unladylike behaviours or body postures, such as sweating rather than 'perspiring', grunting rather than sighing, sitting with legs open instead of legs closed and so on. Note, too, that the fighting styles of these women also correspond to these dictates, the fluid, flowing, more 'feminine' movements of martial arts often chosen above 'macho' guns and punches. The traditional heroic qualities of toughness and resolve are reframed in relation to gender-biased notions of decorum: grace and dignity; perfect hair and make-up; and unconvincing physical action. This reframing of traditional heroic qualities in the contemporary representation of the action heroine has a direct relationship to current ideas about postfeminism and female self-definition that requires clarification.

POSTFEMINISM AND THE ACTION WOMAN

The contemporary female action hero's sexualised brand of physical empowerment locates her in close proximity with key postfeminist discourses around choice, power and sexuality. Postfeminism in this manifestation defines itself against a negative conception of second-wave feminism, which is seen as obsolete and even obstructive to women's contemporary needs and desires. In an astute summation that merits quoting at length, Diane Negra explains that

> post-feminism trades on a notion of feminism as rigid, serious, anti-sex and romance, difficult and extremist. In contrast, postfeminism offers the pleasure and comfort of (re)claiming an identity uncomplicated by gender politics, postmodernism, or institutional critique . . . From the late 1990s renaissance in female-centered television series to the prolific pipeline of Hollywood 'chick flicks,' to the heightened emphasis on celebrity consumerism, and the emergence of a new wave of female advice gurus/lifestyle icons, the popular culture landscape has seldom been as dominated as it is today by fantasies and fears about women's 'life choices'. (Negra 2009: 2)

One of these choices is presented as the reclamation of one's 'true' femininity, reclaimed, that is, from the strictures imposed by feminism. Thus the enfranchised woman is free to participate in the pleasurable consumption of normatively feminine clothing, accessories, cosmetics and personal grooming products not because she feels compelled to by a culture accustomed to sexu-alising women, but because, to take the tagline from a ubiquitous hair product advertisement, 'you're worth it'. She is also free to express her feminine sexu-ality, empowered to take pleasure in participating in the sexualised display of her body either for personal or romantic purposes, because she is doing it for herself. In the media, lifestyle magazines and films, '[m]eanings of choice and individual freedom become wed to images of sexuality in which women appar-ently choose to be seen as sexual objects because it suits their liberated inter-ests', as Robert Goldman et al. explain (1991: 338). However, these discourses of self-realisation can also be seen as forceful attempts to assimilate feminist ideas about equality and empowerment in the service of interpolating women back into the sexual and economic hierarchies of consumer capitalism.

These accounts allow us to locate the contemporary action heroine in rela-tion to other developments in media and consumer culture, as well as putting the move from the troubling musculinity of Ripley and Sarah Connor to the appealing hyper-femininity of contemporary heroines in the context of the wider discursive shift from a 'difficult', serious feminism to an accommodat-ing, allegedly 'positive' postfeminism. Certainly the contemporary action heroine deserves the postfeminist moniker in her ability to 'have it all' (Tasker 2004: 9). In an essay on what he enthusiastically terms 'action babe cinema', Marc O'Day interprets the action heroine's dual status as active subject and sexual object as an overturning of the traditional gender binary because the films *assume that women are powerful* without resorting to explanatory devices to justify her physical aggression (such as an intense maternal drive, mental instability or trauma) (O'Day 2004: 216, emphasis in original). I would want to problematise the assumption that explanatory devices are not present in such films: in *Elektra* for example, the heroine's skills were the result of training by her fatherly mentor, and she is motivated in the present by a maternal desire to protect a threatened young girl; the girl's father is also present, construct-ing a potential family unit for Elektra (Jennifer Garner) to join. In addition as we have seen, female aggression in these films is qualified in other ways, as fantasy, as comedy, as artifice and in a compensatory form of sexual display. The contemporary action heroine does seem to 'have it all' in some ways: expensive cars, clothing, travel, homes and often high-paying jobs are all on show in films like *Elektra*, *Kill Bill* (2003), *Underworld*, *Charlie's Angels* and *Mr & Mrs Smith*. The iconography of affluence provides aspirational visions that integrate the films into wider consumer culture and postfeminist discourse. As this list of luxury items illustrates, fantasies of monetary empowerment and the trappings of an elevated social status are mapped onto fantasies of physi-cal empowerment. It also serves to illustrate that postfeminism's discourses of choice and self-realisation are only applicable to and available to women of particular socio-economic status: white, middle-class women (Projansky

2001: 70). The 'action babes' we have been discussing are usually affluent white women, and, just as in some parts of Western society, their empowerment is often achieved at the price of women of other ethnicities: in *Aeon Flux* Sithandra, played by an actress of part-Nigerian descent (Sophie Okonedo), dies protecting her white colleague Aeon (Charlize Theron) and Puerto Rican marine Rain (Michelle Rodriguez) dies to make way for Alice (Milla Jovovich) in *Resident Evil*. Contained in various ways, then, these female action heroes are also less progressive than they might first appear.

As further confirmation of this it is worth considering the narrative's frequent function as a further containing frame in 'action babe' cinema. Here too the women's independence and empowerment is qualified, this time by narrative process. The most striking form of this is the supplanting of the female hero with a male hero. Where the active woman co-exists alongside and coaches a central male protagonist into becoming powerful she is most likely to have to 'make way' for him, often through death. In the Introduction I mentioned Trinity's trajectory from action hero and mentor to sidekick and love interest in *The Matrix*, but in *Matrix Revolutions* (2003) she must make way for him completely when she is killed in a crash. In *Wanted* highly skilled contract killer Fox (Angelina Jolie) helps recruit and train newcomer Wesley (James McAvoy), but at the film's end commits suicide to save Wesley's life and free him from the grip of a rogue assassins' organisation. Some films posit a villain who illustrates the danger of 'too much' female agency, power or independence. The villain of *Charlie's Angels: Full Throttle* is a rogue Angel (Demi Moore) who has forsaken Charlie's paternal leadership: she is characterised as a revenge-obsessed loner, and is pathologised through her 'masculine' love of guns (rather than the more graceful, 'ladylike' martial arts of the Angels) and a hint, in her final battle, of lesbianism.[6] In *X-Men: The Last Stand* (2006) the timid Jean Grey is driven mad by telepathic and telekinetic powers that she is unable to control, becoming a divided but monstrous and murderous figure who must be killed off. But the most prevalent narrative containment strategy is a familiar one that was also mobilised in earlier periods of Hollywood history, for example, in the screwball comedy cycle. Exemplified by such films as *The Awful Truth* (1937) and *Bringing Up Baby* (1938) the cycle usually paired a weak, hesitant man with a dominant and often physically active woman.[7] Such pairings' apparent gender reversal is undercut by narrative resolutions in which the heroine is contained inside marriage, thus serving 'to revivify the institution of marriage and traditional gender relations' (Neale 2000: 70).[8] In a strikingly similar fashion, the narrative containment of the contemporary action heroine often takes the form of a movement into, or a return to, the heterosexual couple, to marriage, or to the family unit (or all three), a strategy that gives the lie to the independence these powerful women appear to embody. Some are already daughters, groomed for action by influential father figures in films like *Elektra*, *Kill Bill*, the *Charlie's Angels* films, *Lara Croft: Tomb Raider* and the *Resident Evil* franchise. Others are already wives, like in *Mr & Mrs Smith*, *Hancock* (2008) and the *Fantastic Four* films. Some are transformed into wives and/or mother figures at the narrative's close, as is the case in *Kill Bill: Vol 2* (Quentin Tarantino, 2004), *Elektra* and *Aeon Flux*. Most striking towards the end of the decade has been a flurry of action romantic comedies where this narrative containment *is* the narrative set-up; the dramatic tension arises from the woman's predicament of being romantically involved with an action hero, in films like *Killers* (2010), *Knight and Day* (2010) and *The Bounty Hunter* (2010). While the earlier *Mr and Mrs Smith* (2005) gave an egalitarian spin to the concept – both were equally efficient trained killers – these later films position the female as the weaker figure who has to 'learn' from their mentor/action hero boyfriend how to be physically aggressive.

In a contemporary Western culture frequently characterised as postfeminist then, these women seem to represent the 'acceptable face' of female empowerment: predominantly white, heterosexual, sexualised, affluent, normatively feminine and usually contained if not initially then by the narrative closure within a heterosexual union or family unit. And they also present sanitised versions of female physicality, the biological and psychological realities of physical exertion, stress and violence elided. As a result these 'action babes' dampen the action body's potential to be a site of vivid sensorial investment in the work of the body. But is contemporary action cinema's representation of active female physicality as homogeneous as I have suggested? Are there other ways of showing the female action hero that are evident elsewhere in action cinema, or indeed within some of the 'action babe' films we have been looking at? I want to look now at representational tendencies that do not quite fit into the 'action babe' category.

ONSCREEN PHYSICALITY

The publicity poster campaign for the first of the *Kill Bill* films (Quentin Tarantino, 2003, 2004) presents us with a protagonist who seems readily to correspond to the sexualised object/active subject dualism of the action heroines in films like *Charlie's Angels*, *Lara Croft: Tomb Raider* and *Resident Evil* (incidentally an impression the teaser trailer does not disabuse us of).[9] The poster shows 'the Bride' (Uma Thurman) in a figure-hugging yellow and black leather motorcycling suit, standing nonchalantly holding a samurai sword. The outfit and Thurman's shoulder length hair foreground her conventionally feminine attributes, but the image also suggests her fighting potential, the clothes referencing the yellow and black tracksuit Bruce Lee wears in his last, unfinished film *Game of Death* (1972),[10] while the samurai sword evokes both the Japanese samurai film and the active heroines common in Chinese and Hong Kong swordplay films.[11] The opening of the film, however, confronts us with and radically undercuts the 'action babe' expectations the poster has fostered. The first three shots, humorously intertextual, give little sign of what will shortly follow. First, a (fake) 'ShawScope' logo that refers to the Shaw Brothers, a key producer of Hong Kong martial arts films in the 1970s; next, a 1970s-style scratchy 'Our Feature Presentation' logo, as if we were sitting in a local cinema thirty or so years ago; then a sly *Star Trek* reference as the phrase 'Revenge is a dish best served cold', appearing in white type on a black background, is credited as 'an old Klingon proverb'. During this and two further intertitles ('Miramax Films Present' and 'A Band Apart') we hear – rather than see – the Bride for the first time, not talking but panting: great, gulping, rasping, whimpering breaths. There follows a cut to an extreme close-up of the Bride's face: she has been brutally beaten and is fighting for air. Feet (shown in a brief cutaway) approach. A man (identified as Bill by the napkin he uses to wipe her face) talks quietly about this moment representing him at his 'most masochistic', and then, just as she shakily tells him 'it's your baby', he shoots her in the head. This is a raw image, a close-up of her bloodied face soaked in sweat and swollen with bruises, her hair matted with blood, showing her shaking and squirming in pain. It visually and aurally articulates her extreme physical suffering in emphatic terms, while also spatially situating the spectator in uncomfortable, intimate audio–visual proximity to it. It represents not

The Bride defies gravity getting to the second level of the House of Blue Leaves in *Kill Bill Vol. 1*

only an emphatic contradiction of our 'action babe' expectations, but also a reversal of the conventional first appearance of the action hero as an intact, assured and attractive figure.[12]

The first full scene continues to play with and undermine the conventions I have suggested constitute the presentation of the 'action babe'. We have moved to a different moment in time: the Bride looks physically intact and healthy as she pulls up in front of a neat, colourful suburban home, toys strewn about the front lawn, flowers blooming under the windows. She rings the bell and as the female occupant of the home opens the door, clearly expecting someone else, a brief flashback shows the woman punching a battered and heavily pregnant Bride to the floor and thus offers motivation for the Bride's present animosity. We will later learn that this is Vernita Green (Vivica A. Fox), one of a team of assassins led by Bill (David Carradine) who subjected the Bride to a beating and tried to kill her. Back in the present the Bride punches Vernita so that she falls backwards into the house and as the door closes behind them they commence an urgent, often close-quarters fight, using knives and household items as well as their bodies. After some time a school bus pulls up outside indicating the arrival of Vernita's four-year-old daughter, Nikki (Ambrosia Kelley). Vernita sends the girl to her room, and the two women move into the kitchen to pause for coffee, debating the rights and wrongs of the Bride's attempts at retribution. Under cover of making Nikki an afternoon snack Vernita shoots at the Bride using a gun secreted inside a box of Cheerios children's breakfast cereal. She misses (her skill is knives, not guns), and before she can pull the trigger again the Bride has thrown a knife into her heart. Nikki is standing silently in the doorway, having witnessed her mother's death: the Bride says she can come and find her when she is older if she 'still feels raw about it', and leaves.

The disjunction between the suburban family house setting and the no-holds-barred fight to the death going on within it – which trashes the tidy, well-kept domestic interior – generates a gallows humour that seems at first glance similar to the strategy of containing female physical action within a comic, fantastical frame that we observed at work in *Charlie's Angels: Full Throttle*. And yet in contrast to the heavily signalled artifice of the Angels' movements in the Mongolian sequence, which dissipates our sense of their bodies as powerful, exerting physical presences, this scene's presentation brings us into close proximity with a much more naturalistic depiction of the female body in action. In wider shots the women's thrusts and lunges are marked by vocal sounds which seem to correspond closely to those that would issue from a real-world body under similar duress, with no attempt to 'feminise' those sounds by modulating them into the sighs and gasps I identified in Chapter 3. Close-ups don't just highlight impacts but pick out signs of exertion at moments of concentrated effort when the women are using all their strength against each other. Early in the scene the Bride traps Vernita in a head-lock and the editing dissects the act in a series of close-ups that redouble our attention to the body. First comes a medium frontal close-up of both women grimacing in the headlock and a jump cut to a slightly closer but more mobile view which makes the sweat on their faces, wet fringes stuck to foreheads and facial bruising more visible. Vernita is gurgling and strug-gling for breath, the Bride is breathing heavily with the effort of maintaining advantage. A series of extreme close-ups follow: the first shows Vernita's hand trying to rip the Bride's hand away, and picks out beads of sweat, popping veins and straining muscles on both their hands. The second and third move between the two women's twisting, sweating faces before more shots of hands, of Vernita thumping and pulling at the Bride's arm in a vain attempt to loosen it from her neck. Such filmmaking choices move us into close sensory as well as optical proximity to these exerting bodies. The sense of the physical work and bodily consequences of violent action is intensified by the inclusion of sights and sounds that have a tactile quality, bringing us nearer to these onscreen bodies' experiences (see Marks 2000: 127–93).[13] As the Bride squeezes Vernita's neck we hear her leather jacket's fabric squeak-ing as it stretches, a sound that appeals to our own body-memories of material stretching against the skin during physical exertion or extension. Glass tables, shelves and picture frames are quickly smashed as the fight develops, scatter-ing shards everywhere: several shots highlight the vulnerability of human skin by showing a hand, face or body being pricked by or crunched against these sharp, penetrating surfaces, again sensations we can imagine based on our own embodied experiences in the world. The use of glass here recalls a similar strategy in *Die Hard* (1988) when John McClane must walk across shattered glass with bare feet, communicating in a toe-curling, exquisitely vivid way the hero's capacity for physical endurance. By the end of the scene the two women's groomed, feminine presentation, as well as the iconography of the affluent woman's family home, has been thoroughly broken down, setting them at a distance from normative constructions of femininity not just in their physical exertions but in terms of 'appearances'.

The film puts in place an explanatory device that explains the Bride's violent acts, but this revenge motivation is almost fetishistically overdeter-mined so as to self-reflexively undermine the device's containing effects. Not only does the Deadly Viper Assassin Squad attempt to kill the Bride after a prolonged and distressing gang beating, they also massacre her whole wedding party, including her fiancé and her friends. She was pregnant at the time, so it appears (for most of the first film) that as a result of the attack they have also killed her baby. She survives, but does not regain consciousness for four years; in the intervening period while she is comatose she is repeatedly raped and pimped out to other men by a hospital orderly. She also subsequently overhears the hospital orderly's remarks that the physical trauma of the original assassination attempt has left her unable to have further children. These traumatic events explicitly position her as the hero of a female revenge narrative, like the protagonists of films such as *I Spit On Your Grave* (1978) and *Ms 45* (1981), which depict raped women so traumatised and angered by their experiences that they are driven to kill their rapist (and/or other men). But the events also read as a series of horrors perpetrated against her, horrors that only continue within the timeframe the two *Kill Bill* films depict as she is shot, stabbed, sliced and buried alive. Thus she is also constructed as an active female survivor like those in slasher movies such as *The Texas Chain Saw Massacre* (1974), *Halloween* (1978) and *The Texas Chainsaw Massacre 2* (1986), that Carol Clover calls the 'Final Girl' (Clover 1992: 35). The Final Girl's physical aggression is motivated (or we might say explained) by the trauma of watching her friends die horribly, and is directed at the killer himself at the end of the film; in this way she embodies both 'suffering victim and avenging hero' (ibid.: 17). Both the heroine of rape revenge and the vengeful Final Girl are inextricably linked by an anger that then enables their physical aggression. The Bride's past experiences and the violent episodes we are party to in the present locate the Bride in this tradition of angry, suffering, survivor figures. However, the overdetermined nature of the Bride's multiple motivating traumas makes allusions to these earlier moments in film history at which women were physically aggressive register merely as homage. Nevertheless they do refer us to previous different ways to depict and frame female exertion and aggression, something that, as I will shortly suggest, the film is very much interested in exploring.[14]

The Bride might therefore be seen as a progressive representation of the female action hero, rooted in real-world physics and physiology, crediting the female body with a convincing capacity for physical action that works against traditional gendered expectations of the kind that motivate McCarthy's scepticism at *Salt*. But this is only half the story. Alongside the series of action sequences in the *Kill Bill* films that direct us towards the naturalistic depiction of her pain, endurance and violent exertions (being shot and buried alive, her training with Pai Mei, her fight with Elle and so on), other sequences adopt a very different stylistic and tonal register. Scenes of her acquiring transport, hotel accommodation and clothing with ease (a motorcycle, cars, various flights, various outfits), and being able to take her samurai sword on a flight as a carry-on item, place us back in the world of the impossibly affluent 'action babe'. Action sequences like the massacre of the Crazy-88 Gang at the House of Blue Leaves restaurant similarly move the physical action into a fantastical register, not just through the hyperbolically stylised, credulity-stretching bloody violence often associated with Tarantino's directorial style. In several ways the sequence works to point up the artifice of the fighting.

The interior design of the brightly coloured, well-lit hall where the massacre happens combines mock exterior features (plants, bamboo trees, a pond, roof canopies, mock street lamps) with other elements that foreground the space's constructed artifice: a stage, an ornamental Zen stone and sand garden under a glass floor, parasols and chandeliers. Evoking the ostentatious stages for significant confrontations in kung fu movies like *Fist of Fury* (1972), the House of Blue Leaves also brings to mind other artistic forms where precise choreography and stylised forms of physical movement are crucial, such as Western musical theatre or Chinese opera. The samurai swordfight between the Bride and the Crazy-88 Gang necessitates controlled, but graceful and fluid physical movements from her that might bring to mind the 'ladylike' fighting style of the Angels. The swooshing and clashing of metal, and the 'pause/burst/pause' pattern of the fight moves and combinations, lend an expressive audio-visual rhythm to the sequence that emphasises highly choreographed rather than naturalistic modes of human motion, a sense heightened by the obvious use of wire work to create bodies that occasionally seem weightless, such as when the Bride and her pursuer Johnny Mo (Gordon Liu) reach the upper level of the House by 'running' up the walls.[15] The impression of a series of dance 'numbers' is strengthened by occasional use of frontal framing in combination with dramatic lighting or colour (the Bride's bright yellow costume; the section of the fight that is silhouetted against a primary-coloured background), and the way the scene is set to a series of pieces of music, roughly one for each stage. Such presentational conventions operate as explicit homages to the wire work-enabled spectacles of Chinese and Hong Kong swordplay movies, such as the Tsui Hark-produced *Swordsman* (1990, 1992) and *Once Upon a Time in China* series (1991–1997) and later cross-overs like *Crouching Tiger, Hidden Dragon* (Ang Lee, 2000) and *Hero* (Yimou Zhang, 2002). But they also distance us from the work of the action body, from an embodied connection to the actual exertions that make its movements possible. Thus the scene's fantasies of empowerment are experienced at a distance, 'over there' rather than 'here'.

Kill Bill Vols 1 and *2* display a central, unyielding tension between two radically different modes of presentation, a tension that they make no attempt to resolve. Indeed I would suggest that the films are fascinated by the possibilities and problems of displaying female physical violence onscreen. Some of their scenes locate impossible physical feats in an explicitly fantasy context. Other scenes authenticate the Bride's active body in biologically credible terms, bringing us into close proximity and sensory engagement with its exertions and achievements. While this has been taken as a symptom of Tarantino's contrary, provocative approach to filmmaking, the representational and tonal tension in *Kill Bill* also embodies contrasting tendencies evident in wider US cinema about how to depict female physical action: credible or incredible, realistic or comical-fantastical, normatively feminine or not. As the first half of this chapter demonstrated, the tendency most popular in the 2000s has been that seen in the 'action babe' films. In the context of postfeminist discourses of choice and consumerism, these 'action babes' embody fantasies of empowerment that are not just physical but socio-economic, and represent a sanitised picture of female perpetrated violence, but within the containing frame of overt fantasy settings. In this dominant representational mode images of physical stress and extension and the actual biological consequences of violence are suppressed. But these untidy signs of female physical agency are finding their way onto screens at the margins of mainstream Hollywood. Films like *Monster* (2003), *Hard Candy* (2005) and *The Brave One* (2007) continue the approach evident in some parts of the *Kill Bill* films by forcing the spectator into close proximity with a viscerally realistic physicality, aggression and rage. Only *The Brave One* (as a clear example of a vigilante film in the tradition of the *Death Wish* series)[16] has a direct generic relationship to action cinema, although the other two feature revenge as a motivator for physical aggression; all three were small films at the margins of mainstream production.[17] The question posed by the marginal presence of these alternative depictions is whether the much more naturalistic, credible images of active female physicality they provide will find their way back into the action cinema. Although 'action babe' cinema has been quite homogeneous in its containing strategies, I want to suggest that as the decade has progressed, the polarised nature of the opposition between 'action babe' cinema and other modes of representing female physicality is beginning to break down. Naturalistic portrayals of active female bodies exerting and under stress are starting to appear in mainstream action cinema, for example the literal and brutal punch-up between John (Brad Pitt) and Jane (Angelina Jolie) in *Mr and Mrs Smith*, the rough, physical fight between terrorists and FBI agent Janet Mayes (Jennifer Garner) as part of a rescue mission in *The Kingdom* (2007), and the explicit foregrounding of Alice (Milla Jovovich)'s rage – and raw, 'unladylike' screams – in *Resident Evil: Extinction* (2007). This may well be a case of Hollywood trying to assimilate alternative depictions back into the mainstream, in the process containing any radical force those depictions might have had, but I would like to end the chapter by introducing an optimistic note. Images of credibly powerful, convincingly physically potent women in action have the potential to leave 'lasting impression[s]' (to use Tasker's phrase (1993: 140)), because they engage the senses of the spectator much more directly. In this way our memories of our embodied experiences of these women's physically empowered actions might help these representations outlive and exceed the containing frames that mainstream action cinema tries to impose, prompting less talk of gender switches and more space for women to be active in action cinema without their presence being qualified.

NOTES

1. Tasker notes that active heroines are usually located within narratives that 'repeatedly seek to explain her (and to explain her away)' (Tasker 1998: 69).
2. The phrase is proposed by O'Day (2004), in an account that I will be engaging with later in the chapter. In what follows I will continue to use O'Day's 'action babe' moniker to help distinguish this mode of depicting the female action heroine from other modes, particularly given the phrase's fitting connotations of objectification, visual assessment and gender stereotyping.
3. The term 'containment strategy' is used by Ed Guerrero in relation to portrayals of African Americans, but the concept is also relevant in relation to portrayals of women (see Guerrero 1993: 244).
4. The exploitation movies of the late 1960s and early 1970s took advantage of the relaxation of censorship to provide products targeted at a large youth market that was not being catered for by mainstream Hollywood products (Hillier 1993: 38–49; Neale 2000: 121). While each exploitation movie had to deliver a certain quota of sex, violence and nudity, beyond that directors appear to have had some creative freedom during this period, able to include references to social issues such as rape, abortion or domestic violence within the narrative, if in rather lurid terms. So for example *Caged Heat* addresses themes of brutality and exploitation in a women's prison, but this is the catalyst for an action sequence at the film's climax initiated by and fully participated in by women. A bunch of female ex-cons take up rifles and guns and storm the prison where their friend is being brutalised by the prison doctor, blowing away the prison officers who try to stop them.
5. For example, in *Fantastic Four* Sue Storm (Jessica Alba)'s invisibility power is unstable, affected by her emotional state. In one sequence she becomes visible in front of a crowd of people after she has stripped to her underwear.
6. In a pause in the face-off between Moore's ex-Angel and Diaz's Angel, she leans into Diaz and lingeringly licks her face in a parodic performance of lesbian desire.
7. In *Bringing Up Baby*, for example, Katharine Hepburn's character is permitted agency – her actions drive the narrative – and a physicalised performance that would be deemed 'unladylike' in other generic contexts, playing golf, climbing buildings, driving cars and dragging a leopard around, in marked contrast to the male character's passive, reactive role.
8. There have been other kinds of narrative containment too; the *femmes fatales* of 1940s *film noir*, who used their sexuality to control weak, often paranoid men to criminal ends, were usually locked up or killed by the narrative's end, in films like *The Lady from Shanghai* (Orson Welles, 1941), *Double Indemnity* (Billy Wilder, 1944), and *Out of the Past* (Jacques Tourneur, 1947).
9. See '*Kill Bill 1* teaser trailer' on Buena Vista Home Entertainment's 2005 DVD release *The Kill Bill Collection*. The trailer judiciously edits material from the film so that, despite showing some fight excerpts in which Thurman's clothes are bloodied, her face and those of the Bride's female opponents are generally free from blood, and there is no inkling of the image of the brutalised body the opening will provide.
10. Bruce Lee died before *Game of Death* could be finished. Several versions of the film have been released, intercutting footage of Lee with a range of look-alikes and doubles, including *Game of Death* (Robert Crouse, 1978).
11. The samurai sword signals Tarantino's efforts to associate the Bride with female warriors in non-Western traditions of martial arts cinema. Chinese and Hong Kong swordplay movies, or *wuxia pian*, were heavily influenced by Japanese samurai films. They presented

tales of chivalrous swordfighters in ancient, fantasy-filled settings, where the quality
of the swordplay itself was the key visual signifier of the central protagonist's heroism.
As Stephen Teo points out, in 'their heyday (from 1966 to 1972), some of the best
wuxia movies emphasised the skill of the swordfighter, male and female', and one of
the 'established types' of this genre was the swordswoman (Teo 1997: 99). Alongside
swordplay movies developed the *gung fu pian*, or kung fu movie, and here women have
also featured as action heroines. Kwai-Cheung Lo has noted the way that Hong Kong's
'women actioner films as such have provided a model for many recent Hollywood
blockbusters' featuring action heroines (Lo 2007: 126).

12. This convention holds true most of the time in action cinema, with some exceptions (such
as *Spider-Man*, for instance) and is certainly rigorously adhered to in the female action
film.

13. Laura U. Marks' work on haptic visuality helps us to see how such images, with their
emphasis on tactility, 'bring the image closer to the body and the other senses' (Marks
2000: 152).

14. The rape revenge films and slasher movies mentioned deploy a number of filmic strategies
to encourage an embodied engagement with the onscreen body, including judicious use
of Steadicam work to 'embody' a killer's gaze, and close-ups that pick out the visceral
consequences of violence or the physiological and psychological responses of the female
protagonist to the horrors she is forced to witness and the violence she is driven to
perpetrate.

15. Bordwell notes that Hong Kong cinema makes use of this heavily stylised choreographic
strategy to create a sense of speed and skill during fight sequences: 'Very often the
performers' movements are not continuous . . . The result is an overall flow that harbors
a percussive rhythm. The short pauses articulate stages of action, giving them a staccato
efficiency. The static instants also make the movements seem more rapid by contrast'
(Bordwell 2000: 221).

16. The series starred Charles Bronson and began with *Death Wish* (Michael Winner, 1974),
in which architect Paul Kersey (Bronson) goes on a vengeful rampage against the low-lives
of New York after his wife is murdered by street criminals. The film generated four direct
sequels and other vigilante films.

17. All three were independent productions targeted at a cross-over art cinema / mainstream
audience.

CHAPTER 5

Action men

BEING A MAN ABOUT IT

In the Introduction I noted that the approach of the millennium prompted a series of films, including *The Truman Show*, *Fight Club*, *The Matrix*, *Dark City* and *eXistenZ*, which depicted a crisis of masculine control. David Bordwell has wryly described this crisis as 'evidently one of the longest-running crises in history' (Bordwell 2006: 104), but as Martin Fradley argues, while 'a rhetorically compelling and suitably angst-filled narrative of white male decentring and decline has become one of *the* master narratives in post-1960s American culture' this discourse had become 'especially pronounced in the 1990s' (Fradley 2004: 239). Reflecting cultural anxieties that extended beyond gender, such as media saturation and the growing ubiquity of digital technologies and commodity fetishism, the films also expressed an uncertainty about the possibility of a heroic male masculinity that flowed from debates and socio-cultural developments around gender identity that took place during the 1980s and 1990s, and which are worth reviewing here in order to provide some context for the consideration of 2000s male action heroes that follows.

The pumped-up strong bodies of 1980s action cinema epitomised by *Rambo: First Blood Part II*, *Commando* (1985) and *Predator* (1987) had looked suddenly out of place in the aftermath of the 1980s AIDS epidemic, which was repeatedly visualised in the mainstream press as an emaciated male death. Health could no longer be 'read' in the male body's external physical structures and appearance, rendering the macho body-builder physique redundant as a symbol of male vitality and strength. At the same time government reticence in the face of the epidemic fired up a queer activism that pushed gay and queer identities and representations much further into the public eye, driven by an emergent queer theory that laid bare the constructed nature of traditional gender identities and the fluid possibilities of queering gender and sex roles.

Women's growing presence and empowerment in the workplace persisted into the 1990s as second wave feminism's legacy continued to be felt, and this coincided with a collapse of skilled and unskilled manual labour – as computers hastened automation – that moved many men into sedentary white collar office jobs. In this context, anxieties thrived amongst men and within the culture at large about the stability of traditional notions of masculinity. The decade was bookended by two publications that summed up this sense of crisis and garnered much media attention: Robert Bly's *Iron John: A Book About Men* (1990), the catalyst for a men's movement speaking to men in crisis, and Susan Faludi's book *Stiffed: The Betrayal of Modern Man* (1999), which documented men's reflections on the causes of their perceived disenfranchisement. The books both revealed in their different ways 'backlash anxieties that straight white men had lost out not only to women, but also other minority groups', producing a 'rhetoric of white male victimization' (Rehling 2009: 25). Two cultural figures emerged from this narrative of victimisation: the iconographic figure of the 'angry white male' personified by D-FENS (Michael Douglas) in Joel Schumacher's 1993 film *Falling Down*, and the 'New Man', a figure forged in the men's movement's focus on self-questioning, self-reflection and acknowledging emotions.

Falling Down's angry white male self-consciously demonstrated the problem of the moral basis on which the white male could 'act out'; in the face of the abstract cultural, economic and corporate forces that were the real contributing factors to his frustrated disenfranchisement, D-FENS is forced to find individual people on whom to take his frustration out, most of whom are arguably equally if not more disenfranchised, and who receive a punishment from D-FENS that is excessive in relation to their 'sins'. Action cinema's desire to construct a reasonably compelling moral justification for violence thus prompted a move away from the angry white male to the sensitive 'New Man', who found his cinematic equivalent in older, thoughtful figures in positions of paternal authority, such as Clint Eastwood as a troubled secret service agent in *In The Line of Fire* (1993), Tommy Lee Jones as an Emergency Management director in *Volcano* (1997), Harrison Ford as a CIA Analyst in *Patriot Games* (1992) and *Clear and Present Danger* (1994) and as the US President in *Air Force One* (1997).[1] These older men's physiques are also indicative of a negotiation over the body image of the hero which was evident in other strands of action cinema across the decade. The context for this negotiation was the shifts in body images in the media more generally, especially in relation to issues of gender, sexuality and health, in response to the mixture of socio–cultural factors glossed above. Style magazines promoted androgynous, 'genderless' bodies, and constructed a fashionable body shaped by so-called 'heroin chic': an undernourished physical frame, pale skin, and static and lifeless rather than energised and vigorous in appearance (see Blanchard 1997). Correspondingly in action cinema the inflated musculature of Stallone and Schwarzenegger looked increasingly anomalous, and was replaced by the thinner, less muscular physique of actors like Bruce Willis, Tom Cruise, Keanu Reeves and Nicholas Cage. By 1991, Schwarzenegger's terminator killing machine had already been refigured as protector and stand-in father-figure in *Terminator 2: Judgment Day* (James Cameron, 1991); by the time of *Terminator 3: Rise of the Machines* (Jonathan Mostow, 2003) Schwarzenegger's character is explicitly described as an obsolete model superceded by a much more effective female terminator machine.

The strident discourses of male victimisation and crisis – in both cinema and the wider culture – with which the 1990s ended found their equally strident manifestation and riposte in Ridley Scott's *Gladiator* (2000), which heralded the new decade with a forceful declaration of male power and moral certitude. The film charts both its protagonist's profound disenfranchisement and his subsequent remasculinisation through violence. Respected Roman general Maximus (Russell Crowe) is at the film's beginning poised (albeit unwillingly) to become emperor, selected by leader Marcus Aurelius (Richard Harris) over Aurelius's own son, the Machiavellian Commodus (Joaquin Phoenix). When Commodus discovers this he murders Aurelius, has Maximus's wife and son killed, and becomes emperor himself. Maximus is pitched into grief-ridden slavery, and must fight his way through the ranks of gladiators in order eventually to face again the man responsible for his family's murder. The film first depicts Maximus's abject victimisation by visually literalising his being brought low: he responds to the loss of his wife and son by fainting – usually posited as a symptom of female hysteria, and thus figuring his disempowerment as a form of feminisation – and is then bodily strapped down flat during his transportation by his new slave owners, his agency and power radically constrained. His narrative of becoming-powerful is dramatised as an emphatic rising-up from this position of stasis and weakness. In the gladiatorial ring we witness the escalation of his determination, fighting and leadership skills, his ability to rise above others as they are felled by his penetrating swordsmanship and aggressive fighting style, and the visible 'hardening up' of the body as he graduates from flimsy, breachable sackcloth to a leather tunic and a single metal shoulder plate to the glinting, hard surfaces of his full armour, sword and shield. This rising-up is underpinned by a moral dimension – he rises back to the status of respected hero by ridding Rome of the poisonously dictatorial Commodus in a staged challenge between the two. Commodus had attempted to seal Maximus's fate by stabbing him in the back before the fight. But even while dying from the wound Maximus manages to kill Commodus, saving Lucille and her son from his perverse machinations, and reinstalling the Senate to Rome before he 'returns' to his dead family. Maximus's moral certitude and moral victory are thus emphatically overstated, reliant on the overdetermined demonisation of Commodus as his self-regarding, ruthless, jealous, murderous and sexually perverse opposite.[2] In Maximus's valiant death is thus conflated the victory of male physicality, redemption through violence, and the reinstatement of white, male heterosexuality and the rule of law.

Gladiator marked an emphatic return to the explicit spectacularisation of the male body that was a key characteristic of the action films of the 1980s. The 1980s male hero displayed a pumped-up, hyper-muscular body that declared its own power and impenetrability even as the hysterical over-determination of that body revealed anxieties about its capacity to remain intact and in control. As Peter Lehman has observed, all visual representations of masculinity are polarised between the spectacular assertion of phallic power and the corresponding collapse of that power, but in 1980s action cinema this resulted in a white male body constructed as 'both powerful and suffering', heroically enduring victimisation and torture (what Tasker calls 'metonymic representations of castration') before the final victory is enacted (Lehman 1993: 31, Tasker 1993: 127).[3] *Gladiator*'s narrative of becoming operates in the same way: Maximus's suffering is repeatedly extended in psychological and physical ways by the scheming Commodus, and he becomes the apotheosis of Tasker's 'powerful and suffering' hero as he overcomes Commodus while suffering the pain of his own slow death. Fradley finds a 'distinctly phallic metaphor' in this 'fall, abjection and subsequent rise of white masculinity', but the film itself displays no such self-awareness (Fradley 2004: 240). While the 1980s heroic body was often framed by 'a humour which is centred on the performance of gendered identity' (Tasker 1993: 127), *Gladiator*'s spectacle of masculine power is deadly serious, a sincere assertion of morality and the rightness of a mightily physical male body, rather than a knowing performance of gender. It rehearses in overdetermined ways male victimisation and loss of power, but it also represents an attempt to reject these discourses of male 'weakness' by eulogising an explicitly physicalised spectacle of male power. *Gladiator* is vehemently nostalgic for a mythical past moment at which 'the physical values of masculinity were assured, a time when women's role was marginal . . . [and] before the impact of technology that questioned the relevance of physical strength to male identity', a time when the male body was 'untainted by commodity culture and consumerism', as Nicola Rehling has argued (Rehling 2009: 108–9). However, the fact that Maximus must die – partly so that he does not become tainted by the politicking of Rome, it seems – acknowledges the impossibility of this construction of masculinity in a contemporary setting.

Gladiator's massive popularity was a key factor in the resurgence of the historical epic in films like *The Last Samurai* (2003), *Troy* (2004), *Alexander* (2004) and *Kingdom of Heaven* (2005), although each was in its own way narratively preoccupied with the passing of this particular brand of heroic masculinity, even as they celebrated it. Clearly spectators' desire to witness fantasies of empowerment embodied through this vigorous mode of masculine physicality had not dissipated, and the epic male body persists throughout the 2000s. However, the cycle's manifestations later in the decade, in films like *300* (2006), *Beowulf* (2007), *Prince of Persia: The Sands of Time* (2010) and *Clash of the Titans* (2010) display a less serious and more knowing attitude to the construction of this epic male body. Their publicity heralds their origins in fictional and culturally playful source texts: videogames, graphic novels or cult B-movies. The films themselves feature ironic dialogue about gender performativity alongside their hyperbolic declarations of machismo, and they foreground their diegetic artifice with exhibitionist special effects sequences. In this way the films locate their tales of masculine power-under-duress in spaces more explicitly marked as fantasy, and their pumped-up bodies inside a knowing frame that acknowledges cultural negotiations and debates about the construction of masculinity. This shift in the tone of such representations does not simply mark the usual trajectory of a generic cycle towards revisionism and self-referentiality, but is indicative of a wider playfulness in the construction of 2000s male heroism, a playfulness that had its origins in the anxieties and debates of the 1990s.

PLAYFUL MASCULINITIES

The Transporter ends with a high-speed vehicular chase, a fitting finale to a film about an ex-military man, Frank, who transports people and things for money in a much admired (within the film) and much fetishised (by the film) black executive car. But the penultimate action sequence finds Frank in a seaside bus depot, facing henchmen intent on making sure he cannot reach criminal businessman Mr Kwai (Ric Young), stop his human trafficking operation and rescue Kwai's daughter Lai (Qi Shu). Frank has just lost his jersey in a prior scrap with several Kwai footsoldiers in the cramped spaces between and inside the parked buses, so when he reaches the bus depot he must confront his next attacker bare chested. The man is tall, at least a foot taller than Frank, and fully clothed, so that Frank's bare skin registers his vulnerability in relation to his larger (and thus potentially more powerful) opponent. Frank bests him in a dirty fistfight – ears and genitalia as much targets as heads, stomachs and legs – but the man manages to pull Frank into a headlock as five new thugs run forward with pipes and iron bars. Fending them off with kicks initially, Frank kicks over a barrel of oil so that it spills all over the floor, forcing the men to lose their footing. Using one of the depot uprights as leverage, Frank then slams himself and his tall captor down onto the ground, loosening the headlock which allows him to wriggle free. Frank rolls over to another drum of oil and pours it all over himself. The oil makes it impossible for the thugs to grab hold of Frank's body, while he himself works with the slippery surface to build up momentum for spinning kicks and swift, sliding body movements to outwit the oncomers. Ever resourceful, Frank rolls out of the oil and rips the pedals and pedal clips off a nearby bicycle. He clicks his shoes into the clips so that he now has full purchase on the slick floor, and proceeds to high-kick each of the men into submission. There is a coda to the sequence: as the final thug falls, three more men arrive, this time armed. Frank is forced to use his tall attacker as a human shield as he smashes backwards through a bus depot window and into the water below. The armed men continue shooting at Frank, who shields himself behind the tall attacker's now limp body. In response Kwai's men throw a barrel of gasoline into the water, setting its surface ablaze. Frank is running out of air and must swim further to escape, so he presses his face against his human shield and in a striking inversion of the kiss of life, sucks the air our of the dead man's lungs so that he can swim to safety.

This is the second time Frank's naked torso has been displayed by the film. Earlier he and Lai had to dive through the water underneath Frank's house to escape an attack by Kwai's men, and had to find dry clothes at a neighbouring house. There the sight of Frank's torso (combined with his new status as her protector) prompted romantic feelings in Lai; as a result the display of naked male flesh was framed and justified by the presence of a desiring heterosexual gaze. In the bus depot sequence no such 'guarantee' of Frank's heterosexuality is present in the fictional world, and Frank's nakedness risks generating connotations of other kinds of desiring gaze, particularly since it is placed within a strictly homosocial space. The film does apply some 'macho' connotations to his nakedness. The narrative motivation for his bare chest is his combat ingenuity: he takes his jersey off in a single smooth movement so that he can use it to catch two attackers round the neck, pulling them close so he can dispatch them with a double punch to their heads in the fight between the buses. The film has exchanged Frank's usual costume of suit and tie for the bare-chested fighting style of the martial arts expert, epitomised in Bruce Lee's iconic pose of battle-readiness, which Statham mimics here. Frank's dirtied face and torso also recall the paint-daubed skin of the combat soldier, camouflaged for battle. In this way the film reiterates Frank's skill and versatility as a fighter, able to mix his fighting styles to suit the occasion. But the sequence also brings other kinds of association to bear as the fight progresses, which seem to undercut the traditional constructions of fighting masculinity already mentioned. Oil, usually used for the inside of machines, is here poured over the body, coating it in a glistening film that calls up the oiled male figures of certain strands of homosexual and heterosexual pornography in which the male body is located as a passive object of sexual desire. Moreover, as the men struggle for purchase in the oil slick, accompanied by the sounds of squirting sludge and wet skin

Frank uses his clothes as defensive and offensive weapons in *Transporter 3*

contacts on the soundtrack, the fight increasingly resembles the eroticised objectification of female mud wrestling. Presenting the naked torso within a scene of physical combat is one of the ways Steve Neale suggests the action film suppresses the erotic component of male display in a homosocial environment (Neale 1983: 12). But this frame cannot – and I would argue is not intended to – fully contain the connotations of heterosexual and homosexual erotic display mobilised by the presence of the oil in combination with Frank's nakedness. Indeed, the sequence seems instead to be interested in playful references to constructions of masculinity that are different, in terms of physicality and sexuality, from the traditional explicitly heterosexual, macho male action hero. For example, there is a reference to the fluid grace of the male tap dancer: when Frank dons the pedal clips and steps menacingly back into the oil towards his opponents, he seems to dance towards the men (building to a turn worthy of Fred Astaire, but which ends in a deadening kick), the pedals clicking beneath his feet like tap shoes. Later, in the water, as he takes the air from the dead thug's lungs, the image reads in every way like a lingering kiss between the two men. Both instances, like the staging of the oil fight, exceed the frame of narrative motivation and the traditional terms of the construction of the action hero's masculinity.

Even with the alibi of a nifty fight move Frank's willingness to take off his shirt shows he is comfortable with displaying his body, despite the aggressive homosocial spaces through which he must move. Rather than suggesting that Frank is therefore occupying a passive position as eroticised object normally reserved for women, we should see this instead in the context of a contemporary Western culture in which the display of the male body is commonplace. Paul Smith argues that

> [t]here exists a whole cultural production around the exhibition of the male body in the media – not just in film, but in television, sports, advertising, and so on – and this objectification has even been evident throughout the history of Hollywood itself, while evidently having been intensified in recent years. Scarcely any of this plethora of images depend upon the feminization of the male. (Smith 1993: 158)

Written in 1993, Smith's words ring even more true today, given the proliferation of advertising platforms and the ever-increasing ubiquity of images stoking our consumer culture. Smith admits that such displays risk a 'possible disturbance in the field of sexuality' that must be mitigated against, but interestingly *The Transporter* seems less invested in this type of mitigation than we might expect (ibid.: 160). I have suggested that the bus depot action sequence refers us to homosexual and heterosexual economies of erotic consumption of the male form, and to less overtly masculinised forms of physical movement.

This is notably not 'offset' by the heavily emphasised heterosexist and homo-phobic pronouncements typical of some strands of action cinema, deployed to shore up the hero's heterosexuality at moments where he displays his body. A small amount of rather perfunctory off-setting occurs in the briefly-drawn implication that Frank and Lai have offscreen sex, but it is not dwelt upon; the pre-emptive kiss is rather chaste by all accounts and is prefaced by Frank's per-sistent protestations that he doesn't like 'complications' (read 'women'). At the same time, this is a man who is very particular about his sartorial choices and the upkeep of his smart, expensive car and spotless garage, and who keeps an unassuming but chic *pension* in Marseilles. This kind of attention to detail, to personal grooming and to life's pleasures distinguishes Frank from the action heroes of 1980s and 1990s action cinema (who even in their nurturing mani-festations were tough and fairly macho in attitude), and moves him closer to a set of characteristics stereotypically associated with the male homosexual. In this way Frank seems to exemplify the 'metrosexual male', a term first coined by British cultural commentator Mark Simpson in 1994, and elaborated in his 2002 article, 'Meet the metrosexual'. Simpson argued that by the mid-1990s advertisers and lifestyle magazines were targeting a new consumer figure, the affluent male who is particular about his appearance, and less concerned than older generations about policing the traditional boundaries of sexual desire.

> The typical metrosexual is a young man with money to spend, living in or within easy reach of a metropolis – because that's where all the best shops, clubs, gyms and hairdressers are. He might be officially gay, straight or bisexual, but this is utterly immaterial because he has clearly taken himself as his own love object and pleasure as his sexual preference. (Simpson 2002: paragraph 7)

The British footballer David Beckham is a key figure in Simpson's account, sporting frequent new haircuts, a moisturised complexion and the odd item of traditionally female clothing in the name of fashion, happy to advertise a range of consumer products, and comfortable with displaying his body to both male and female admirers as part of his sponsorship duties. In a similar way Frank confidently embraces the luxuries he owns, those things that mark his exist-ence within an individualist, pervasive consumer culture, is happy to display his body to both women and men, and is comfortable enough about his own sexuality to 'kiss' a man for the pragmatic reason of acquiring oxygen.

The film's ease at presenting us with this metrosexual male and his naked flesh is for David Greven a sign of the queering of representation that develops during the 1990s and 2000s following the increased visibility of queer identi-ties in the media and an explosion of queer films in the 1990s, an idea we will return to in Chapter 6 (Greven 2009: 6). Certainly Frank in *The Transporter* is an example of a contemporary action hero who appears more 'relaxed' and reticent about the need continually to re-assert his heterosexual credentials, either in dress, word or deed, within films that are more explicitly knowing in their references to alternative constructions of masculinity and sexuality. We might think here of Vin Diesel's flamboyant outfits and bodily display in the *xXx* films (2002, 2005), 'evil' Peter Parker (Tobey Maguire)'s lively dance performance to a jazz number in *Spider-Man 3* (2007), or the spandex, leather costumes and buff bodies in *Daredevil* (2003), *Beowulf* and the *Fantastic Four* films, although each displays varying levels of self-consciousness. In the two *Transporter* sequels Frank continues to take his clothes off, and his attention to sartorial details becomes even more pronounced: in both films he stops a fight from starting until he has hung his jacket up to avoid it being damaged, and in *Transporter 3* during a garage fight sequence Frank uses his jacket, shirt, tie and another man's belt variously to strangle, lasso and whip his opponents. But there is a difference between knowingly referencing homosexual and heterosexual economies of erotic consumption and elements of the gay male stereotype, and openly acknowledging the possibility of homosexual interaction. As David Greven observes, '[m]asculinity has become self-aware, yet it still clings to strategies of disavowal' (ibid.: 242). The veneer of cool, metrosexual consumerism is explicitly marked as a performance in the films, one that keeps criminal clients at a distance, conceals Frank's activities from the prying eyes of the police, and hides his emotions from prospective 'complications'. At the same time, underneath the sharp suits and expensive accoutrements is the body of a highly effective fighter. Frank can perform different layers of playful masculinity and the film allows us to be complicit in these knowing performances through its use of excess (like the oil in the bus depot) and through characters' ironic asides. But in place of open protestations, Frank's fighting prowess operates as the guarantee that he is, under the façade of metrosexual consumer, a normative, physically powerful construction of heterosexual masculinity. This is a playful masculinity that is, then, carefully qualified.

FRAMING UNCERTAINTY

A playful knowingness is also evident in the 2000s superhero cycle. For example the male heroes in *X-Men* and *Hancock* comment overtly on the rather camp costumes they have been asked to wear, outfits that would normally be a naturalised element in the fictional world of such films. More often it is the male hero's narrative of becoming that is the subject of knowing humour, perhaps inevitably given the superhero narrative's concern with origin stories that often show the hero discovering and struggling to control his new powers. In *Fantastic Four* Johnny Storm (Chris Evans) discovers his ability to generate fire on a skiing trip with his girlfriend. Johnny has been buried by an avalanche when he turns into a human flame; he ends up in a pool of hot water and invites his disconcerted girlfriend to join him. In *Superman Returns* (2006) Superman remembers his early teens, running at superhuman speeds and jumping huge distances through the fields around his adoptive parents' farm. Misjudging a jump between one farm building and the next, the young hero-to-be crashes clumsily into a rooftop weather vane, through a barn roof and is about to slam into the ground at high speed when he discovers his ability to resist gravity: rather than hitting the ground he is surprised to find he is hovering just above it. Back in the present Superman smiles at the memory, and then throws a ball so far that his faithful labrador can only watch it disappear into the distance with a regretful whimper. Here knowing humour does a significant amount of work, acknowledging the audience's extra-textual awareness of the superhero narrative (and its real-world impossibility), and of the alternative masculinities that might be implied by the costumes and bodies in question, as well as representing one of the protagonist's strategies for coping with his own unruly body. However, implicit in this dynamic of learning to cope that structures the superhero's origin story is an uncertainty that can continue to pervade this particular construction of masculinity, despite its overt empowerment.

The superhero cycle has been one of the most commercially successful manifestations of (predominantly) male heroism in the 2000s, spawning serial blockbusters like *X-Men*, *Spider-Man* and the *Fantastic Four*; the recent *Batman* films *Batman Begins* (2005) and *The Dark Knight* (2008); and films such as *Superman Returns* (2006), *Daredevil* (2003) and the *Blade* (1998, 2002, 2004) movies. While some of these feature women in ensemble casts, the most focused dramatic attention is usually paid to the male figures such as Wolverine (Hugh Jackman), the hero with no memory of his past and a fiery temper, in *X-Men*. These films' popularity proceeds in part from their special effects displays, which can convey super-powers with a photorealism not possible in earlier decades, thanks to advances in digital imaging technologies which gathered pace across the 1990s and into the 2000s. Like other fantasy films superhero movies also have the potential to achieve broad audience appeal drawing on familiar source materials with established fan bases of younger newcomers and adults 'for whom the originals have become the stuff of fond nostalgia' (King and Krzywinska 2000: 62). Kathy Smith suggests that in the 2000s fantasy films performed a further function: that in the wake of the events of 9/11 they met the needs of audiences seeking a ' "guaranteed" fantasy, the reality of which was securely beyond imagination' after the real-world horrors of 9/11 (Smith 2005: 69–70). King is sceptical, pointing out that 'any shift in the centre of gravity towards more all-out fantasy, in the shape of blockbuster franchises such as *The Lord of the Rings* and *Harry Potter* series, was already in train well before the events of September 2001' (King 2005: 56).[4] Nevertheless it is likely that the ongoing popularity of the superhero film through the 2000s represents a desire amongst audiences to explore heroism and its motivations in a context safely divorced from the ethical dilemmas and complications of real-world politics and war in Iraq and Afghanistan, a phenomenon I will return to in Chapter 8. What interests me in this chapter is the way in which the superhero movie permits a particular mode of heroic masculinity that is explicitly uncertain, one that brings together playful knowingness with a sense of the powerful male body as unruly.

In *Spider-Man* shy awkward teenager Peter Parker gains his powers after being bitten by a genetically modified spider on a school visit. This results in a number of unexpected changes to his body as his powers begin to manifest themselves. He looks in the mirror to find he has a newly muscular body; he then checks under the briefs he is wearing, and looks very pleased with what he finds there. But he is also ejaculating white, glutinous webbing from his wrists in an initially uncontrolled fashion, and his powers fluctuate depending on his mood. The gaining and discovery of powers plays here like the typical growing pains and physical discoveries of puberty (albeit in a fantasy context) including analogies for the specifically male pubertal issues of premature ejaculation and erectile unpredictability. As the narrative progresses, Parker displays uncertainty about how he should use his new powers, makes mistakes including one which causes the death of his uncle, and almost rejects the path of heroism completely. The film thus presents us with a complicated figure of heroic masculinity, a physically powerful, heroic male who is also the fey, hesitant, self-questioning and emotional teenager, but also constructs power as in itself potentially dangerous. This divided masculinity – extremely powerful but unstable or questioning – is also to be found even in those superhero films in which the hero is beyond his teenage years: Wolverine's struggles with his identity and his nature in the *X-Men* films, taking in a crush on a female member of the team, unpredictable rages and competing father figures; Bruce Banner's crisis of control over his body and his temperament in both *Hulk* (2003) and *The Incredible Hulk* (2008); and the Batman's struggle to overcome his inner demons and master his body in *Batman Begins*. The source material contributes significantly to this construction of masculinity; the films have chosen superhero characters for whom crisis or uncertainty is an integral part of their mythos, such as the adolescent, stumbling *Spider-Man* (first appearance 1962), the unstable *Incredible Hulk* (a scientist damaged by radioactive rays transformed into a giant, primitive monster during bouts of uncontrollable rage, first appearance 1962), and the *X-Men* (first appearance 1963) who developed powers at puberty that forced them into a marginalised position in society. But the superhero is in any case almost always a divided figure, particularly in comic books from the 1960s onwards: the body's excessive allocation of power exceeds conventional social and physical frameworks, constructing the superhero as unpredictable and marginalised as well as empowered. As Scott Bukatman has pointed out superhero comic books thus present 'body narratives, bodily fantasies, that incorporate (incarnate) aggrandizement and anxiety, mastery and trauma', with the body of the superhero functioning as the locus for uncertainty and crisis (Bukatman [1994] 2003: 49). Such connotations also pertain to the cinematic superhero, particularly with the deployment of digital imaging that can photorealistically depict the physical instability, metamorphosis and mutancy that is the outward sign of the hero's inner turmoil. Despite the often simplistic morality of these films' villain-hunting endeavours and the superhuman powers displayed by the heroes, the films offer a masculinity defined by its anxious uncertainty, not simply about how to wield power in literal terms (a consideration safely located in an explicitly fictional universe) but about being in the world, about the emotional decisions involved in being among people. Uncertainties and problems with clear real-world application find their place alongside the more abstract theme of power gained and lost, framed within films that are 'only' entertainment, fantasy, the stuff of comic books.[5]

TEEN HEROES AND FATHER FIGURES

This desire to place the exploration of anxieties about male power and judgment within a frame that suggests these are not serious anxieties also seems to drive another set of films that have enjoyed sustained popularity in the 2000s: those featuring young male protagonists, like *The Guardian* (2006), *Live Free or Die Hard*, *Jumper* (2008), *Eagle Eye* (2008), *Zombieland* (2009), the *Transformers* franchise (2007, 2009) and the recent *Scott Pilgrim vs the World* (2010). Clearly designed to extend the appeal of the action film to an even younger audience, these films are also intended to retain older action fans, thus maximising box office potential. The young male heroes in these films display a different brand of playful masculinity than that found in the *Transporter* films, not least because these characters do not have extreme physical strength or agility (although the hero of *Jumper* has a supernatural ability to teleport). Instead they are teenaged, fairly unathletic 'average Joes', plucked from their banal everyday concerns and thrust into a set of circumstances much larger than themselves which they respond to with wry commentary. In *Transformers* Sam Witwicky (Shia Labeouf) purchases a second-hand car that is unbeknownst to him an extraterrestrial robot sent to ask for Sam's help in an intergalactic war between good robots ('Autobots') and bad robots ('Decepticons') that is about to reach Earth. Sam is in possession of a pair of his explorer ancestor's spectacles upon which is a code that reveals the location of a powerful energy cube that the Autobots must prevent the Decepticons from acquiring. Unaware of his car's secret, Sam is traumatised to see it drive away from his home, apparently unmanned, and gives chase on his rickety bicycle to a deserted haulage yard. On the way he calls the police, performing an exaggerated impression of police intercom dialogue gleaned from films and television shows to comedic effect ('Mobilise all units. Bring *everyone*'). At the haulage yard he discovers the car transformed into a towering robot that is projecting a message into the sky. After a staggered pause in which he simply takes in the image, Sam's response is to record a video message on his phone which once again moves the scene into a comic register. As he documents what he thinks are his 'last words on Earth' he tells his parents he loves them and then offers a convoluted apology for the pornographic magazines ('Busty Beauties') they will find under his bed. A slapstick chase between Sam and the yard guard dogs follows before the police apprehend him. Here and throughout the two *Transformers* films Sam supplies the chatter of the comic fool but also the awed reactions of characters caught up in something larger than themselves, in both ways embodying a playful knowingness about the impossibility of the circumstances being presented. Sam is, then, an interesting hero figure for an action movie. He is radically disempowered, like any teenager at the mercy of parents, the school bully and his own hormones, and as events develop also at the mercy of police, secret service agents and the robots that have invaded his life. He is only important by association (his ancestor's spectacles) rather than possessing physical agency himself, and is plagued by the same self-questioning and lack of confidence as any teenager. The hero is depicted at the age when it is 'natural' and expected that a man would be unsure of himself, would show weakness or uncertainty, would sometimes fail. Here heroism derives from surviving and personal conviction, rather than physical action, from trying things and failing, rather than not participating. Anxieties about failure, about power and its loss are thus explored at a distance, projected onto pubescent masculinity rather than being applied to an adult masculinity.

These teenaged heroes are usually teamed up with a young woman who operates as a comic foil and romantic interest, or an older man who passes on his knowledge to the younger man. In *Transformers* it is Mikaela Bane (Megan Fox), Sam's crush but also an extremely competent car mechanic who has learned both the trade and some additional tricks from her father. Her skills will be crucial in the final robot battle when she hotwires a pickup truck, loads up a damaged Autobot and drives the truck backwards through the battle so that the Autobot can fire his cannons into the fight. In so doing she rescues a team of special forces soldiers who have become cornered and are about to perish at the hands of the Decepticons. Nevertheless her experiences of the narrative developments are usually only displayed in relation to Sam, and her agency in the film is quite minimal. Similarly Millie (Rachel Bilson) in *Jumper* must simply watch and wait to see if David (Hayden Christensen) can resolve his difficulties, since she herself does not share his ability to jump through space and time. Predictably she moves into the position of maiden in distress in the film's denouement, a position devoid of agency. It is a different matter when the teenaged male is paired with an older man in films like *The Guardian* and *Live Free or Die Hard*. The older man is usually played by an actor associated with earlier periods of action cinema: in *The Guardian* it is Kevin Costner teaching Ashton Kutcher's character how to be a rescue diver; in *Live Free or Die Hard* it is Bruce Willis putting his young charge Justin Long in protective custody and along the way teaching him about being physically assertive. This means that the older man can still possess agency and physical power within the narrative, although there is an open acknowledgment that they are not as powerful as they once were. The generational difference produces tension between the pair through the first two-thirds of the film, during which the older hero figure gets the opportunity to display his physical power while attempting to teach the reluctant youth. Then comes the moment when the younger man must prove himself, showing what he has learnt: in *The Guardian* when Jake (Kutcher) must dive alone, without Randall (Costner), and in *Live Free or Die Hard* when Farrell (Long) manages to shoot a gun to successfully ward off an attacker. Such father–son relationships are a familiar Hollywood trope, but in movies where heroes are getting younger, these character relationships reassert a patriarchal lineage that frames the teenager's hesitancy and fear within a longer tradition of stable empowerment. Notably also the older hero figure takes on the physical feats that the teenager would normally have to do, subjected to physical strain while the young hero is relegated to the position of spectator. Perhaps driven by the cultural taboo of subjecting young adults to cruelty, the result is films in which the stakes for heroic action are less emphatically experienced.

If the teen hero movie offers a space in which an uncertain heroic masculinity can be rehearsed at a safe distance from adult masculinity (and often in the safe context of explicit fantasy settings), then a similar impulse drives those films that feature older male heroes. Several 1980s action stars have been staging returns to their former roles, like Arnold Schwarzenegger in *Terminator 3*, Stallone directing and starring in *Rocky Balboa* (2006) and *Rambo* (2008), and a plethora of action stars in *The Expendables*. These films construct conflicts that require raw firepower or manpower rather than technological wizardry or diplomatic negotiation to solve them, relocating the solution to the narrative problem squarely in the pumped-up bodies of these ageing heroes, and displaying a nostalgia for a past in which the justification for violence seemed more straightforward. Often this justification is very conventionally gendered: in both *Rambo* and *The Expendables* hundreds of enemy soldiers die violently to make possible the rescue of a woman in danger, while in *Terminator 3* and *Live Free or Die Hard* the threatening spectre of female physical empowerment must be eradicated with excessive violence (the female terminator blown up by a bomb thrust into her mouth, the villainous female martial arts expert crushed under an exploding truck). These films also contain explicit acknowledgment of the age of their heroes, from John McClane's constant refrain that he's getting too old for this in *Live Free or Die Hard* to Lee (Jason Statham)'s repeated suggestion that Barney (Stallone) isn't as fast as he used to be, a playful knowingness which rests on an ageing masculinity rather than alternative masculinities. And yet this gentle acknowledgment that masculine power is not infinite is married with fantasies of empowerment that assert the exact opposite as the films redefine the age limits within which bodies can be active in the visual economy of the action film. This contradiction is often left unresolved at the narrative's end: in *The Guardian* and *Terminator 3* the older hero dies, making way for the younger hero, but in films like *Die Hard* and *The Expendables* there is a strong sense that these characters will continue. Perhaps this is better read as a desire to continue, an attachment to the fantasy of continuing mastery rather than a denial of the frailties of the human form.

PROLIFERATING MASCULINITIES

In the 2000s the manifestations of heroic masculinity seemed to proliferate into a variety of contexts, and into a number of different forms. And yet the proliferation was less diverse than one might think at first glance: most male heroes in the 2000s are white, and while often playfully knowing display the same anxieties that had been found in the millennial male-hero-in-crisis films of the 1990s. What is noticeable is the effort to frame such anxieties, locating them in an explicitly fantasy context like the superhero film, or within a teenaged masculinity in films like *Transformers*, or in a nostalgically recalled past where the justification for violence was a simpler affair. Looking at the decade in this way it makes sense that there is still also a strand of films that overtly confronts crisis and anxiety, either in a generalised way in the resurgent disaster cycle (*The Day After Tomorrow* (2004), *War of the Worlds* (2005), *2012* (2009)) where the male protagonist is most often desperately trying to save his family, or the paranoid male heroes who are witnesses of trauma in *I Am Legend* (2007), *The Happening* (2008), *Cloverfield* (2008) and *The Book of Eli* (2010), or damaged psyches and compromised bodies in *Minority Report* (2002), *Max Payne* (2008), *Gamer* (2009), *Surrogates* (2009) and *Inception* (2010). This trend bears the marks of the 1990s cultural preoccupation with male victimisation, some of the conditions of which are still with us, such as loss of jobs due to technologisation, a rampant consumer culture and persisting negotiations around sexual and gender identity. In its basic concern with power, how to use it and the risk of losing that power, such films are also in a longer tradition, representing a thematic concern that has returned repeatedly in the action film. Nevertheless the paranoia about and dramatic enactments of loss of control that these films rehearse would seem to be driven in large part by the combination of factors that have been experienced by US citizens since 9/11: an increased sense of the threat of terrorism at home and abroad, lack of say in government surveillance and military action, and a resulting generalised sense of fear and disempowerment. Some films have emerged during the same period that I would suggest try to counter these anxieties by positing a hyper-masculine figure, either visually or metaphorically. In *Crank* (Mark Neveldine and Brian Taylor, 2006) for example, the narrative set-up seems designed to permit the male hero to be violent and sexually aggressive. Chev Chelios (Jason Statham) has been injected with a high-tech, slow-acting poison by his enemies, and in order to survive long enough to take revenge and perhaps find an antidote he must keep his heart rate extremely high. He tries to achieve this by exacting bloody violence, driving extremely fast, engaging in rough (and very public) sex and drug taking. *Shoot 'em Up* (Michael Davis, 2007) similarly conflates sexual agency and violent physical aggression in a striking shootout scene. Hitman Smith (Clive Owen) is having sex with rescued prostitute Donna (Monica Bellucci) when several henchmen of the local ganglord Hertz (Paul Giamatti) crash into the room. Smith grabs his revolver and manages to shoot all of the attackers without pausing sexual intercourse, even though he has to change position several times. Indeed as the last henchman is killed Smith also manages to bring Donna to orgasm, the double meaning of the word climax literalised. These films present themselves as action comedies, but in my view they are deadly serious in their promotion of an archetypal masculinity that is, despite the 'knowing winks', violent, aggressive and sexually dominant. How these and the other proliferating masculinities of the last decade will develop in future cinematic representations will be interesting to see.

NOTES

1. See Chapman 1988, Jeffords 1993 and Pfeil 1995.
2. Commodus' incestuous desires for his sister Lucille (Connie Nielsen) contrast with Maximus' normative heterosexuality, which is guaranteed by his attachment to his dead wife and his own attraction to Lucille.
3. Paul Smith calls this process the 'orthodox codes of the action narrative', codes he describes as 'objectification and eroticisation, followed by near destruction and final hypostasisation [a making concrete, making apparent] of the male body' (Smith 1993: 161).

4. The *Harry Potter* films have the following release dates and are listed in the Filmography: 2001, 2002, 2004, 2005, 2007, 2009, 2010, 2011.
5. The obvious exception to this construction of superhero masculinity is *Iron Man* (2008), which is closer to the self-conscious playfulness of *The Transporter* in its depiction of Tony Starck (Robert Downey Junior)'s trajectory from arms dealer to superhero. We will come back to *Iron Man* briefly in Chapter 8.

CHAPTER 6

Race in the action film

Transformers (Michael Bay, 2007) opens with a racially mixed group of US Special Operations soldiers engaged in lively banter on an air transport over Qatar, reminiscing about their shared homeland which, they reveal, means different things to each of them. The brief scene establishes that the men – an African American, a Latin American and two Anglo Americans from different regions of the US – have a history together as a military unit and have developed a teasing but affectionate camaraderie that transcends their racial and regional differences. This depiction of multiracial harmony reflects the increased racial mix of the urban action movie over the previous decade that Beltrán (2005) has observed, but is also an expression of Hollywood's adherence to the 'melting pot' myth that the US is 'a model of multiculturalism and globalism', a place where people of different backgrounds can co-exist peacefully (Beltrán and Fojas 2008: 18). And yet the scene also explicitly foregrounds ethnic and cultural difference as a cause of frustration. The Latin American soldier 'Fig' (short for Figueroa, and played by Amaury Nolasco) is wishing he could eat a plate of his mother's alligator meat when African American Epps (Tyrese Gibson) interrupts to register his disgust at such a gastronomic prospect. Fig counters by pointing out pragmatically that the alligators have the most succulent meat, and then slips into further description in Spanish. Epps objects ('English, please') and Anglo American Captain Lennox (Josh Duhamel) backs Epps up with: 'English. I mean, how many times? We don't speak Spanish, I told you that.' The 'we' here is significant. It isolates Fig from the rest of the group as someone who has not yet displayed the correct behaviours to allow him to assimilate into the US 'melting pot' successfully. As Gina Marchetti has pointed out, access to the 'melting pot' (and its promises of socio-economic ascendance enshrined in the mythology of the American Dream) 'has a price: the rejection of any marker of "foreignness" – for example, a language, a religion, or a culture' (Marchetti 1991: 278).

Here Fig must give up his Spanish and his talk of alligator meat to assimilate fully into the unit, and by implication, into mainstream US culture. The film seems keen to highlight the men's 'colour blind' racial integration, perhaps as an attempt to suggest that the film itself will be 'colour blind' (indeed claims to progressiveness of this kind are not uncommon in contemporary mainstream filmmaking). But the explicit foregrounding of Fig's 'disruptive' culturally-specific references preserves and characterises racial and ethnic difference as a 'challenge' to be surmounted, rather than as a diversity of heritages to be embraced. There is nothing natural about this characterisation of racial difference as being problematic, even though it is naturalised (that is, made to seem natural) by the banal subject-matter of the conversation and the fact that both the African American and the Anglo Americans react similarly. It is salutary to remind ourselves that the men's objections to Fig have been designed in by the film, so that it is the film that inserts the idea that racial and cultural difference is significant, and implies that racial and cultural hierarchies are required to manage such difference.

The film subsequently solidifies into a racial hierarchy that positions a white male at its pinnacle. The racially integrated military team are not the focus of the narrative that follows: instead the Anglo American teenager Sam Witwicky proves to be the key to stopping the robot war which is about to descend on Earth, and he and his romantic interest Mikaela Banes become the central protagonists.[1] The military unit are designated as helpers, lending their military weight and protection to the young pair and the friendly robots when they can. Fig leaves the screen early, seriously injured in one of the initial robot attacks on the military but his final fate not clarified. Meanwhile Epps and Lennox become the familiar white/black buddy pairing (see Tasker 1993: 43–7; Willis 1997: 27–59; Guerrero 1993; Gates 2004), co-ordinating the rest of the Special Ops team. Other non-white characters that appear in the film occupy minor roles as enablers, but these enablers' characterisation rests primarily on broad racial stereotyping that is deployed to generate humour. For example the expansive African American car salesman, played by comedian Bernie Mac, who furnishes Sam Witwicky with his first second-hand car (which turns out to be a robot in disguise) is derogatory about the country his name refers to ('Bobby Bolivia – like the country except without the runs'), while dressing up his Latino employees as clowns. When Captain Lennox tries to ring through to the Pentagon to alert them to the fact that his team is under attack, an Indian call centre worker is unreasonably obstructive while picking his nose in a bored fashion. Later a white Australian telecommunications whizz-kid (Rachael Taylor) working for the Pentagon calls in on an African American friend (Anthony Anderson) to get some expert help with decoding a robot transmission. He and his brother are very overweight, obsessed with dance competition videogames, and emit high-pitched squeals at the sight of FBI agents invading their house, while fretting about what their cantankerous grandmother is going to make of the mess. Such details are played for laughs but display a casual racism in their invocation of racial stereotypes overlaid with hints of effeminacy, emasculation and a predisposition towards panic or confusion. In particular Bobby Bolivia and the two gamer brothers' behaviour and domestic arrangements call up the racist 'coon' and 'mammy' types Donald Bogle identified in Hollywood cinema of the first half of the twentieth century, which are clearly still relevant to today's cinematic representations (Bogle 2000: 7–9). The purpose seems to be to set these peripheral non-white actors apart from Sam Witwicky, whose appeal as a protagonist is based in part on lively verbal and sometimes physical humour, by mobilising negative African American stereotypes to make them seem more ridiculous than Sam. But they are also set apart through their enabler roles, in an action movie tradition of marginalised 'black helpers' (Tasker 1993: 36) that assist the white hero's narrative of becoming; what James Snead called 'the loyal sidekick/retainer' (Snead 1994: 139). The non-white representations depicted in *Transformers* thus vividly illustrate what Kobena Mercer calls the 'regulative function of the stereotype' in assigning markers of race and ethnicity to Hollywood's roster of secondary characters, using performance style and dramatisation as well as narrative function to place the non-white characters 'below' the Anglo American Sam Witwicky in the film's representational hierarchy (Mercer 1994: 199). Thus the film illustrates the way in which, in contemporary action cinema, 'ideologies of white superiority and non-white subordination continue to have a powerful influence, even while the casting, production design and other manifest components of the films promote a multicultural aesthetic', as Mary Beltrán has pointed out (Beltrán 2005: 63).

The ethnicity of the action hero still frequently 'defaults' to Anglo American, and non-white and non-Anglo characters remain on the sidelines, only permitted to be active and heroic in the context of a larger group, such as the roles played by African Americans Halle Berry in the *X-Men* films and Laurence Fishburne and Jada Pinkett Smith in the *Matrix* franchise, and Chinese American Lucy Liu in the *Charlie's Angels* films. As we see in the case of Figueroa in *Transformers*, the sacrificed helper trope also persists, and is a subject I will return to later in the chapter. And yet, as is attested by the careers of people like Vin Diesel, Will Smith, Wesley Snipes and Dwayne 'The Rock' Johnson, space has opened up for some non-white actors to assume the central role of action hero, while placement within the increasingly common multiple protagonist movie does not in itself make it inevitable that non-white and non-Anglo characters will be subordinate to white characters. Having begun by looking at the way in which racial stereotyping can dog minor characters in the action film, the rest of this chapter will investigate the textual negotiations that take place when a non-white or non-Anglo person is placed at the centre of the contemporary action film. In the space available it will not be possible to address all branches of this topic, but my hope is that this chapter will encourage increased awareness of these textual negotiations around race and ethnicity in the action film that can then be applied and developed further. I have chosen to focus on three areas of enquiry: the African American action hero; the Latin American action hero, and the non-Anglo white action hero, as they manifest in contemporary action cinema.

AFRICAN AMERICANS IN AND OUT OF ACTION

Far from being a mere descriptor of character physiognomy, race must be recognized and acknowledged for its structural as well as thematic centrality to the narrative transactions or narrative situations of popular films today. (Everett 1995–6: 27)

Blackness has a particular valence in US culture which is a direct result of it being co-opted to shore up the category of whiteness. Sharon Willis famously declared that whiteness 'has had a hard time seeing *itself* at all', and as Richard Dyer has pointed out, what is at stake in this studied invisibility is the protection and projection of whiteness as the norm against which non-whites can be declared 'raced' (Willis 1997: 3, italics in original; Dyer 1997: 1–3).[2] For white Americans this project has been of particular importance in the face of various demographic shifts that have challenged the idea of the white majority and indeed the coherence of white identity. Since the end of the nineteenth century repeated waves of non-white immigrants and movements of non-whites into urban centres have caused significant increases in people of non-white ethnicities in cities and at a national level; as of 2009 non-whites make up one-third of the North American population.[3] Over the same period immigration from Southern and Eastern European countries has problematised the fixity and singularity of white identity.

Joshua David Bellin has noted how African Americans were positioned 'as *the* fetishised racial "Other"' in the quest to 'sanctify and safeguard the prerogatives of whiteness' in the first third of the twentieth century, but his comments are equally applicable to subsequent periods of US history and cultural production, including Hollywood cinema (Bellin 2005: 36). Jude Davies and Carol R. Smith suggest that

Hollywood represents all ethnic identities according to semiotic codes, the most obvious of which are ethnic stereotypes . . . All of these have performed both representative and transactional functions, but blackness has fulfilled a specific function as the pre-eminent signifier of otherness, in defining the norm by what it is not, and thereby as a means of binding together disparate [white] ethnicities into a dominant American identity. (Davies and Smith 1997: 52)

Many of the meanings associated with blackness in dominant culture are written specifically across the body, an emphasis on physicality that 'does not allow Blacks to be anything other than their bodies' (Dyer 1993: 103). This emphasis does, however, make the African American a good 'fit' for the universe of action cinema, which is itself predicated on a preoccupation with physicality and the body as spectacle (Tasker 1993: 35). As a result in the 1980s and 1990s, while African Americans continued to fulfil their 'helper' role in 1980s films like *Commando*, *Predator* and *Die Hard*, they were also making their way to the centre ground of the action film, in the 'protective custody' of white heroes in buddy action films like *48 Hrs* (1982) and *Lethal Weapon* (1987), and then as the singular action hero of *Predator 2* (1990). Across the 1990s African Americans continued to prosper in the action genre, and although some were still in the 'custody' of either white men (*Die Hard: With a Vengeance* (1995), *Men in Black* (1997)) or white females in a run of detective thrillers such as *Kiss the Girls* (1997), *The Bone Collector* (1999) and *Along Came a Spider* (2001), Will Smith's growing public profile as a popular rapper and television sitcom star encouraged movie executives to place him as the action hero in films like *Bad Boys* (1995) and *Enemy of the State* (1998) (as well as the hugely successful ensemble hit *Independence Day*).

These different permutations of the African American presence in the action film – helper, buddy or sole action hero – continue into the 2000s: black helpers are still popular in films like *xXx*, *Lara Croft Tomb Raider: The Cradle of Life*, *Batman Begins* and *The Dark Knight* (2008), buddy films such as *Men in Black II* (2002) and *Miami Vice* (2006) are less frequent, and the number of films in which an African American male takes on the role of sole action hero have increased, like the *Blade* franchise, *Man on Fire* (2004), *Déjà Vu* (2006), *I, Robot* and *Hancock*. Moreover, the multiple protagonist, multi-ethnic film format has provided a further space for African Americans, in films like *S.W.A.T.*, *Mindhunters* (2004), *The Kingdom* (2007) and *The Expendables*. Before we look at the racial negotiations that take place in action films with an African American at their centre, it is worth pausing to note the negotiations around gender that have already taken place before the action hero takes to the screen. Missing from this picture are physically active African American women. With the exception of ensemble piece *Set It Off* (1996), Angela Bassett's active role in *Strange Days* (1995) and the marginal parts for Jada Pinkett Smith in the *Matrix* sequels and Halle Berry in the *X-Men* franchise in the 2000s, African American action women are notoriously absent from action cinema. The movement to the centre has been taken up almost exclusively by African American men, quite a contrast with the growth in the numbers of white action heroines described in Chapter 4, and the increased visibility of Latin American action heroines across the same period. In this small survey, then, African American women emerge as the most marginalised group, testament to the 'reciprocal structuring of racial and sexual difference that is articulated in cultural representations' (Willis 1997: 21). Kimberly Springer posits that the violent African American woman calls up the stereotype of the 'Sapphire', a castrating, verbally and physically assertive figure, who is demonised (or made to seem comic) in both African American and white culture. Springer discusses the invocations of the 'Sapphire' type in *Waiting to Exhale* (1995) and *Set It Off*, but she can also be found in other films like *I, Robot* and *Bad Boys II* (2003) as minor characters (Springer 2001; see also hooks 1981 and Jewell 1993).[4] It is, it seems, simply 'too much' to permit a woman to possess both narrative agency and express her heroism through physical aggression onscreen if she is African American, thus her potential presence must be elided. With this absence very much present in our minds, let us now look at the kinds of racial – and gender – negotiations we see in action films with an African American male at their centre.

OTHERNESS AND *I, ROBOT*

In Chapter 1 we discussed *I, Robot* in relation to narrative but here I want to turn attention to the representational strategies the film displays. As I set out in Chapter 1 the first three scenes of the film – which show Spooner in his apartment, on the street and at his grandmother's place – establish a significant amount of narrative information about the hero, including the fact that he is divorced and harbours a distrust for robots; but they also locate these facts in relation to his ethnicity.

Rather than presenting a hero whose African American ethnicity is not acknowledged, for example in the service of a white liberal impulse to be 'blind' to racial differences, *I, Robot* swiftly and overtly attempts to connect Spooner to cultural signifiers of 'African American-ness.'[5] He has a copy of Arthur Ashe's *A Hard Road to Glory: A History of the African American Athlete in Basketball* (1988) on his bedside table when he wakes, and puts on some classic, celebrated soul music, Stevie Wonder's *Superstition* (from the Motown label's stable of primarily African American musicians) as he showers; fully dressed, his 'vintage' 2004 Converse trainers along with his leather jacket, hat and clothing reference contemporary African American urban fashion. A street scene follows as Spooner makes his way to his grandmother's house. In contrast to the unfortunate erasure of African Americans from the Washington DC crowd scenes in *Minority Report*, which generated the impression of a 'white' city that bears no relation to the demographics of the real Washington, *I, Robot* establishes its futuristic Chicago as equally ethnically mixed as its real-world counterpart.[6] Spooner displays an ease and confidence moving around its crowded streets, and has a network of street contacts such as the smart-talking Farber. This ease is naturalised by the way that African American culture has been in representational terms 'not only linked but specifically identified with the city', as Paula J. Massood has observed, but Spooner's street smarts also associate him with the detective figures of blaxploitation films like *Shaft* (1971) and *Truck Turner* (1974), whose experiences of growing up in the black urban 'ghetto' gave them insider knowledge that aided their detection quests, and the figure of the black informant or go-between, who has historically provided 'a way for the white heroes of crime narratives to tap into the secret world of black criminality' (Tasker 1993: 36).[7] The film also connects Spooner in these opening sequences to an idea of African American community. His visit to his grandmother – replete with signifiers of 'homeliness' like the busy kitchen, warm welcoming décor and bustling grandmother who scolds him for not talking to his ex-wife – confirm him as part of a larger network of familial connections. What is odd is that this impression that he is connected to a wider African American community is not pursued or developed as the film progresses: apart from his grandmother no other family members or African American friends appear. At the same time the emphasis on his street smarts is also left undeveloped, since Spooner does not draw on his street knowledge in his investigation and his informant Farber provides no meaningful insights either. The foregrounding of Spooner's 'African-Americanness' through these means and the subsequent failure to make any of them (family connections, street knowledge) pertinent to the investigation and its resolution makes more sense once we take into account the film's thematic concern with difference.[8]

Spooner is summoned from beyond the grave (via a message left for the police) by white mentor Dr Lanning, to begin an investigation into Lanning's apparent suicide and potential murder. It is an investigation that takes Spooner away from the ethnically mixed environs of the street and police headquarters into spaces of white privilege: the penthouse office of the CEO of US Robotics Lawrence Robertson (Bruce Greenwood) ('richest man in the world'), the pristine laboratories and expensive apartment of Dr Susan Calvin, the wood-panelled grandeur of Dr Lanning's mansion-like home. In these spaces Spooner's 'African-Americanness' is used to mark him out from his surroundings, allowing the film to register him as a fish out of water and to invoke the real-world disenfranchisement of many African Americans who would not 'normally' be able to access these spaces. This invocation's purpose begins to reveal itself in Spooner's conversation with Lawrence Robertson (US Robotics CEO). In it Spooner offers a critique of the ubiquitous presence of robots in the city, describing it as 'shitting on the little man', that is, taking jobs from humans who are in manual or service roles, a sentiment that correlates to the reality that African Americans suffer a higher rate of unemployment than any other ethnic group in the US.[9] The film uses Spooner's 'African-Americanness' – and certain generalisations about African American culture and experience – to lend force to his narratively pertinent distrust of robots (which leads him to see the real threat the new NS-5 robots pose before the humans around him do). As a result of the film's foregrounding of his 'African-Americanness' in the opening scenes, Spooner/Smith's black body functions as a marker of racial difference that the film utilises in the service of its own narrative preoccupation with difference (in contrast the white characters appear to be intended to register simply as 'just people' as Dyer would say (Dyer 1997: 1)). The theme of distrusting the 'other' runs through the film, but the status of 'other' is assigned here to robotic technologies, rather than humans of a particular ethnic group. It is 2037 and robot numbers are increasing in urban areas, so that soon there will be 'one robot to every five humans'. The question of whether they are safe presences or some kind of threat drives both Spooner and the detective narrative. In exploring this theme the film maps real-world manifestations of and responses to racism onto the robots: Spooner shows a seemingly irrational distrust of the robots that is immune to the weight of evidence that they are perfectly safe, while Robertson accuses him of being prejudiced and suggests, 'You know, I suspect you simply don't like their *kind*.' In a distorted reversal of the phenomena of white characters co-opting black culture for their own ends that both Willis and Krin Gabbard have identified in recent Hollywood cinema, here white prejudice against non-whites is mapped onto – and performed by – an African American character (see Willis 1997: 209–16 and Gabbard 2004). This lends an extra resonance to the expression of his prejudice and his pursuit of the truth, as well as the predicament of the robot under suspicion, Sonny, who protests his innocence but is being pursued by Spooner because of the man's prejudice. This is a disingenuous racial displacement, which invokes racism and ethnic difference while divesting them of their real-world social and political implications and materiality. Spooner/Smith's body becomes a trigger to call to mind this real-world context, 'African-Americanness' simply 'an image, a cultural icon' functioning in the service of the story, rather than a real-world ethnic identity (Willis 1997: 211).

In her writing on 1980s action cinema Tasker notes that 'the positioning of black performers at the centre of the action narrative usually involves a renegotiation, and reaffirmation of the existence of the margins' (Tasker 1993: 37). We can see the same process at work in *I, Robot*. With an African American at its centre it isn't just the otherness of robots that is pointed up in the film's early scenes, but that of women too. After Spooner's rather fraught conversation with Robertson he is assigned Dr Susan Calvin to show him around

US Robotics and answer any questions pertinent to the investigation. She is serious in attitude and severe in appearance, hair scraped back off her face, a buttoned-up suit masking her bodily curves and showing very little of her skin. Spooner fails to raise a smile with some sexual innuendo, and then tries a different tack: 'So you're a shrink, huh? My ex-wife would sure be glad I'm talking to you. You don't know her, do you?' The joke doesn't wash with Dr Calvin, but Spooner's jesting suggestion that she might know his ex-wife raises the spectre of a network of unco-operative, independent women who communicate with each other. This passing and absurd suggestion of a networked femininity finds a more concrete realisation in what Dr Calvin shows Spooner next: the 'brain' of the building, which has been allocated a female moniker (and voice and visage), V.I.K.I or 'Virtual Interactive Kinetic Intelligence'. This female 'brain' is networked with all the city's computerised and technologised systems, including security. Spooner's response again betrays an anxiety that is female centred: 'She? That's a she? I definitely need to get out more.'

A representational hierarchy is developing, then, that is both raced and gendered in particular ways. Moreover, as I've started to suggest, the robots do not sit outside of this representational hierarchy. Sonny, Lanning's personal robot, becomes the prime suspect when he is discovered by Spooner and Calvin hiding at the crime scene. His indeterminate status, as either a murderer or an accused innocent, a threat to or a friend of human beings, seems to manifest itself at the level of representation as a gendered indeterminacy. Sonny is one of the new 'NS-5' robots whose faces are softer-featured and curvier than their blocky, square-jawed predecessors. When Sonny is taken in for questioning these feminine attributes of appearance are matched by a voice that, though male, is high and soft – that is, rather effeminate. Narratively such details of characterisation seem to be motivated by the fact that Sonny is the first robot to feel emotions, thus connecting him to the traditional conception of women being 'in touch with their feelings'. And yet the indeterminacy of his gender attributes leaves open the question of where this robot suspect should be placed in the film's race/gender hierarchy: masculine hero or feminine villain? The narrative denouement makes this hierarchy clear: it is the massively networked female 'brain', V.I.K.I., who is found to be the real villain, planning to put Chicago under martial law to protect humans from themselves, regardless of the cost to human lives. Spooner and his two feminine helpers, Sonny and Calvin, work together to inject V.I.K.I. with 'nanites' that infect her system and shut her down, while the NS-5 robots are sent away for storage. The immediate threat has been eradicated, but as in many Hollywood narratives, the wider socio-political issues the film invokes remain in place, both diegetically (it's not clear how Chicago will function after the sudden removal of the co-ordinating super-computer; Sonny is likely to struggle to find an outlet for his rapidly developing artificial intelligence) and extra-diegetically, in that the racial tensions and racially-based socio-economic inequalities the film uses as metaphors remain in place in the real world.

RACIAL HIERARCHIES IN *AVATAR*

> I was hoping for some sort of tactical plan that didn't involve martyrdom.
>
> Trudy Chacon (Michelle Rodriguez) in *Avatar* (2009)

Late on in *Avatar*, Jake and his colleagues Chacon and Spellman (Joel Moore) are discussing how they will continue their resistance campaign against the corporation that is oppressing the Na'vi, when they learn that the corporation is planning an all-out military attack. Chacon's response, quoted above, is one of a series of tough wisecracks she makes that diegetically signal her courage in the face of worsening odds. But extra-diegetically the words resonate with an uncomfortable truth. Tasker notes that 1980s action cinema perpetuated the 'cinematic convention, that the black man is willing to sacrifice himself for the white hero', and Kathleen Newman observes a similar trope enacted by Latino characters in mixed race ensemble films from the same period (Tasker 1993: 36; Newman 1992: 59–73). As we saw in the Figueroa example from *Transformers*, it is still common for a Latino or Latina character to have to die or make way to enable a white character's ascendancy, a function Michelle Rodriguez fulfils in *Resident Evil* and *Fast and Furious* as well as *Avatar*.[10] Trudy Chacon's words prefigure her fate. In the final air battle between the company and the Na'vi Jake is about to be shot out of the sky by Colonel Quarich (Stephen Lang) when Chacon appears in a war-painted armed helicopter, pulling the Colonel into a dog fight and drawing fire away from Jake. Using her flying skill she manages to evade and return fire (with the memorable line 'You're not the only one with a gun, bitch') for a while but the Colonel's assault is too intense, and her craft is hit. She is turning to withdraw from the fight when the Colonel decides to finish her off with a precisely aimed rocket blast. There are no reaction shots from the other characters, in fact no-one seems to witness her death at all. Having been instrumental in helping Jake escape the company base so that he can participate in the final resistance battle, and having saved his life, Chacon becomes an oddly unmourned footnote in the progression towards narrative resolution. We might compare, for instance, the lingering treatment of the death of Dr Grace Augustine (Sigourney Weaver), that of Na'vi patriarch Eytukan (Wes Studi), or the multiple shot slow motion sequence depicting the death fall of Na'vi commander Tsu'tey (Laz Alonso). As in *Transformers* there is a racialised hierarchy here, one that preserves a white man's place at the top – albeit in a racial 'disguise' with his blue Na'vi body – but locates the Latino character near the bottom, below other non-white groups.

Latina Trudy Chacon is marginalised as the white Avatar pilots discuss strategy in *Avatar*

It is worth taking a moment to consider the racial politics of *Avatar* as a whole. In my discussion of the film's racial hierarchy I locate the Na'vi as non-white because they are constructed by the narrative set-up as the racial 'other' to which the white corporation has positioned itself in antagonistic relationship. For example we arrive in the foreign territory of Pandora with the white hero, and are promptly informed by Colonel Quarich that 'out there beyond that fence, every living thing that crawls, flies or squats in the mud wants to kill you'. The Na'vi get special mention: 'They're fond of arrows dipped in a neurotoxin that'll stop your heart in one minute.' Given that the Na'vi are digitally constructed bodies made up of a combination of motion and facial capture of a live actor with a computer generated Na'vi body, and the fact that the Na'vi are a fictional alien race, the facial structures and voice performances deployed to bring them to life could have been drawn from actors of a range of ethnicities, including white ethnicities. But instead the choice is made to characterise the Na'vis' appearance as a combination of the iconography of traditional Native American dress and weaponry with some African facial characteristics, and all but one of the voice actors playing Na'vi characters are African American (the exception is Wes Studi who is Native American).[11] So the Na'vis' narrative status as racial others is expressed through the very precise and racialised selection of actors of non-white ethnicity, a filmmaking decision that conforms to and naturalises a white, Anglo American perspective on racial otherness and which seems to prove the longevity of Anna Everett's assertion, that 'it is still the white, bourgeois male to whom Hollywood narratives about race are being addressed' (Everett 1995–6: 29).

As we noted in Chapter 1, through his Na'vi body Jake begins to assimilate into Na'vi life and culture, so that when the corporation's desire to move the Na'vi away from their homes and holy sites manifests as violence, Jake switches sides and combines his human military training and his newfound Na'vi skills to overcome the human forces. Jake thus steps into the tradition of 'American hero-as-Indian-fighter' that Richard Slotkin describes in *Gunfighter Nation* (1992: 15). In his discussion of the frontier romance novels of nineteenth-century writer James Fenimore Cooper Slotkin elaborates on this figure:

> As the 'man who knows Indians,' the frontier hero stands between the opposed worlds of savagery and civilization, acting sometimes as mediator or interpreter between races and cultures but more often as civilization's most effective instrument against savagery – a man who knows how to think and fight like an Indian, to turn their own methods against them. (ibid.: 16)

Avatar draws heavily on this archetype but with some important changes. Human corporations are characterised as the savage force in Pandora, their disregard for Na'vi lives and culture manifesting in racist speech and actions we are invited to condemn as they initiate the violent ethnic cleansing that sees the Na'vi gassed out, firebombed and shot at. Within the terms of this opposition the Na'vi and their human sympathisers are the civilising force, and it is Jake's combined human and Na'vi skills that make him the most effective instrument against the ecological and corporate savagery the corporation is guilty of. Jake thus atones for his early betrayal of the Na'vi, redeeming himself through his choice to live alongside them. These narrative and racial negotiations prompt Annalee Newitz to suggest that *Avatar* represents a 'white guilt fantasy' that she defines in the following way:

> It's not just a wish to be absolved of the crimes whites have committed against people of color; it's not just a wish to join the side of moral justice in battle. It's a wish to lead people of color from the inside rather than from the (oppressive, white) outside. (Newitz 2009: paragraphs 3, 9)

While the title of Newitz's *Avatar* essay is a question – 'When Will White People Stop Making Movies Like *Avatar*?' – Everett supplied the answer in her own essay on race and narrative in the mid-1990s, in which she argues that, we must see the racial discourses in films and in all our media for what they are: significations of the return of the nation's repressed ideology of white supremacy replete with its concomitant pleasure in constructing, containing, and ultimately consuming the other. (Everett 1995–6: 37)

Critiques of capitalism, ecological destruction and military intervention, and promotion of interracial and intercultural tolerance and respect are all readable in *Avatar*, but its insistence on a racial hierarchy that places the white man's experience above the Na'vi and other ethnicities is also difficult to ignore. Jake ends the film a leader of the Na'vi people, reacquiring power 'inside' the non-white community after hundreds of the Na'vi have sacrificed themselves in the final battle under his captaincy, a rather excessive example of the sacrificed helper trope I mentioned earlier. The Latina character, who already occupied a marginalised position within the narrative, excluded from the whites-only privilege of accessing Na'vi avatars (Jake, Norm and Grace are all white), does not even make it to the end of the film. We might well ask why not. Setting aside the sacrificed helper trope for a moment, Chacon is characterised as a tough-talking woman, a good pilot respected by her male colleagues, a 'Macho Latina' (Tolchin 2007: 192) holding her own in a male military environment, her military combats and Ray-Ban Aviator sunglasses (a reference back to the heroic pilots of *Top Gun* (1986)) reinforcing these character aspects.[12] In Cameron's *Aliens* this kind of female character took centre-stage, but Ripley was white. Here Chacon remains marginalised despite the diegetic fact that she is a good fighter, and despite the extra-diegetic fact that it is a rather small part for a Hollywood actress who is increasingly well known. As a Macho Latina, Chacon finds herself at the bottom of both a racialised hierarchy and a gendered hierarchy, dying while not only the white male Jake but his non-white Na'vi wife and mother-in-law survive. As in *Aliens*, in which the Macho Latina Private Vasquez (Jenette Goldstein) is also a sacrificial helper, *Avatar* ends with a family headed by a white hero.

MULTIRACIAL ACTION AND ETHNIC INDETERMINACY

Vin Diesel is a multiracial male film star who seems to have no such problems accessing and occupying the centre stage in action cinema. Of African American and Italian American descent, Diesel's visual appearance communicates an ethnic indeterminacy that each of his films manages in different ways, and which some actively thematise (for example *Pitch Black* (2000) and *The Chronicles of Riddick* (2004), a process that has also prompted scholarly interest (see Beltrán 2005 and 2008, Barnes 2008 and Greven 2009). He has carved out a space as an action hero in a series of multiracial, multiple protagonist urban action films, most prominently the *Fast and Furious* franchise, which are a relatively recent trend in action cinema, as Beltrán has pointed out:

> in the mid- to late 1990s, the racial mix of the urban action film changed dramatically. African Americans, Asians, and other nonwhites, both men and women, began to appear as Hollywood action movie protagonists . . . [this] arguably reflected not only diegetic and industrial evolutions but also shifts in cultural assumptions. Given that popular notions of bodily mastery, confidence, and mobility are still largely tied to white male bodies, this trend implied both a challenge to the hegemonic status quo and a redefinition of the qualities required of contemporary, urban-centered heroes. (Beltrán 2005: 54)

This increased racial mix can be seen in action films both within and beyond the urban action cycle, for example in *Rollerball* (2002), *Mindhunters* (2004), *S.W.A.T.* (2003), *Doom, Sunshine* (2007), *Street Kings* (2008), *Gamer* (2009) and *G.I. Joe: The Rise of Cobra* (2009). Often this context permits traditionally marginalised or stereotyped people of colour to be depicted in a more 'rounded', more fully psychologised way. Other films present themselves as racially mixed but instead draw together a cluster of simplistic racialised stereotypes to fight alongside a white hero or group, a trend I call 'mix-and-match': recent examples include *The Expendables* (in which the dialogue persistently emphasises Jet Li as small in stature and his character as obsessed with getting 'more money' for his family) and *Predators* (2010) (in which Danny Trejo plays a Mexican drugs cartel enforcer, Lewis Ozawa Changchien plays a Yakuza gangster and Alice Braga plays a South American freedom fighter). Within these multiracial frames Vin Diesel's ethnic indeterminacy has a particular valency. Greven suggests that his racial ambiguity (which he alleges Diesel has fostered by eliding his African American heritage in the construction of his star image) 'could be said to constitute omission by its refusal to represent, reveal, claim, or embody racial identity', but it also provides filmmakers with opportunities to contain the anxiety that multiraciality might generate (Greven 2009: 189). In her analysis of Diesel's role in *The Fast and the Furious* (2001), for example, Beltrán observes that his ethnic indeterminacy serves two functions: to confer upon him a 'cultural competency' that allows him to communicate effectively with people of a range of ethnicities, a prized skill in the multicultural narrative setting, and to confer upon him a 'symbolic whiteness' (Beltrán 2005: 59). In the film Diesel plays Dom, a significant player in the illegal street racer subculture which Anglo American police officer Brian O'Conner (Paul Walker) is trying to infiltrate as part of an investigation into stolen goods. Brian's ticket into the street racing scene is his driving ability, which exceeds that of all the other drivers apart from Dom. But Brian also needs Dom's 'cultural competency' to get information from other people for his undercover investigation, and as the narrative progresses the two men team up to find the real culprits together. In this way, despite its

> progressive, color-blind [*sic*] elements, *The Fast and The Furious* privileges a white-centrist perspective and notions of natural white superiority. Perhaps most notably, white characters are posited as dominant within a subculture in which they are often absent or marginal. (Beltrán 2005: 59)

As in *Avatar* 'ideologies of white superiority and non-white subordination continue to have a powerful influence' (ibid.: 62), and Beltrán's account gives a compelling sense of how Diesel's ethnic indeterminacy, framed as an almost-whiteness, is integral to the film's project to appear progressive but also to reassure white audiences. What I would like to do in the remaining paragraphs is to use Diesel to consider the chapter's theme of racial representation and racialised hierarchies from a further angle; that is, to understand what part white ethnicities play in contemporary action cinema's representational hierarchies.

WHITE ETHNICITIES IN THE ACTION FILM

A year after *The Fast and the Furious* Diesel starred in *xXx* (2002), playing an extreme sports enthusiast and petty criminal called Xander Cage who is co-opted by the US National Security Agency (NSA) to infiltrate a Russian gang based in Prague. Aside from his physical capacity for action, the idea of cultural competency seems to travel with Diesel from *The Fast and the Furious* into *xXx*: thrown together with other NSA recruits he gains their trust with conversation, and much more significantly he eschews agency practice and the advice of local secret police to talk his way straight into the Russian crime ring. If this cultural competency proceeds in representational terms from his ethnic indeterminacy, *xXx* is equally invested in Diesel's 'symbolic whiteness'. Before Xander takes up the mission his NSA superior Gibbons (Samuel L. Jackson) suggests that he has been chosen because the Russians are 'Dangerous, dirty, tattooed, uncivilised. Your kind of people.' Given that Gibbons is African American and the Russian gang are white Europeans this makes clear that the film seeks to align its action hero in racial terms with the Russian gang. What the exchange also reminds us is that negative connotations can accrue to the category of whiteness. Earlier in the chapter we noted the reality that the category of whiteness is made up of a disparate cluster of white ethnicities (not least due to the history of immigration from Central and Eastern European countries), a fact that problematises the ongoing dominant cultural project to construct whiteness as 'non-raced' (Dyer 1997: 2). Richard Dyer goes further, to suggest that this unmarked quality of whiteness has generated an anxiety in Western white culture about the 'emptiness of whiteness' and a fear of 'white death', manifested as much in Herman Melville's *Moby-Dick* (1851) as it is in vampire and zombie films and science fiction movies like *Blade Runner* (1982) and the *Alien* films (1979, 1986, 1992, 1997) (Dyer 1997: 217). So, for example, Dyer describes how whiteness registers in the vampire film:

> In the act of vampirism, white society (the vampire) feeds off itself (his/ her victims) and threatens to destroy itself. All of this is so menacing that it is often ascribed to those who are not mainstream whites – Jews (see Gelder 1994: 13–17), South East Europeans (Transylvania in *Dracula* and its derivatives), the denizens of New Orleans (Anne Rice's *Vampire Chronicles*). Horror films have their cake and eat it: they give us the horror of whiteness while at the same time ascribing it to those who are liminally white. The terror of whiteness, of being without life, of causing death, is both vividly conveyed and disowned. (ibid.: 210)

As Dyer's reference to *Moby-Dick* is no doubt intended to imply, this terror of whiteness also has its roots in the American Gothic tradition of Melville, Nathaniel Hawthorne and Edgar Allan Poe, that dramatised the cultural deadlock between the lingering presence of a decadent, restrictive, decaying Old European culture and the pioneering spirit of nation building in the New World, a deadlock Andrew Britton has suggested also animates certain strands of 1970s US horror cinema (Britton 2009: 69). In this formulation a European whiteness is the site of horror.

I want to suggest that the process of evoking a terrifying whiteness and then disowning it that Dyer describes – and which finds a particularly gruesome contemporary manifestation in the white European murderers of the so-called 'torture porn' cycle (such as the Slovakia-based *Hostel* films (2005, 2007) and *The Human Centipede (First Sequence)* (2009) set in Germany) – is also quite common in the contemporary action film. Action cinema has long incorporated white Europeans as villains, as the James Bond franchise and *Die Hard* movies attest. In *xXx* the villains embody the abject whiteness Dyer proposes. The Russian gang is led by Yorgi (Marton Czorkas), a megalomaniac whose plan to throw the world into anarchy involves poisoning cities wholesale across the globe using an armed solar-powered submarine called, perhaps fittingly given our earlier reference to *Moby-Dick*, 'Ahab'. Yorgi and his colleagues speak with thick, stereotypical Russian accents, and their pallid faces and sombre monochrome costuming – all long coats and leather – associate them with cinematic representations of vampirism. These are whites as bringers of death: Yorgi with his deadly submarine, Kirill (Werner Daehn) with his compulsive smoking about which he says 'I like smoke better than air . . . I will still do it after it kills me,' and Kolya (Petra Jákl) with his enthusiasm for defying death (he is a fan of Xander's extreme sports stunts which have been broadcast on the Internet). When the Ahab submarine is finished Yorgi steps behind a screen with his men and releases an airborne poison into the room to kill the scores of scientists who built the vessel and its payload, looking on with heartless amusement as the scientists beg to be rescued and slowly succumb to the fumes. In contrast Xander Cage looks on with horror, hands shaking, breathing ragged. The often racialised opposition between hero and villain here distinguishes between two forms of whiteness: the extreme, abject European whiteness of Yorgi and his men, and Xander's symbolic whiteness. Because of its ability metaphorically to represent US 'melting pot' mythology, Diesel's ethnic indeterminacy comes into play to register this whiteness as American (in contrast to the European whiteness). Earlier in the film the 'Americanness' of Xander's is underlined in a scene in which Yorgi and he drink vodka together. Yorgi is drunk and insists on talking ebulliently at Xander in Russian; in response Xander begins to deliver a loud version of the patriotic song 'America the Beautiful' until Yorgi switches back to English. This joking face-off between American and European whiteness is but a precursor to the battle of wills between Xander and Yorgi with which the film will culminate. The movement of Diesel to the top of the racial hierarchy thus provides *xXx* with the opportunity to explore abject, European whiteness as a site of otherness and villainy.[13] This same conception of European whiteness works to preclude white European action heroes in 2000s action cinema. After the likes of Arnold Schwarzenegger and Christopher Lambert in the 1980s, European heroes are notably absent from the landscape of 2000s US action cinema. The exception is Milla Jovovich in the *Resident Evil* films (2002, 2004, 2007, 2010), although her status in the sequels as an experimental subject, carrier of the zombie virus and subsequent clone reintroduces abject European whiteness in her construction as a hybrid of heroism and hidden monstrosity.

With the advent of what Beltrán calls the 'utopic multiculturalism' of the urban action movie's contemporary manifestation (2005: 59), it is tempting to claim that a progressive agenda might be emerging in what has traditionally been a racially conservative strand of Hollywood filmmaking. While it is important to celebrate the potential for progressive representations of marginalised groups that recent developments have afforded, it is also necessary to be alert to action cinema's continued interest in 'nourish[ing] racial hierarchies without calling attention to itself' (Gabbard 2004: 16), racial hierarchies that too often simply reconfirm white dominance or, in seeking to move one ethnic group into the position of action hero, relegate other ethnic groups in problematic ways. As a result, and as I hope the analyses offered here have demonstrated, such hierarchies and the power relationships they foster can be complex and demand our attention. The disingenuous attempt by action spoof *Tropic Thunder* (2008) to locate the racist mimicry of African American identity in the cinematic past is just one facet of a contemporary Hollywood that is, in the words of Hamid Naficy and Teshome Gabriel, still invested in 'coopting differences, effacing histories and conflictual relations of forces' (Naficy and Gabriel 1993: x); our jobs, as students of action cinema, is to remain alert to that project and its consequences for representation.

NOTES

1. While designated as Anglo American within the film's representational hierarchy, the actors' ancestry is more complex in reality: Shia LeBoeuf is French Cajun while Megan Fox is of Irish, French and Cherokee descent. This is a perfect example of Hollywood's erasure of the complexity of ethnic heritage.
2. A burgeoning field of 'whiteness studies' developed over the 1990s, including scholars such as hooks 1991, 1992 'Madonna', 1992 'Representations', Pfeil 1995, Dyer 1997, and Willis 1997.
3. See US Census Bureau 'QuickFacts' about the US, accessed 1 July 2010 at http://quickfacts.census.gov/qfd/states/00000.html
4. In *I, Robot* the Sapphire type surfaces in the street scene where Detective Spooner tackles a robot to the floor suspecting that it has snatched a human's purse: in fact the robot is running towards its owner with a purse containing her asthma inhaler. The woman is verbally assertive, telling Spooner off in no uncertain terms. In *Bad Boys II* the type appears in the television store scene (which will be discussed further in Chapter 7), as a loud mother who harangues the store owner about the kinds of images that have been allowed to play on the store televisions.
5. On 'blindness' to racial difference amongst whites and its implications see hooks 1992, 'Representations' and Dyer 1997.
6. As of the US Census in 2000, Chicago's demographics showed 42 per cent of people identified as white, 37 per cent identified as black, and 26 per cent as hispanic. See US Census Bureau 'QuickFacts' about Chicago, accessed 1 July 2010 at http://quickfacts.census.gov/qfd/states/17/1714000.html. In relation to *Minority Report*, it is worth noting how significant the contrast is between the white majority in the fictional crowd scenes and the reality that, in 2000, 60 per cent of Washington's inhabitants identified as black, compared to 30 per cent white. See US Census Bureau 'QuickFacts' about Washington DC, accessed 7 September 2005 at http://quickfacts.census.gov/qfd/states/11/1150000.html
7. Massood cites the following reasons for this identification of African Americans with the city: 'the history of African American movement and migration, and the rising importance of urban spaces in Black life contributed to contemporary Black popular culture, especially (though not limited to) the cinematic representation of African American urban experiences' (Massood 2003: 204).
8. This invoking and then disavowal of African American community links *I, Robot* to the liberal films of the postwar period, such as the Sidney Poitier vehicles *Guess Who's Coming*

to Dinner and *In the Heat of the Night* (both 1967), which presented a positive depiction of the African American male but isolated him from the wider African American community. Manthia Diawara suggests that such films 'serve the function of plotting Black people in White space and White power, keeping the real contours of the Black community outside Hollywood' (Diawara 1993: 12). Contemporary films that could be said to do the same include *Hancock*, *Book of Eli* and the *Blade* films.

9. See 'Employment status by race' table for 2009 in the 'Race and Hispanic or Latino Ethnicity' section of the US Bureau of Labor Statistics webpages, accessed 1 July 2010 at http://www.bls.gov/cps/demographics.htm#race

10. Rodriguez' character Letty is assassinated because of her association with Vin Diesel's ethnically indeterminate Dom; he then pairs up with Anglo Brian (Paul Walker) to avenge the assassination. So here the Latina Letty's death makes way for the Anglo and his ethnically indeterminate partner.

11. The *Transformers* films also conflate alien otherness with racialised notions of otherness in the use of African American voice actors (and stereotyped vocal performances) for some of the Autobot robots. The sequel's comedic pair of robots called 'Skids' and 'Mudflap' drew particular fire. See staff article 'Is *Transformers: Revenge of the Fallen* racist?' in *The Week* for a useful summary of these reactions (accessed 15 February 2010 at http://theweek. com/article/index/97976/Is_Transformers_Revenge_of_the_Fallen_racist).

12. See also Beltrán (2004, 2008) for an elaboration of the critical issues circulating around the Macho Latina or *más macha*.

13. The hierarchy also includes an African American enabler, the mysterious Gibbons, and Yelena (Asia Argento), a Russian spy working undercover as a member of Yorgi's gang and subsequently Xander's allie. In the film's white versus white structure Yelena functions like the traditional black informant or go-between character Tasker identifies (1993: 36), connecting Xander to Yorgi's world and giving him information about it that he can use in his mission. Interestingly her government have stopped giving her orders, so she is happy to take on Xander's instructions, and at the end of the film she enthusiastically assimilates into the US melting pot, having got permission from Gibbons.

CHAPTER 7

Homosexuality in the action film

In *Bad Boys II* (Michael Bay, 2003) two narcotics cops are having a heart to heart on a couch in a deserted side-room of a television store. They have sought refuge there because the shop floor is in uproar: the videotape confiscated from a local criminal that they have been playing on the shop's televisions (the nearest playback facilities they could find) contained pornographic images which have now been projected onto all of the televisions at once, in front of surprised customers and a very angry shop owner. Marcus (Martin Lawrence) wants to talk: he has been struggling to manage his temper and his nerves as a result of a series of stressful incidents in their current investigation, which culminated in his detective partner Mike (Will Smith) accidentally shooting him in the backside during a firefight with some people they wanted to question. Marcus complains that 'My ass still hurts from what you did to it the other night.' Mike tries to account for the accident, saying 'Hey, it got rough. I mean, we got caught up in the moment, shit got crazy . . . you know how I get.' Marcus nods but it is his next line that makes clear why he is so fretful, as he explains, 'When you popped me from behind I think you damaged some nerves. Now I can't . . . I can't even get an erection.' Unbeknown to the pair, their conversation is being filmed on a camera that has been left on a stand in the room, and being broadcast live to the same television screens that had previously been showing pornography. To the store customers, who don't have the benefit of the context the narrative has provided to us, Mike and Marcus' conversation sounds like a frank conversation between two gay lovers about their sex life. Frequent cutaways to store customers make this clear: a concerned mother covers her two small boys' ears; a young man shopping with his girlfriend looks disconcerted; an older gay couple sympathise ('That poor man is pouring out his heart'). When Mike objects to Marcus sharing about his erectile dysfunction ('We're partners, but we are partners with *bounda-ries*'), the gay couple deliver their verdict on what they perceive is one lover's heartless disregard for the other's feelings ('He's a mean fuck'). It is intended as a comic scene, humour generated by the disjunction between what the men appear to be saying and what they are actually talking about, which intensifies as the conversation becomes more intimate.

The two heterosexual male heroes are momentarily misrecognised as gay, and unwittingly 'perform' homosexuality to the watching store customers. The scene's comic *frisson* derives not simply from the fact that it is a variation on the longstanding comic trope of straight men 'playing gay' (see Barrios 2005), but also from the film's assumption of the impossibility of an openly gay action hero. This assumption seems to find its validation when one surveys the landscape of contemporary US action cinema: while – as we saw in Chapters 4 and 6 – white women and African American and Latino men have established themselves as action heroes in a growing number of films over the last decade, there are no openly gay action heroes (two exceptions might be asserted – the detective thriller *Kiss Kiss Bang Bang* (2005) and historical epic *Alexander* – both of which I will turn to later in the chapter). Films in other production sectors and other genres have placed gay men and occasionally lesbians at the centre of their narratives and enjoyed box office success (such as studio and studio independent releases like *Monster* (2003), *De-Lovely* (2004), *Capote* (2005), *Brokeback Mountain* (2005) and *Milk* (2008), comedies featuring homosexual main characters, like *The Next Best Thing* (2000) and *I Love You Phillip Morris* (2009), and gay-themed comedies such as *I Now Pronounce You Chuck and Larry* (2007), *I Love You, Man* (2009) and *Humpday* (2009)), so this apparent omission in the action cinema of the 2000s demands attention.[1] In the light of recent (albeit partial) advances in gay rights and, following the emergence of the New Queer Cinema indie movement in the early 1990s, the mainstreaming of queer cinema's themes through the late 1990s and into the 2000s, what is preventing openly gay action heroes from entering action cinema?[2] Taking as its inspiration Andrea Weiss' insight that we should consider 'invisibility as well as visibility as a form of representation' (Weiss 1992: 2), this chapter seeks to address these issues by mapping out homosexuality's status as both presence and absence in contemporary action cinema, as well as documenting how the films themselves speak to this presence/absence.

HISTORY AND HOMOSOCIALITY

As Parker Tyler and Vito Russo were the first to document, due to the strictures of the Hays Production Code which prohibited explicit or implied reference to homosexuality, male homosexuality in classical Hollywood cinema was implied rather than stated, if it was present at all. The gay man's presence was signalled through particular elements of costume, gesture and expression such as a limp wrist, a flower in the lapel or a fey manner, which structured homo-sexuality's outward sign as a form of gender inversion (effeminacy rather than normative masculinity). Such figures found their way into movies as comic relief, as demonised villains or as sympathetic characters whose sexual 'devi-ancy' was most often punished by a tragic death (see Tyler 1993, Russo 1987).[3] As earlier chapters have illustrated, the same strategies of containment applied in the representation of other 'minority' groups such as women and people of colour can be seen in the history of Hollywood representations of homosexu-ality: comic framing, marginalisation, containing forms of narrative closure and demonisation. The conflation of conventionally conceptualised gendered behaviour with sexual orientation evident in classical Hollywood – that the gay man 'must be' depicted as effeminate, the gay woman as mannish – illustrates the extent to which homosexuality was policed in this period in relation to a strict gender binary. Judith Butler suggests that the principles of gender normativity also structure homophobia; that 'the homophobic terror over performing homosexual acts, where it exists, is often also a terror over losing proper gender ("no longer being a real or proper man" or "no longer being a real or proper woman")' (Butler 1993: 27). The effeminate 'demonized gay or proto-gay villain' in films like *Silence of the Lambs* (1991) and *In the Line of Fire* (1993) in more recent cinematic history speak to the continued persistence of such anxieties and the strategies deployed to answer them (Pfeil 1995: 244). As Benshoff and Griffin argue, the normative gender binary is mapped onto a 'straight–gay binary' that cannot account for the variety of gendered identities and sexualities that comprise human nature (Benshoff and Griffin 2006: 4–8). One of the things this chapter is interested in exploring is how this 'straight–gay binary' and its imposition or regulation impacts on the representations that emerge in contemporary action cinema.

The action film provides a fertile ground for the anxieties about losing one's proper gender that Butler describes. Action cinema is traditionally masculin-ist, heavily invested in reinforcing dominant constructions of masculinity as active, physically strong, rational and powerful, values which, as we have seen, are predominantly embodied in the figure of the white heterosexual male. In its preoccupation with demonstrating these masculinist values the action film often excludes women or consigns them to the periphery of the space of action, as onlookers or passive victims, while groups of heterosexual men occupy the centre. In these homosocial groupings and pairings men bond, share intense physical experiences with each other, and trade looks while showing off their physiques, their weapons and their athletic capacities to each other. As a result, as Tasker has pointed out, 'the homoeroticism surrounding male action stars is a constant presence, acknowledged and played with by films which . . . simul-taneously deploy an anxious disavowal of gay desire' (Tasker 1993: 29). In her groundbreaking works *Between Men* (1985) and *The Epistemology of the Closet*

(1990) Eve Kosofsky Sedgwick notes the slippage of signification inherent in homosociality and the problems it poses for heterosexual men seeking to define themselves as such. There are, she notes, 'important correspondences and similarities between the most sanctioned forms of male-homosocial bonding, and the most reprobated expressions of male homosexual sociality' (Sedgwick 1985: 89). Sedgwick argues that from the eighteenth century onwards in England and the US the urgent necessity to distinguish between the two has meant that homosociality has been 'brutally structured' by homophobia (Sedgwick 1990: 185). This has been equally true of homosociality in the action film's recent past, as a brief discussion of 1980s action cinema will demonstrate. In 1980s action films featuring male pairings or groups, homophobia found expression in a number of ways: Tasker notes that some films like *Lock Up* (1989) and *Death Warrant* (1990) 'express[ed] images of homosexuality [only] in terms of the threat of violent rape' (Tasker 1993: 29), while in other films like *Dressed to Kill* (1980), *Mad Max 2: The Road Warrior* (1981) and *Commando* (1985) the villain was either an explicit or implied homosexual; in each case the villainous homosexual functions as what Robin Wood calls a 'disclaimer' to reassure us that 'our boys are not like *that*' (Wood 1986: 229). In addition, derogatory dialogue references to 'fags' and 'queers' found their way into films like *Commando* and *Lethal Weapon* (1987) (indeed Cynthia Fuchs hyperbolically suggests that the latter film is 'rife with homophobic verbal ejaculation' (Fuchs 1993: 199)). Further strategies to disavow the homoerotic potential in action cinema's homosocial groupings include the peripheral or off-screen women characters featured as love interests in order to guarantee the male heroes' heterosexuality (Wood 1986: 229). In addition, in Cynthia Fuchs' discussion of interracial buddy films like *Lethal Weapon* (including *Off Limits* (1988), *Black Rain* (1989) and *Lethal Weapon 2* (1989)) she suggests that they foreground the racial difference between the two male leads in order to efface the possibility of homosexual interaction. As Fuchs explains, '[a]s the interracial cop-buddy film sustains its extralegal, politically progressive veneer, it also represses and recuperates the most threatening, invisible (non) difference of homosexuality' (ibid.: 197). This brief historicisation allows us to place current practices of presenting and policing homosociality into context.

POLICING HOMOSOCIALITY NOW

Homosociality is still a key feature of action cinema, and to assess how its potential for homoeroticism is handled it is useful to return our attention to *Bad Boys II* and the scene with which I opened this chapter. The film replaces the interracial buddy relationship with an all-African American pairing, but beyond that follows the formula faithfully, giving us a mismatched pair working through an investigation, and including the familiar trope of the complicating personal relationship that creates tensions between the pair. Here that complication is Marcus' sister Syd (Gabrielle Union), whom Mike is secretly dating, a fact that they are keeping from Marcus. Syd is also a district attorney working undercover on the same case as them, and when she is kidnapped both men have to put their differences aside in order to save her. While Mike is the foil for Marcus' more overtly comedic performance, the pair's differences are elaborated primarily in terms of – and thus foreground – their heterosexuality: Marcus is married while Mike is more of a ladies' man; Marcus' stress is affecting his ability to have successful sexual intercourse, while Mike is in a sexually fulfilling relationship with Syd. This works to mitigate the way in which their bickering often makes them sound like they are 'an old married couple'. It is in this context that the scene in the television store unfolds. It is unusual in its open acknowledgment of the possibility of a lived homosexual domesticity, performed unwittingly and momentarily by Mike and Marcus and given a real-world correspondence by the two gay men shopping together for televisions. That said, the two gay customers are constructed in terms of the familiar stereotype of the effeminate homosexual male, including effeminate gestures (sunglasses dangled from one hand), earrings, flamboyant shirts and a camp vocal performance. Marcus may be pouring his heart out on the couch in a whining voice with tears running down his face, but the explicitly effeminate presence of the gay customers ensures that the elements of Marcus' performance that might be seen as 'unmanly' are not associated with effeminacy, because it is manifested in a more pronounced way elsewhere in the scene. Moreover, the performance of homosexuality that Mike and Marcus are unwittingly producing is heavily foregrounded as a performance, that is as a conversation that has been mediated so that its content registers differently. The scene alternates close-ups of the pair with wider shots of the room that carefully include cameras in both the foreground and the background of the shot; a pronounced dolly forward into a close-up of the camera recording the conversation; and frequent shots of the pair's image on television screens around the store. The frequent cutaways to the watching store customers also underline the mediated status of the conversation and its potential to generate misunderstanding. Through these strategies the scene literalises the buddy movie's homoeroticism while directing us away from it, inviting the audience to focus on the distance between the misinterpretation (embodied by the overly effeminate 'real' homosexuals) and the 'guaranteed' reality of Mike and Marcus's oft-reinforced heterosexuality. Indeed the scene attempts to reverse the traditional dynamics of the buddy movie, in which homoeroticism is the secret that must be disavowed, by constructing heterosexuality as the 'secret reality' being obscured by the television. The placing of the audience in the reassuring position of privileged knowledge (in terms of narrative information and genre conventions), able to laugh at the store customers' misrecognition, and enjoy the momentary acknowledgment of the buddy movie's inherent homoeroticism, naturalises and reaffirms Mike and Marcus's heterosexuality. In this way the scene approaches its subject matter in a manner remarkably similar to that identified by Sharon Willis as being at work in *Lethal Weapon 2*, which:

> exhibits a particularly – and jocularly – anxious fascination with its own homoerotic subtext . . . Such [direct reference] seems designed to diffuse and contain the overtly homoerotic charge these scenes produce – to offer and then withdraw the lure of homoeroticism. (Willis 1997: 28–9)

The real performance here is arguably the film's – the performance of a relaxed, knowing admission of the homoeroticism inherent in the buddy formula, located in the open acknowledgment of the everyday reality of homosexuality, which in fact operates as an extended and overdetermined disavowal of the possibility of homosexual relations between the two men. Indeed the conversation between the pair ends with Mike re-emphasising the 'boundaries' of their relationship to make clear its platonic nature, drawing to a close the film's momentary performance of the 'other option'.

What Willis describes as the offer and then withdrawal of the 'lure of homoeroticism', or, put another way, the acknowledgment and then disavowal of homoeroticism, is also present in other films, such as Guy Ritchie's 2009 production of *Sherlock Holmes*. In the film (as in Sir Arthur Conan Doyle's stories) Holmes (Robert Downey Junior) and Watson (Jude Law) share a house as well as solving crimes together, and while their investigations are presented very much in an action mode – involving frequent fights and shoot-outs – their partnership is also depicted in terms of domesticated cohabitation. While Watson is Holmes' action side-kick in the action sequences, in the scenes at the house he occupies the role of a wife, opening the blinds when Holmes is sitting at home in the dark, arranging food and drink for him and encouraging him to get out of the house more, turning off the oven when he leaves it on, and returning his pistol to him when he leaves it at home. Once again the homoerotic subtext finds its way to the textual level, performed by the male leads not simply in their domestic arrangements but also the moments at which the dialogue shifts to homoerotically charged innuendo. When Holmes and Watson are working to get Irene Adler (Rachel McAdams) down from a butcher's hook and Holmes needs something to hoist himself up with, he removes Watson's belt from his trousers with the quip 'don't get excited'; later, after Watson has been seriously injured during the course of the investigation, Holmes wakes from a fitful sleep to find a recovered Watson sitting smiling at him. Watson declares somewhat wryly 'You look gorgeous,' while Holmes retorts, 'Somehow I knew you wouldn't leave.' The film also frames the men's close bond by linking them with two women: Watson's fiancée Mary (Kelly Reilly) and Holmes' old flame Irene. Their performance of a homoerotic domesticity and their compulsion to pair with each other (Holmes' reluctance for Watson to leave for marriage, Watson's repeated impulse to join Holmes on his latest scheme) is thus knowingly remarked upon in the film for comic effect but underpinned by their heterosexuality. Other films that include a female love interest with the sole purpose of guaranteeing the heterosexuality of the male protagonists include: *Fast and Furious* (2009), in which Dom's girlfriend Letty spends an intimate night with him before being abruptly removed from the narrative, leaving Dom and his old partner Brian (Paul Walker) free to team up again to fight a new set of criminals; *The Departed* (2006), in which police psychiatrist Madolyn (Vera Farmiga) is girl-friend of one of the two male protagonists and the psychiatrist to the other; and *Troy*, *Kingdom of Heaven*, *Miami Vice* and *The Expendables*. Elsewhere and sometimes in the same films homophobic expressions work to differenti-ate the men speaking from the homosexual 'other' the expressions construct. So in S.W.A.T. (2003) a meeting between estranged erstwhile police partners Street (Colin Farrell) and Gamble (Jeremy Renner) in a bar quickly turns ugly, Street gesturing towards Gamble's friend and asking 'Is this your girlfriend?' prompting the man to respond 'No, but you can be my bitch.' Homosexual acts are constructed only as demeaning or horrifying; in *Hancock* (2008) the titular super-powered hero's worst punishment for trouble-making prison inmates is to force them to ape a homosexual sex act, by pushing one man's head into the other's anus. Earlier Hancock has made clear his opinion of superheroes in costumes: when his soon-to-be public relations consultant Ray (Jason Bateman) holds up a series of comic book heroes for his perusal, Hancock's verdict is 'Homo. Homo in red. Norwegian homo.' Hancock's use of homophobic language mitigates against accusations that Hancock is unmanly when he adopts a similar costume for crime-fighting duties. These familiar endeavours to regulate the representation of homosociality by shoring up male heroes' heterosexuality, disavowing homoeroticism and demonising homosexuality continue to be prevalent in contemporary action cinema, and demonstrate the way in which homosexuality often functions as a structuring absence in these films.

'DON'T ASK, DON'T TELL': CONTAINING ONSCREEN HOMOSEXUALITY

One of the most common ways in which Hollywood action cinema 'contains' homosexuality in representational terms is, as we have seen, by removing it completely from the screen and thus from the space of action. In the following section I want to suggest that where homosexual characters *are* present in action cinema, their depiction and framing is frequently marked by the same homophobic anxieties that structure the onscreen management of homosocial groups. I want to start by looking at two films in which men who indulge in homosexual activity occupy the role of male hero.

Alexander (2004) is Oliver Stone's retelling of the life of the Macedonian King Alexander the Great, who conquered the Persian Empire by the time he was 25 in 331 BC. The historical record is inconclusive about whether Alexander (played by Colin Farrell in the film) was bisexual, but the film asserts his bisexuality, showing not just Alexander's marriage to two women but implying a sexual relationship with a Persian manservant called Bagoas (Francisco Bosch) and hinting at the consummation of his close lifelong friendship with his general Hephaestion (Jared Leto). *Alexander* thus follows in the footsteps of a number of films that carve out a space to depict homosexuality as a practical reality because they are based on historical figures of record, such as *Capote* and *Milk* – and we could also include *The Hours* (2002), *Frida* (2002) and *Monster* (2003) – although as Benshoff and Griffin have noted, homosexuality is equally as often 'written out of [other] films based on real-life queers', such as *A Beautiful Mind* (2001) and *Troy* (2004) (Benshoff and Griffin 2006: 263). However in this film the non-heteronormative aspects of Alexander's bisexuality are heavily contained and qualified. In the original theatrical release of the film Alexander's sexual relationship with Bagoas is communicated by implication (and, one might say, innuendo): one public, chaste kiss, Bagoas' evident irritation when he is dismissed from Alexander's bedchamber because Hephaestion is staying instead, and later in the movie a shot of Alexander beckoning to Bagoas to join him in his bed. The representation of his friendship with Hephaestion is even more oblique, a puzzling decision given that this is suggested as Alexander's most significant relationship. At several points they exchange words of love and commitment to each other. For example, when Hephaestion stays the night, they are shown conversing intensely on a balcony, looking into each others' tear-filled eyes while exchanging the following words:

> Alexander: I trust only you in this world. I've missed you. I need you. It is you I love, Hephaestion, no other.
> Hephaestion: [. . .] Like a deer listening in the wind you strike me still, Alexander. You have eyes like no other. You are everything I care for. And by the sweet breath of Aphrodite I'm so jealous of losing you to the world you want so badly.
> Alexander: You'll never lose me, Hephaestion. I'll always be with you, to the end.

The dialogue is worth quoting at length because it signals aspects of their relationship that the film itself is unwilling to visualise. Their mutual love for each other is evident, but other phrases indicate that this love extends beyond platonic friendship. Alexander's words 'I've missed you. I need you' remain ambiguous until framed by Hephaestion's subsequent lines ('like a deer', 'you strike me still', 'eyes like no other'), which through their relaxed eulogising about physical attributes confirm the pair's shared sexual attraction. Yet this verbal openness (which does not characterise Alexander's wordless relationship with Bagoas) is not matched by what we are shown. The scene ends with a fully clothed embrace on the balcony rather than any confirmatory images of the bedchamber, and in the film as a whole the pair are only ever shown embracing, with no kisses or further signs of physical intimacy being offered, leaving their relationship oddly unclarified in sexual terms. In direct and dramatic contrast, the consummation of Alexander's marriage to Roxanna (Rosario Dawson) – which in narrative terms does not supplant his associations with Hephaestion and Bagoas – is an explicit depiction of emphatic heterosexual intercourse. In this way the homosexual aspects of Alexander's life are relegated, moved offscreen, as if the film has hesitated in the act of articulating them.[4]

Shane Black's *Kiss Kiss Bang Bang* (2005) is at once more upfront and more elliptical about the sexual preferences of one of its two male protagonists. A *film noir* pastiche, it follows heterosexual New York thief Harry Lockhart (Robert Downey Junior), who is mistaken for an actor and whisked off to Los Angeles to star as a police officer in a new movie. His preparation for the part includes shadowing a private detective who happens to be gay – 'Gay Perry' (Val Kilmer). Even before Harry has spent his first night shadowing Perry, the film swiftly introduces an old school friend into the narrative to establish his heterosexual credentials: Harmony (Michelle Monaghan) is a girl Harry used to be in love with at school who has been trying to make it as an actress in Hollywood for the last five years. She remains a presence as the narrative progresses by being somehow connected to the case that Perry and Harry stumble upon on their first night working together. Perry is matter of fact about his homosexuality, and although it is used as the pay-off for a couple of jokes it does not result in his visual representation being obviously stereotyped. However, where Harry is permitted to pursue (albeit not very successfully) his romantic desires onscreen, Perry's practising of his sexuality is hidden from view and not mentioned in dialogue. Like the gay best friends and neighbours of 1990s cinema (see Benshoff 2009: 199), Perry is not permitted to demonstrate sexual agency and is utterly divorced from any form of gay community or gay club scene. Despite Perry's sexuality being contained in this way, the film still creates opportunities for Harry to express revulsion at it. During their shared reminiscences about school crushes Harry visibly – and audibly – grimaces when Perry mentions a boy's name; after Perry and he pretend to make out in order to escape detection by a police patrol car Harry recoils in disgust, spitting on the floor; and later when Harry tries to revive an unconscious and injured Perry using the mouth to mouth resuscitation technique he falls back, similarly repulsed, because blood has started to pour involuntarily out of Perry's mouth. This final example is revealing; the scene gives Harry a cause for disgust not directly connected to the confrontation of homosexual desire but which is crucially still located in the gay body. In offering an unapologetic gay man as a character, the film matches him with a male character who is permitted to be sporadically but openly homophobic.

Elsewhere, the tradition of demonising homosexuality by presenting villains who are gay or connotatively homosexual in stereotypical terms (that is, their homosexuality is implied, as in the Hays Production Code era) is alive and well. In the science fiction action film *Gamer* (2009) a megalomaniac called Ken Castle (Michael C. Hall) has invented two televised games that have become hugely successful: in 'Society' players outside the game can control human beings inside the game and make them do whatever they want; in the federal-backed 'Slayers' players can control convicts in a similar fashion, engaging them in bloody war games with each other. Now Castle wants to put all human beings under his own personal control, using the game mechanism, nanites that convert the brain either to be controlled or to send commands remotely. The hero Kable (Gerard Butler) was convicted of a crime he didn't commit and is now stuck in the 'Slayers' game, trying to survive long enough to escape and be reunited with his wife and child, an endeavour which will eventually lead him into direct confrontation with Castle. Aside from his family, Kable's heterosexuality is marked by the stereotypical iconography of the tough-guy: he is well-built, has a beard, is armed with large guns, sports militaristic combat-wear and moves with a combat-ready gait. In contrast Castle's characterisation constructs him as connotatively homosexual: he has a soft voice, wears costumes that include feminine touches (slacks with espadrilles during a television interview; later a classical Mandarin blouse), and is an adept dancer. This last fact is revealed in the first phase of Castle and Kable's final confrontation. Kable has broken into Castle's base and locates him in a hall, accompanied by a line of henchmen. Using the same technology that the 'Society' and 'Slayers' games rely on, Castle controls all of his men at once, demonstrating this with a musical number in which his burly henchmen incongruously echo his hip-swaying movements with varying degrees of success. Lip-synching to Sammy Davis Jr's version of 'I've Got You Under My Skin' Castle shimmies and prowls, the song lyrics seemingly directed at Kable as well as commenting ironically on the predicament of the men under his control. In this way the film maps homosexuality (and, given the song lyrics, homosexual desire) onto murderous megalomania. A similar representational move occurs in Zack Snyder's two recent blockbusters, *300* (2006) and *Watchmen* (2009). The former offers a fictionalised depiction of the Battle of Thermopylae in 480 BC, in which King Leonidas led 300 Spartan soldiers to hold off a massive Persian army. The heroic Spartans are hyper-masculine, with highly muscular physiques, rugged beards and spears cocked and ready for battle. The homoerotic potential in these hyperbolic representations is significant because the Spartans' costumes of capes, leather shorts and sandals leave their torso and legs constantly exposed and therefore on display to other men, both Spartan and Persian. The film negotiates this homoeroticism by openly acknowledging it – the Spartans jokingly accuse each other of being 'boy-lovers' for example – and then by disavowing it, supplying a villain onto whom the homosexuality latent in homoeroticism can be projected. Persian king Xerxes is coded particularly vehemently in terms of stereotyped homosexuality. After the Spartans have shown their strength and stamina in battle with the Persians, and repelled every messenger who has asked on Xerxes' behalf for them to surrender, Xerxes himself comes forward to meet Leonidas. He is carried on a giant gold staircase adorned with lion and antelope statues and a huge gold sun that shines behind him. Xerxes pauses as if to be admired, before sashaying down the staircase towards Leonidas. Xerxes' costume is limited to a gold codpiece and chains of gold and jewels that are draped across his head and body, along with some glittering facial piercing and heavy make-up around the eyes and on the lips. His body is slim, much less muscular than the Spartans', which increases the feminising effect to which the make-up and ostentatious jewellery are already contributing. Xerxes' performance style, body piercings and bejewelled costume generate associations with stereotypes of homosexuality, transvestism, transexuality and S&M iconography.

Xerxes and Leonidas meet in *300*

As Xerxes makes his final offer to Leonidas to become one of his generals and help him take over the world (on the condition that Sparta surrenders to him), Xerxes' hubris and megalomania are mapped onto this outrageously stereotyped display of homosexuality.

In *Watchmen* the villain is Ozymandias, a slim, self-regarding, pristine and rather flamboyantly dressed character who is obsessed with ending the Cold War by visiting mass destruction on the world's largest cities. If there were any doubt about whether he is gay, the film supplies its confirmation in a scene where his computer is broken into, revealing a folder titled 'Boys' sitting prominently on the desktop. Once again the aim seems to be to set Ozymandias apart from *Watchmen*'s other softly-spoken character, Dr Manhattan (Billy Crudup), a former human scientist who has transformed into a super-powered giant as a result of a nuclear accident and now manifests as a naked, hairless, blue figure who has cut himself off from the world and is noticeably uninterested in his girlfriend. Other 'gay villains' include Hollywood Jack (Timothy Olyphant) in *A Man Apart* (2003), Charlie Prince (Ben Foster) or 'Charlie Princess' as one character calls him in *3:10 to Yuma* (2007), and the Eastern European gay couple (played by Callum Keith Rennie and Fagin Woodcock) in *The X Files: I Want to Believe* (2008) who abduct women so that one of the men can swap his male body for a woman's. Even from the briefest of summaries we can see how this last example conflates murdering, transgender identity, homosexuality and racial 'otherness' together in this villainous couple. David Greven adds Satan (Rosalinda Celentano) in *The Passion of the Christ* (2004) to this list, a representation he labels homophobic because the devil is imagined,

> as an androgynous youth whose temptations of Jesus carry with them the dread, disturbing whiff of sexual perversity. Played by a young Italian actress . . . Satan serves as effeminate or androgynous counterpoint to the already inherently feminine and feminized form of Jesus. (Greven 2009: 207)

Greven's verdict neatly sums up the anxieties that drive both the elision of homosexuality from Hollywood action films and the ways in which it is characterised and structures the representational hierarchy when it is included. In the next section of the chapter I want to look at the way in which certain action films deploy homosexuality in a further way: as metaphor.

HOMOSEXUALITY AS METAPHOR

In *Spider-Man 3* (2007) Peter Parker aka Spider-Man (Tobey Maguire) is living what seems to have become a complicated life. His public success as the crime-fighting Spider-Man has made him rather self-regarding, which is affecting his relationship with Mary-Jane (Kirsten Dunst). He is estranged from his best friend Harry (James Franco), and a newcomer – Eddie Brock (Topher Grace) – is competing for the staff photographer job at the *Daily Bugle* that he has always coveted. A meteor crashes into a park where Peter and Mary-Jane are star-gazing, excreting an oily black substance, later identified as a symbiote, that finds its way into Peter's apartment. It attacks Peter while he is sleeping, and when he wakes up he is no longer in his bed. The camera pulls out from a microscopic close-up of Spider-Man's eye cover to frame his head; it then spins backwards and reorients so that we see that Spider-Man is in fact suspended upside down, looking at his reflected double in the glass frontage of an office block. The film at this moment makes explicit what will be its major thematic concern and structuring narrative principle: the double and the destabilising effects of its presence. Peter/Spider-Man has a number of doubles in the film: the vengeful Harry, who has his own secret identity and special powers as the New Goblin; Eddie Brock, the up and coming photographer who wants the staff job because he is, just like Peter, planning to get married, and who is taking the same kinds of photographs as Peter; and Peter's own double nature, heroic but self-regarding (Mary-Jane also has a double: Gwen (Bryce Dallas Howard), who Spider-Man has recently rescued). The symbiote's effect initially seems positive in that it makes Peter/Spider-Man feel quicker and stronger, but in fact it inflames his negative personality traits, in particular his narcissism and his aggression, transforming him into a cruel, violent version of himself. The two sequences that signal Peter's transformation into his own dark double are, however, rather different in tone from other parts of the film. The first shows him swaggering down the street, clicking his fingers and thrusting his pelvis suggestively at passing women, the second takes place in a jazz club in which he dances with Gwen to make Mary-Jane jealous. Here Peter's narcissism reaches its peak (the film ensures we know that Peter's cocky self-confidence does not correlate to the actual impression he is making; as he clicks at women on the street they recoil from him in bemusement or disdain), and the film chooses to manifest this as an excessive theatricality. Peter uses flamboyant gestures in the street scene, and in the jazz club delivers an elaborate, exuberant dance routine to play off Gwen and Mary-Jane against each other. The camp tone of both scenes is superfluous – in that Peter's arrogance and egotism could have been communicated without it – but its presence is revealing. In accordance with the dominant gender binary and the conventional representation of heroic gender, the slim, fresh-faced and occasionally still hesitant Peter registers as a rather feminised male hero, albeit 'redeemed' by his alter-ego's super-abilities. If the meteor substance magnifies existing traits, then it also seems to magnify this emasculated, feminine side; Peter is transformed into a theatrical figure that draws on the stereotype of the flamboyant homosexual. The fact that all this takes place in New York's theatre district (theatre an art form that has a reputation for attracting a high proportion of gay people) further underlines this association. These moments also draw surreptitiously on the historical association of narcissism with homosexuality, which have been 'inextricably linked' since Freud's 1914 essay 'On Narcissism: An Introduction' (Greven 2009: 22). In a pathologised version of same-sex desire, as the symbiote's effects intensify Peter is increasingly in love with his dark self. He is forced to confront his destructive personality when he accidentally hits Mary-Jane during a brawl at the jazz club, and he runs to the privacy of a nearby church bell-tower to try to remove the symbiote. Coincidentally his other double Brock is depressed and praying in the same church, and hears Peter's cries as he struggles to rip off his symbiote-infected suit. Coming to investigate he is at the bottom of the bell-tower when the symbiote disengages from Peter; it falls onto Brock and takes him over, turning him into a monstrous version of Spider-Man. This destructive transference of glutinous material from one man to another itself resonates with a fear of same-sex desire and intercourse, a fear the film manages by killing off all Peter's male doubles – evil Peter, Brock and Harry – by the film's end, and by fading out on the heterosexual couple, Peter and Mary-Jane, reunited in a slow dance at the jazz club. The film thus draws on pathologised conceptions of homosexuality in complex ways in its dramatisation of Peter's crisis.

Aside from the negative association of the superhero with a flamboyant homosexuality, an association also suggested in Hancock's dismissal of comic book heroes as 'homos' discussed earlier, the potential to mobilise homosexuality as a metaphor in more progressive ways remains, even in the superhero movie. In their excessive allocation of power, and because their bodies exceed conventional physical (and therefore also social) frameworks, superheroes are usually forced to negotiate different, and often more marginalised, ways of being in the world, to occupy the position of 'other' as well as hero. The dynamics of superhero narratives, the fact that the heroes must hide a part of who they are or 'come out' to those around them (in films like *Superman Returns* (2006), *Iron Man* (2008), *Hulk* (2003), *The Incredible Hulk* (2008), *Batman Begins* and *The Dark Knight*), correlates their experiences closely with key milestones of homosexual experience. One franchise that explicitly mobilises this correlation is the *X-Men* franchise (2000, 2003, 2006, 2009); in the films' large cast of mutant heroes there are always characters in the process of embodying typical homosexual milestones: hiding one's true self, repressing 'urges', coming out, negotiating a place in the community and freely expressing oneself. Alienated from society by their mutant tendencies, in key scenes the mutants repeatedly have to try to 'pass' as conventional humans, struggle to gain their families' understanding when they 'come out' as different, and campaign for tolerance and equal right for mutants, echoing similar gay rights campaigns. Like homosexuals the mutants are forced to establish safe spaces like Xavier's school where they can be themselves and express their tendencies without censure. Underlying the events of each film is the threat of governmental and legislative action against the mutant population; characters are regularly distracted by television reports of pro- or anti-mutant demonstrations, campaign speeches, votes and debates. The mutants are threatened with and subjected to potential registration, incarceration, experimentation, isolation, abuse and misunderstanding. In a sense it is quite a mechanistic use of the metaphor, but what makes it distinctive is the franchise's attempt to encourage particular kinds of response to the narrative of marginalisation it presents. Mutants are not positioned within the narrative as exceptions or aberrations: mutancy manifests at puberty, thus linking it to other natural bodily changes at that period of human development; and the films also include a signature sequence which emphasises that the mutants are commonplace. In each film Professor Xavier (Patrick Stewart) uses a machine called Cerebro, which enhances his telepathic powers in order to locate mutants and humans. In a spectacular sequence, upon activation of the machine the walls of the spherical room in which Cerebro is housed appear to fall away, replaced by Xavier's mental images of a constantly shifting three-dimensional map of the world across which a constellation of mutant presences glow; the camera moves dynamically through the space, picking out one mutant after another. What is revealed simultaneously to the spectator and characters watching within the diegesis is a world filled with as many mutants as there are humans. Significantly these mutants are not unusual-looking, and are not captured exhibiting fantastical powers; instead they are simply going about their daily lives like everyone else (walking to work, taking their children to school, greeting friends and so on). In contrast to the localised narratives of *Hulk*, the *Spider-Man* films and other single superhero films, the *X-Men* films imagine a world where mutants are everywhere, where any teenager may develop a mutation. As we watch the mutant heroes fight to save humanity from the misanthropic plans of rogue mutant Magneto (Ian McKellen), the fear and disgust displayed by the human public seems irrational and without basis. At the same time, cruelty towards mutants is demonised by the film, as spectators are forced to share the mutant heroes' experiences of prejudice first-hand – from verbal abuse and police harassment to the mental and physical torture Wolverine is revealed to have been subjected to in *X-Men 2* as a result of villain William Stryker (Brian Cox)'s experiments in a secret military base (clearly intended to echo the Nazi doctors' experiments on homosexuals in the death camps of World War II). Such strategies are used to construct prejudice and intolerance as destructive and counterproductive. Through the Cerebro sequences the films take the unusual step (for mainstream Hollywood cinema) of positing prejudice as a social problem rather than an individual one, so that the corollary promotion of tolerance and community the films engage in has a political aspect. This is, therefore, a more progressive mobilisation of homosexuality as metaphor, likely made possible by the fantastical setting.

THE INVISIBLE WOMEN

Near the beginning of this chapter I quoted Andrea Weiss' encouragement that we need to consider 'invisibility as well as visibility as a form of representation', an observation on the representation of lesbians on screen. In her book *Vampires and Violets* (1992) she makes clear that the key reason for such an approach is the persistent erasure of lesbians from mainstream Hollywood cinema. As Benshoff and Griffin have pointed out, following one or two liberal-minded films of the 1980s, such as *Personal Best* (1982), *Lianna* (1983) and *Silkwood* (1983),

> by the mid-1980s, homosexual characters in Hollywood film were either downplayed or removed altogether. Gay male kissing or overt eroticism was definitely out – as they basically still are in mainstream Hollywood films. Softcore lesbian erotics could be tolerated, but revolutionary dyke characters or queer central characters could not. (Benshoff and Griffin 2006: 189)

Indeed the strategies set out earlier in the chapter in relation to the representation of gay men in cinema also apply to lesbians, including erasure from the screen; the removal or minimisation of lesbianism as source material is moved to the screen (for example in *The Color Purple* (1985), *Fried Green Tomatoes* (1991) and *Boys on the Side* (1995)); and the demonisation of lesbians as obsessive or murderous (in films such as *Windows* (1980), *Black Widow* (1987), *Basic Instinct* (1992) and *Single White Female* (1992)), a trend that appears to have returned with a vengeance in films like *Chloe* (2009) and *The Roommate* (2011). Lesbian lives have been the subject of a small strand of independent filmmaking over the last twenty years (including for example the New Queer Cinema film *Go Fish* (1994) and subsequent movies *High Art* (1998), *But I'm A Cheerleader* (1999) and cross-over success *The Kids Are All Right* (2010)), while in *Kissing Jessica Stein* (2001) and *Imagine Me and You* (2005) studio independents like Fox Searchlight and Focus Features respectively have financed movies aimed at mainstream audiences in which a lesbian relationship is progressed according to the tropes of heterosexual romance. In the action film, lesbians have been few and far between, and when they are present they traditionally function in one of two ways: as sexualised spectacle, or as one of the hero's helpers (for example, Private Vasquez in *Aliens*, or the lesbian police investigator Amy Wallace (Laurie Metcalf) in *Internal Affairs*

(1990). Contemporary action cinema continues these trends with dismaying persistence, providing no lesbian action heroes to speak of (independent cinema provides a space in which to deride this mainstream tendency, of course, as the cheerfully silly lesbian action film *D.E.B.S.* (2004) illustrates), while *Domino* (2005), an action film based on the life of bisexual female bounty hunter Domino Harvey, removes any reference to her lesbian relationships. Where lesbians do appear, they either provide hyper-feminine erotic spectacle (like the harem women in *300*), or they are characters in minor or supporting roles, coded as lesbian by their short haircut, macho behaviour or butch clothing, such as the lesbian control room technician in *Avatar* who, during Jake's escape from the corporation's base, spots that Chacon has started the engine on her vehicle in the hangar without authorisation. Such minor characters are positive presences in that they just 'happen to be gay', but limited in that they often die before the narrative's end. For example, in *Watchmen* the lesbian Minutemen heroine Silhouette (Apollonia Vanova) and her girlfriend (Leah Gibson) don't make it past the credits, a crime scene photograph showing that they were murdered in their bed. In *Matrix: Revolutions* the short-haired ship doctor Maggie (Essie Davis) is murdered by her patient Bane (Ian Bliss) who has been possessed by evil Agent Smith (Hugo Weaving). Later as the machines tunnel through into Zion, the human underground city, married volunteer Zee (Nona Gaye) is partnered up with shaven-headed, muscular and butch-looking Charra (Rachel Blackman) to deploy rockets from a mobile rocket launcher. In the intense battle with the machines they initially enjoy some success, their rockets disrupting the machines' bombardment. However, after one rocket almost hits a major target, airborne machine 'squids' with roving mechanical tentacles turn on Zee and Charra, and while Zee manages to get to safety Charra is pinned and then fatally penetrated by the squids' mechanical claws.

These deaths are part of Hollywood's regulation of female homosociality, which, although it can provide the titillating spectacle of lesbian homoeroticism, must also work to disavow the possibility of actual lesbian interaction. *Resident Evil* is an interesting text in this regard. The film finds Alice (Milla Jovovich) trying to make her way out of the Umbrella corporation facility in which she has been trapped with a group of paramilitaries and hordes of flesh-eating zombies. As each soldier is picked off the group is whittled down to two male colleagues and the tough-talking Macho Latina paramilitary Rain (Michelle Rodriguez), who has had plenty of screen time to demonstrate both her heroism and her combat skills. She and Alice have developed a camaraderie across the film, so that when Rain is bitten by a zombie the race is on to find the antidote. It is located on a train which will also provide the group with an escape route out of the facility. As Alice gently administers the antidote to Rain's arm, they make a pact that it will be Alice who kills Rain if she turns into a zombie – a zombie film trope that connotes a strong friendship has been forged. Rain appears to stop breathing but just as Alice is about to pull the trigger Rain stops her, saying wryly 'I'm not dead yet,' to which Alice replies 'I could kiss you, you bitch.' It is their most intimate moment, the one closest to acknowledging the homoerotic potential of their homosocial pairing, but shortly the antidote will fail and Rain will turn zombie, forcing Alice to shoot her in the head in self-defence. The death is oddly unmotivated in narrative terms: Rain is a relatively sympathetic character, has been tested and survived, and has been treated with the antidote. So why not provide a happy ending for the character? Beltrán suggests that Rain illustrates 'the typical construction of Latina action protagonists as inherently fierce and fearless', but implies that her limited character development and her death are confirmation that 'Hollywood creatives do not quite know what to do with the physically capable Latina protagonist after she's handily escaped a catacomb full of zombies, particularly when she is paired with a white female' (2004: 195). Beltrán is interested in placing the character in relation to the history of Latina/o cinematic representation in the mainstream, but it is the pairing of Rain with a *feminine* white woman that also seems to present the film with a 'problem' it feels it needs to solve. Usually the Macho Latina is paired (if at all) with a male within a mixed race and mixed gender group, as in the *Fast and Furious* franchise or *Predators*, which reassuringly frames the Macho Latina's strength and independence as being containable within a heterosexual union. Here the pairing is with Alice, while Rain pays absolutely no attention to any of the men in the team. The matching of Rain's 'butch' to Alice's 'femme' subversively mimics the heterosexual gender binary, and as such has the potential to raise the spectre of actual homosexual interaction in a way that Alice's pairings with white feminine women in the subsequent sequels do not. I would suggest that it is this, as well as the film's racial hierarchy, that consigns Rain to her tragic end. In what is often described as a progressive era, this film and the others we have discussed in this chapter demonstrate homosexuality's continued function as a structuring absence but also Hollywood's 'resolutely heterosexist' nature (Benshoff and Griffin 2009: 351).

NOTES

1. The narrative function of homosexuality in these listed films does vary, however, and demands a more extended discussion than this chapter on action cinema has space to provide. Readers who wish to pursue this further are directed in the first instance to Harry M. Benshoff and Sean Griffin's useful overview of the history of homosexual and queer representation in US cinema and their discussion of contemporary trends (Benshoff and Griffin 2009: 303–55).

2. For discussion of New Queer Cinema and its consequences for mainstream cinema, see Rich 1992 and 2000, Pidduck 2003, Aaron 2004 and 2006, and Holmlund 2005.

3. Examples would include the 'sissy' characters in films like *Movie Crazy* (1932), *The Gay Divorcee* (1934) and *Adam's Rib* (1949), duplicitous Joel Cairo (Peter Lorre) in *The Maltese Falcon* (1941) and the murderers in *Rope* (1948) and *Strangers on a Train* (1951), or tragic figures such as Plato (Sal Mineo) in *Rebel without a Cause* (1955).

4. There was speculation that Oliver Stone removed some sexual scenes between Alexander and Bagoas from the original theatrical release (see Waxman 2004); it is also clear from the *Alexander Revisited: The Final Cut* version released on DVD in 2007 that Stone had cut a homosexual sex scene between King Philip (Val Kilmer) and his Pausanius (Tony Kebbell) which is restored in the *Final Cut*. Sex scenes between Alexander and Hephaestion do not seem to have been filmed.

CHAPTER 8

Action cinema after 9/11

There has been much debate about whether Hollywood filmmaking changed as a result of the terrorist attacks on 11 September 2001. The images of the attacks on the two towers of the World Trade Center, of impacts, explosions and the scale of destruction captured in bright sunlight by home video and television cameras, were uncomfortably reminiscent of numerous fictional scenes in Hollywood action cinema and disaster movies. The experience of people watching the events unfold in real time on their television sets was one of horror but also of disturbing recognition as they were confronted by images that, in a different context, had provided many of them with pleasure and entertainment. The desirability of violent Hollywood spectacle was suddenly called into question in the most perturbing of ways, prompting calls for a reconsideration of what kinds of entertainment images should be screened in movie theatres.[1] Such reconsideration also seemed fitting in the context of wider newsmedia and political responses to 9/11, which asserted repeatedly 'that the world had been irrevocably changed' (Mulvey 2006: 23). David Holloway has argued that this idea of a changed world was mobilised more for its political utility than its accuracy; that it was used to defend the ' "Bush Doctrine" of pre-emptive war, unilateral policy-making and "regime change" in "rogue states" ', while being inaccurate because the 9/11 attacks were 'just one incident in a much bigger, transnational Islamist insurgency' that had been building throughout the 1990s (Holloway 2008: 4).[2] Wary of being associated with those disconcertingly Hollywood-like images, early responses from studio executives and creatives often chimed with this sense of a changed world. For example, at an Academy of Television Arts and Sciences (ATAS) industry panel called 'Hollywood Goes to War?' on 5 December 2001, ATAS chairman and writer-producer Bryce Zabel declared, 'What we need is a new paradigm' for film and television (Chambers 2002: paragraph 31). Hollywood also held a series of meetings with representatives of the Bush administration to see how they could help, beginning just one month after the attacks.[3] Wheeler Winston Dixon, however, suggests that industry soul-searching about what Americans might want to see at the movie theatre was necessarily driven by economic, as well as patriotic concerns, and initial hesitation about what was appropriate to screen in cinemas was shortlived, due to audiences' quickly re-established appetite for fictionally framed violence:

> In the days and weeks after 9/11, Hollywood momentarily abandoned the hyperviolent spectacles that dominated mainstream late 1990s cinema. Films were temporarily shelved, sequences featuring the World Trade Center were recut, and 'family' films were rushed into release or production ... Predictably, however, this reversal of fortune did not last long, and soon Hollywood was back to work on a series of highly successful 'crash and burn' movies. (Dixon 2004: 3)

Given the emotive nature of 9/11 it is easy to overestimate its effect on Hollywood filmmaking. Still, an analysis based only on the presence or absence of explosive action sequences from the Hollywood release roster, or on the genres that were embraced or rejected, has limitations. It cannot in itself capture fully the nuances of Hollywood's 'processing' of either 9/11 or indeed the Iraq and Afghanistan wars that were begun in its aftermath. This is because such processing can manifest itself in a myriad subtle ways, in shifts for example in the dramatisation of a particular moment, design of narrative elements and plot developments, aspects of characterisation, setting or visual design; certainly scholars like Thomas Elsaesser and Christian Keathley make similar arguments about the effects on US cinema of an equally traumatic period in US history, that of the Vietnam War (see Elsaesser 2004 and Keathley 2004). A complete study of such shifts is beyond the scope of a book focused specifically on contemporary action cinema. But violent spectacle and physical heroism, integral components of the action film, were key aspects of the initial discussion of how 9/11 was experienced, and were also at issue in the two wars that followed it.[4] As a result it is pertinent to enquire as to whether action cinema or certain of its strands have responded to the events of 9/11 and its ramifications. After pursuing this enquiry across action cinema as a whole my focus will turn to those action films that have explicitly striven to negotiate the socio-political and cultural complexities of the post-9/11 world.

HOLLYWOOD AND ACTION CINEMA AFTER 9/11

Heroism is central in the action film, enacted by the hero in exhilaratingly physical ways, his or her violence meted out in the name of justice and moral righteousness. Heroism as a cultural idea gained renewed currency in the immediate aftermath of 9/11. The events prompted an overflowing of praise for the US police, fire and rescue and ambulance service personnel who had risked their lives or died trying to rescue others when the twin towers fell, for the passengers of hijacked United Airlines Flight 93 who hatched a plan to foil the hijackers and perished trying to implement it, and for those who died or whose bravery helped saved lives as events unfolded. Here were acts of human sacrifice and bravery that could be heralded unproblematically as heroic, and which were duly eulogised by US television and print media as well as by politicians and the general public. But this discourse of patriotic heroism was to be tortuously problematised by what happened next. The military interventions initiated by the US and its allies after 9/11 in the name of the 'war on terror' were highly controversial. In the face of anti-war demonstrations the public and legal mandate for war with Iraq was difficult to assemble even before the assertion that Iraq was holding weapons of mass destruction was discredited; the basis for the occupation of Afghanistan seemed equally nebulous. Government reassurances about smart military technologies only targeting the 'real' enemy in Iraq were undermined by emerging details of the scale of civilian Iraqi casualties (estimated deaths range from 34,832 to 793,663 according to Fischer 2008: 3), while the revelations of prisoner mistreatment at Guantànamo Bay in 2002 and Abu Ghraib in 2004 and of the rendition of terror suspects to non-US locations to avoid legal oversight in 2005 called into question the 'heroism' of implicated military personnel and further muddied the notion that the US was fighting a 'just war'. Debates about what US troops are fighting for have continued across the decade, as US military deaths on both fronts have risen inexorably, Iraqi and Afghan civilian casualties increase year on year (de Mistura and Gagnon 2010; Fischer 2008) and the progress of military attempts to quell insurgency and civil unrest in both countries is persistently called into question.[5] In a set of circumstances arguably similar to the Vietnam War, these public, political and media discussions have put significant pressure on the notion of heroism, with its usual assumption of a morally just motivation difficult to square with the realities described above. In the midst of these heated cultural debates would Hollywood change or modify its construction of heroism?

Rebecca Bell-Metereau suggests that Hollywood quickly supplied avenging heroes in a series of military action films such as *Behind Enemy Lines* (US release date November 2001), *Black Hawk Down* (December 2001), *Collateral Damage* (February 2002), *We Were Soldiers* (March 2002), *Windtalkers* (August 2002) and *Tears of the Sun* (March 2003). Bell-Metereau sees these films in relation to media discourse around 9/11:

> One may look at the growing number of militaristic movies, temporarily upstaged by real-life events but waiting in the wings like prima

ballerinas, to see that the media not only reported but helped to create a siege mentality, followed by a reaction of panic and consequent thirst for revenge. (Bell–Metereau 2004: 142)

While I am sympathetic to Bell-Metereau's underlying disappointment with media sensationalism and what she clearly feels are jingoistic action movies, in my view she may be placing too much emphasis on the mere existence of these films, rather than taking into account their relative popularity with audiences. In the years immediately following 9/11 the most popular movies at the box office were in fact fantasy films like *Spider-Man* (2002), the sequels in the *Lord of the Rings* trilogy (2002, 2003), instalments in the *Matrix* (2003), *Harry Potter* (2002), *Star Wars* (2002) and *Pirates of the Caribbean* (2003) franchises, and family or comic films like *Finding Nemo* (2003), *Bruce Almighty* (2003) and *My Big Fat Greek Wedding* (2002). Compared to takings for *Spider-Man* of $404 million and $377 million for *Lord of the Rings: The Return of the King*, the box office returns on the military action films was significantly smaller: for example *Black Hawk Down* took $109 million and *We Were Soldiers* $78.1 million.[6] Similarly, Jonathan Markovitz' suggestion that the 'stark rhetoric of the Bush administration's quest to eradicate "evil" finds a perfect correlate in films that cast A-list Hollywood stars in battles against the calculating and murderous violence of always highly racialized terrorist "others"' certainly applies to the militaristic films and to the fantastical Orcs in the *Lord of the Rings* trilogy, but seems less convincing when applied to *Spider-Man* or *Pirates of the Caribbean: The Curse of the Black Pearl* (Markovitz 2004: 202). Rather than seeing action films as only catering to a desire for revenge, then, it is more accurate to suggest that a particular strand of action cinema (and not its most successful strand at that, in box office terms) may have spoken to audience's desires to experience vicariously US forces' delivery of violent acts of retribution. And yet this, too, is somewhat of a muddied picture. While *Collateral Damage* offers the wish-fulfilment fantasy that a single man can neutralise a terrorist cell that the government has failed to contain, other films like *Black Hawk Down*, *We Were Soldiers* and *The Last Samurai* (2003) locate their heroes in explicitly impossible or futile situations where bravery and patriotic sacrifice are the only options. These films might in fact speak to a need to witness cathartically the act of heroic sacrifice, rather than revenge.

In the years that followed Hollywood and US independent cinema began directly and indirectly to address the post-9/11 world, its faultlines, tensions and human impact, in *Fahrenheit 9/11* (2004), *United 93* (2006), *World Trade Center* (2006), *Munich* (2005), *Redacted* (2007), *Battle for Haditha* (2007), *Rendition* (2007), *Lions for Lambs* (2007) and *Stop-Loss* (2008).[7] In action cinema specifically a small number of films similarly engaged directly with aspects of these issues, such as Spielberg's *War of the Worlds* (2005) which worked through allegory and the puppet satire *Team America: World Police* (2004).[8] What has been more common, however, is for action films to make what Holloway calls 'modish' references to 9/11, Iraq or Afghanistan, or associated locales and themes (Holloway 2008: 75). For example, as we saw in Chapter 5 *Transformers* begins with soldiers travelling to their camp in Qatar in the Middle East: while this refers to the US Air Force's real world co-option of a Qatar air base in December 2002 to support their forward operations in the Middle East, there is no narrative motivation for this part of the story to take place in Qatar, and events move fairly quickly back to US soil. Similarly *Iron Man* (2008) opens in Afghanistan in order to add a modish pertinence to Tony Starck (Robert Downey Jnr)'s arms dealing and his subsequent punishment, his incarceration by terrorists during which he learns the error of his ways. While there is disapproval of the potentially calamitous effects of the cluster bomb-style weaponry Starck is pushing (Starck's narrative trajectory includes realising his weapons are destructive) this is quickly brushed aside. Once Starck escapes the terrorists the significant remaining portion of the film is situated in the US, apart from a brief demonstration of the Iron Man suit's powers saving Afghan civilians from terrorists, a rather simplistic bit of wish-fulfilment quickly upstaged by the intensifying tension between Starck and his US-based enemy. Elsewhere a fatally powerful Dracula rises from an unmarked grave in Iraq in *Blade: Trinity* (2004) and we are informed in *Sherlock Holmes* that Watson was a hero in the Afghan Wars. Michael Wood's observations about the passing references to World War II in early post-war Hollywood seems equally applicable in these examples: 'the world of death and war and menace and disaster is really there, gets a mention, but then is rendered irrelevant by the story or the star or the music' (Wood 1975: 17–18).[9] Attacks on home soil are the subject of *Shooter* (2007), *Vantage Point* (2008) and *Law Abiding Citizen* (2009), while the rogue soldier invoked by the government to explain the atrocities at Guantànamo and Abu Ghraib (Holloway 1998: 47) finds his way into *The Incredible Hulk* (2008), and in police uniform in *Assault on Precinct 13* (2005) and *16 Blocks* (2006). Amidst suspicions about the fabrication of evidence about the mandate for the Iraq war and the reduction of civil liberties flowing from the 2001 Patriot Act, *The Bourne Identity* (2002) and its sequels (2004, 2007) characterise national security as a dirty and often corrupt business with dramatic consequences for the individual. Worth mention too is the low-budget horror actioner *Red Sands* (2009) which follows the rapidly declining fortunes of a unit of US soldiers on patrol in the Middle East. Their desecration of a holy site (a reference to the damage done to Iraq's cultural heritage during the war and occupation) calls forth a malignant spirit which possesses each of them, driving them to kill each other. The sole survivor carries the spirit with him to a US army base, ending the film with the prospect of further destruction-from-within of the military rank and file. In each of these films references to the post-9/11 world are made in a superficial rather than interrogative way to add a sense of currency to the narratives. Other films, such as *The Kingdom*, *The Hurt Locker* and *Green Zone* (2010) place their protagonists in naturalistic Middle East settings and at the apex of conflict in one way or another as they attempt to evoke the intricacies, tensions and pressures of the situation. However, their conventional narrative structures and the inevitable focus on individual dramas risk a failure to express the complexity of this post-9/11 world. Discussing earlier fiction films that try to address socio-political issues, Richard Maltby argues that the inclusion of thematic material that references the real-world context 'establishes a point of contact between the movies' Utopian sensibility and the surrounding social environment of its audience' (Maltby 2003: 269). But he also indicates the problems of this 'Utopian sensibility': using *Mississippi Burning* (1988) as an example he illustrates how the film invited audiences 'to imagine institutionalized racism as if it could be solved by the conventions of a detective story' (ibid.: 269), when of course it could not. How does the relationship between genre conventions, the wish-fulfilment of the action narrative and its physical heroism, and the realities of the post-9/11 world intersect in these latter films?

NEGOTIATING A SPACE FOR ACTION

The Kingdom (Peter Berg, 2007) opens with an extended three-minute montage which combines animated and newsreel footage to construct a timeline that contextualises the fictional narrative. The timeline traces the development of the oil connections between the US and Saudi Arabia across the twentieth century, the establishment of compounds for US oil workers and their families, Osama Bin Laden's increasingly vocal opposition to the US presence, and the series of terrorist bombings that continue beyond 9/11 to attacks on Western compounds in Riyadh and Saudi Arabia (in May and November 2003, although the film does not specify this). This opening is elliptical but works to historicise recent real world terrorist attacks, acknowledging the antagonistic effect of the presence of the US in Saudi Arabia on the emirate's conservative demographic as well as hinting at the extent to which US foreign policy is dictated by its oil interests. It is an unusually frank act of relating the movie's fictional world to the real post 9/11 context, a signal that the film is trying to treat the context with some seriousness, and perhaps an attempt to claim the veracity of the fictional situations it will present. After this documentary-style prologue the film follows four FBI agents as they travel to Saudi Arabia to investigate the three-stage attack on a compound (a daylight shooting and suicide bombing by people dressed as state police, then a bomb detonated later in an ambulance sent to the scene) that has killed US men, women and children and an FBI agent. In a Rapid Deployment Team Briefing in the Washington FBI field office emotions are running high: the FBI officer who perished was a close friend of several present. The prologue has told us that the FBI is the lead agency whenever US citizens are attacked abroad, but political sensitivities are making official access impossible: intelligence analyst Adam Leavitt (Jason Bateman) exclaims, 'If there was ever a time to put boots on Saudi soil, don't you think this is it?' but forensic examiner Janet Mayes (Jennifer Garner) quickly tells him why they are unable to, explaining that 'The Saudi royal family cannot appear as if they are losing control.' Team leader Ronald Fleury (Jamie Foxx) reveals that the US State Department will also not sanction access, to gasps of outrage from the team. The scene asserts the difficulty of creating a space in which heroic action can be taken within the web of pre- and post-9/11 political tensions the prologue has weaved for us. Frequent reaction shots show us how keenly frustrated these men and women are by the constraints imposed by politics. There is a palpable sense of wanting to do something, to retaliate or respond, but not being able to, a desire familiar from initial US reactions to the losses of 9/11. The reaction shots, the death of a colleague and the prologue's explanation of the FBI's mandate in foreign US murders all work to align the audience with the characters' shared assumption that an interventionist approach – similar to the interventionist principle that has underwritten both Iraq and Afghanistan wars – is desirable. So, while careful to acknowledge the relevant political sensitivities through dialogue, the scene in fact prepares us to accept that Saudi reluctance to accommodate more US personnel should be disregarded in the service of creating a space for the FBI characters to act. Thus, by the end of the scene, when Fleury bullishly declares that he is going to get them access, this meets both the characters' and the audience's desires to move events along. Fleury's subsequent ability to leverage a chain of influence that extends through an investigative reporter at *The Washington Post* via the Saudi Arabian ambassador to the Saudi prince to get them on a plane to the attack site the same evening could be read as a critique of the shady dealings necessary in contemporary politics. But given that these unofficial channels enable the US protagonists to take up their desired central role in the investigation, it seems the film is more interested at this stage in substituting the reality of grappling with complex political situations for a fantasy about instant access and instant action. Nevertheless the difficulty of creating a space for heroic action in the post-9/11 context remains a potent theme of the film, which shapes its engagement with real-world issues. A team consisting of Fleury, Leavitt, Mayes and bomb technician Grant Sykes (Chris Cooper) enters the emirate unofficially by plane, but the terms of access have brought their own limitations: monitored by the Saudi National Guard and chaperoned by Saudi state police they have only a five-day window for the investigation, are forbidden from working at night or handling evidence at the attack site, and are unable to question people without their state police chaperones. The US team's reactions when they encounter these restrictions are often vociferous, despite the reality of the risks the restrictions are designed to cope with. Frequent cutaways to potential threats in the surrounding area beyond the compound legitimate the prudence of the state police's stringent security measures and construct such reactions as self-involved, but at the same time the desire for narrative progression works to align the audience with the team's desire simply to get on with what they do best. In a moment that demonstrates the constraining nature of these restrictions, Mayes is conducting a forensic examination of a body killed in the blast when a state police officer starts to protest vehemently. Sergeant Haytham (Ali Suliman) explains that as a female non-Muslim Mayes cannot touch the male Muslim body. She has to guide Haytham to carry out the technically skilled forensic procedures on her behalf. US viewers used to the pleasures of the detection process in police procedurals and crime scene investigation dramas on film and television are likely to perceive these obstructions as unwelcome, interrupting the forward momentum of the detection process and delaying the narrative resolution. Elsewhere the Muslim sensitivities of state police Colonel Faris Al Ghazi (Ashraf Barhom) about appropriate language are ignored and made fun of by the rather bellicose Leavitt and Sykes; depending on your point of view you might read these scenes as the FBI agents' wilful disrespect of a simple, politely-made request or the colonel's oversensitivity on a trivial matter. Thus everyday Muslim beliefs are openly discussed (still unusual in Hollywood), but at the same time the dramatisation of the scenes in which they are referenced leaves open the opportunity to read them as a nuisance or triviality given the narrative importance bestowed on the hunt for the compound attackers. The prologue openly acknowledged the clash of cultures between US compound occupants and conservative Saudis (characterised as an opposition between 'tradition' and 'modernity', a formulation that rather problematically casts the US as progressive modernisers). The film's continued preoccupation with the limits and boundaries that the US protagonists come up against has the capacity to read – and function – as both a progressive awareness-raising discourse on the necessity of tolerance and respect of cultural differences, and as a conservative critique of cultural beliefs that are outmoded and obstructive or counterproductive to justice. In this way the film remains 'open' to politicised interpretations that are strikingly polarised and leaves audiences to choose their position. As Maltby reveals, such a strategy reflects established Hollywood practice when referencing socially or politically sensitive subject-matter: 'displac[ing] responsibility for the interpretation of a movie's content onto its audience' so that studios themselves are not accused of holding partisan political views (Maltby 2003: 275).

This is a multiple protagonist movie in which heroism is necessarily shared as well as individualised, so that *The Kingdom* must negotiate who of the four Americans and their two key Saudi colleagues will be permitted to express physical heroism, and to what extent. The character trajectories that result reveal the competing pulls of the film's attempt to engage with the real-world cultural-political landscape and its adherence to the representational conventions of the action film. The US group is carefully differentiated, bringing various specialisms to the investigation as one might expect, but with a mixed personnel of an African American man, two white men and one white woman that hail from different parts of the US, and have contrasting personality traits. There is already a hierarchy of command: Fleury displays quietly determined composure in his leadership role, which involves co-ordinating the team's activities and liaising with the Saudi state police; the rest of the team act as his advisors and information gatherers. His authority also has the capacity to extend beyond the group, as illustrated by his early success in getting access to the Saudi ambassador but also his later audience with Prince Ahmed Bin Khaled (Omar Berdouni), in which he convinces the prince to loosen the restrictions under which the team is working. Mayes, Sykes and Leavitt have no such influence: Fleury has the power to expand the space of action in a way that the other American characters do not. It is also Fleury who establishes a close working relationship with the team's ally, state police Colonel Al Ghazi, which is crucial in extending still further the team's access to the city spaces outside the compound where the bombers are hiding. The fact that it is the African American team member who achieves this connection with Al Ghazi can once again be read both ways, as an empowered characterisation or as an implicit invocation of racist ideas about people of non-white ethnicities sharing affinities that white people cannot access. The prince's loosening of restrictions frees up the Americans to establish a co-operative relationship with their Saudi colleagues to move the investigation along more quickly, but it is not particularly egalitarian. In taking control of the investigation the Americans co-opt the Saudis as a workforce, with state police officers relegated to excavation workers at the bomb crater, forensic examination assistants, chauffeurs, guides and translators. Thus a racialised hierarchy arises in the film, if we can understand 'race' here in terms of a combination of nationality and ethnicity (a frequent conflation in white racist discourse). The film redirects our attention away from this by focusing much of the dramatic interest in the narrative on the burgeoning relationship between Fleury and Al Ghazi. Initially wary of each other, they become close after each helps the other's investigation, progress Fleury will later use to convince the prince to shift supervision of the investigation from the unsympathetic general of the National Guard to Al Ghazi, thus allowing Fleury and Al Ghazi to work more closely together and more freely.[10] A mutual understanding of their matching team leader roles leads to banter, friendship and the exchanging of first names, and both discover a shared desire to deliver retribution to the bombers. Al Ghazi's declaration of this impulse is interesting as much for what it affirms as what it elides. In a medium close-up he says solemnly:

> I find myself in a place where I no longer care about why we are attacked. I only care that one hundred people woke up a few mornings ago and had no idea it was their last. When we catch the man who murdered these people I don't care to ask even one question. I want to kill him.

Al Ghazi's words echo the eagerness for vengeful action that infused the briefing room in Washington (and which Sykes later suggests Fleury is harbouring to the extent that it might affect his judgment). But the phrases 'I no longer care about why' and 'I don't care to ask even one question' suggest a particular response to terrorism that is uninterested in an analysis of its causes – that violent retribution is the only solution. Echoing the jingoistic aspect of the Bush administration's 'war on terror', Al Ghazi's sentiments also correspond to the action film's convention of resolving the narrative through a culminating violence, while pointing away from the real-world realities of anti-terrorist strategies, which must include intelligence gathering and analysis as well as more direct forms of action. Thus aligned, Al Ghazi moves explicitly into the role of Fleury's partner in the final section of the narrative; as in the buddy action film he backs up Fleury in discussion and pairs with him in combat. He is part of the team, albeit (as in the white/black buddy movie) in the 'custody' of his American friend. In the final action sequence all six of the investigators – the four Americans and the two Saudis – will have the opportunity to give vent to their desire for revenge; to express a violent heroism in place of the more sedentary modes of investigative action they were able to take before.

Leavitt is kidnapped in an attack on the state police motorcade in which the US team is travelling. A chase develops which leads to an apartment block where the bombers are preparing to execute Leavitt on camera. Outside, neighbouring buildings and alleyways erupt as gunfire and rockets assail the team's vehicle from all directions; cornered, the US/Saudi team exit their vehicle and in the ensuing firefight kill fourteen shooters stationed in windows and on rooftops and balconies. Haytham and Sykes stand guard outside and wait for back-up while Fleury, Al Ghazi and Mayes search the building for Leavitt and the bombers. As Fleury and Al Ghazi get waylaid in a gun battle down one corridor, in another Mayes discovers Leavitt and rescues him from his captors. All four converge on a family apartment that has drawn Mayes' attention: inside is Abu Hamza (Hezi Saddiki), the bomber responsible for the compound bombing. As the team attempt to apprehend the bomber Al Ghazi, Abu Hamza and a young member of the Hamza clan are all killed in the crossfire, leaving the Americans and Haytham distraught. Two aspects of this

Al Ghazi and Fleury are strangers who become buddies in *The Kingdom*

denouement are worth highlighting further for what they tell us about the tensions in the film between genre conventions and the real-world context. One is the fatal shooting of Al Ghazi, the most fully realised of the two main Saudi protagonists. His death prompts Fleury to visit Al Ghazi's family and speak to his son, in the same way that he had visited the son of the FBI agent killed in the original bomb attack before he travelled to Riyadh. These mirror scenes at the beginning and end of the film work to emphasise the similarities between the two men, their shared humanity and family values in spite of their different nationalities and religions. Thus Al Ghazi's death appears to be motivated by the film's desire to press home a message about respect and understanding. And yet it also conforms to traditions of racial representation in the action movie, and to the racialised hierarchy I earlier suggested was at work in the film. The Saudi officer must sacrifice himself to the US cause rather than the other way round, and in so doing takes his place in the long tradition, discussed in Chapter 6, of non-white 'helpers' who die for the usually white male hero. As Tasker reminds us, where the central male hero is African American rather than white the racial hierarchy can reassert itself in the hierarchising of more minor roles (Tasker 1993: 37).

The other aspect of this culminating section I want to draw attention to is Mayes' rescue of Leavitt. The only female of the team, Mayes has displayed emotional and physical vulnerability at a number of points in situations where the men have not. She is the only person who cries at the news of the FBI agent's death in the Washington briefing, the only team member to complain of ear drum damage after a gun turret fires loudly near the whole group, and is not physically strong enough to hold onto Leavitt as terrorists drag him from the car in the motorcade attack. Her resilience and physical agency are therefore qualified along traditionally gendered lines, constructing the expectation that there will be limits to her capacity for heroic action as the violence at the apartment block begins to unfold. This expectation is emphatically overturned by the brutally physical fight she wins in order to free Leavitt. Mayes finds the room in which he is being held and shoots three of Leavitt's captors from a hole in the ceiling. A concealed fourth captor drags her bodily through the opening, and throws her into the floor and the wall. Mayes regains advantage by creative means, clinging to the man's shoulders while throwing him off balance by biting his ear and wrestling his gun out of its holster as he repeatedly rams her body against the wall, shooting his ankles before he manages to throw her off. Leavitt in the meantime has loosened his bindings and leaps on the man only to be quickly thrown, but this gives Mayes time to find a flick knife. As the man turns back to Mayes she stabs him in the crotch, leg and chest before pushing him to the ground and plunging the knife into the back of his head, killing him. This is a strenuous, messy, no holds barred fight to the death, Mayes' winded grunts and yells of effort credible in their approximation of the sounds of extreme physical exertion. As we saw in Chapter 4 it is still unusual to see a woman as an active, successful participant in a fight of this nature that is naturalistically rendered. But even though this moment is progressive in terms of gender representation, a nod to the real-world participation of female combatants in Iraq and Afghanistan, it may also have a less progressive function. Throughout the film there are references to Mayes' gendered presence being a 'problem' for the Saudi Muslims. For example, when the prince visits the investigation site Mayes is told she must cover her feminine curves; later she is barred from the men-only audience with the prince at his palace, and in accordance with Muslim teachings she is not permitted to touch a male corpse because she is female. These prohibitions have the effect of sidelining Mayes, but in contrast the narrative denouement self-consciously places her centre stage as a crucial agent in both the Leavitt rescue and the discovery of Abu Hamza. This emphatic reinstatement of Mayes' narrative and physical agency subtly undermines the Muslim prohibitions in favour of a supposedly Western brand of gender equality. These implications of the fight sequence alongside the way in which Muslim principles are trivialised by characters at other moments suggests that the drivers for the film's representational hierarchy are not just issues of gender, race or nationality but religion.

The Kingdom is an unusual action film in that its dramatisation of its fictional events openly and carefully acknowledges the different political, national and cultural perspectives at stake in the complicated real-world context to which it refers. However action cinema's tendency to generate a racialised and gendered hierarchy of representations, alongside its narrative investment in a hero who overcomes enemies with spectacular violence and a refusal to take up clear political positions on the subject-matter (in order to avoid alienating sections of its audience), all shape the film and its sometimes problematic engagement with issues of terrorism, US heroism and national, religious and ethnic distinctions. In the end the film defaults to acting out a simplified version of reality based on wish-fulfilment and the endorsement of redemptive violence: as Melani McAlister has said of the hostage rescue action sub-genre, 'the uncertain and messy outcomes of real-life hostage and terrorist situations [are] reimagined in the simpler language of defined threat and unambiguous victory' (McAlister 2006: 332). Having invoked the complex interconnected factors that gave rise to terrorism, the film's ending elides the wider picture, hinting at a generalised future threat posed by Hamza's radicalised younger family members, but unable to turn to face the multiple challenges posed in Iraq, Afghanistan and in states where other terrorist cells are active. *The Kingdom* demonstrates that Hollywood's narrative and representational conventions struggle to accommodate the real-world complexities of the post-9/11 world, showing ambition in that direction but ultimately failing. The film I want to consider next by way of comparison tries to solve this problem of complex realities by limiting its focus to one group (American soldiers) in one geographical space (Iraq).

CONSTRAINED PERSPECTIVES

The Hurt Locker (Bigelow, 2008) is an independently financed film about a US Explosive Ordinance Disposal (EOD) unit working in Baghdad that was subsequently embraced by Hollywood, winning significant critical praise for its portrait of men under extreme pressure in the field of battle. Among a slew of accolades, its director Kathryn Bigelow and screen writer Mark Boal picked up Academy Awards for their work on the film, which also won Best Picture and three other categories.[11] Although the film was independently financed Bigelow seemed to take a traditional Hollywood line when she stressed that, despite the film's focus on a military campaign that has prompted heavily politicised debate, the film was not intended to be a political statement. Claiming that the film was 'not partisan', she argued instead that it focused on the 'dehumanising and humanising aspects of war' and their effects on the individual.[12] Here Robin Wood's observation that mainstream filmmakers depoliticise their portrayals of socio-political movements or issues by reframing them in terms of individual experience finds its openly acknowledged manifestation in Bigelow's words.[13] How might we test out Bigelow's claims of apoliticality? What kind of hero and setting does the film construct? In contrast to the more wide-ranging discussion of *The Kingdom* in the preceding section, I want to try to answer these questions through a detailed analysis of aspects of *The Hurt Locker*'s visual style.

The opening of the film establishes the nature of the space of action through particular strategies of sound and image. A low, minor-key orchestral chord which will persist through the first moments becomes audible just as an inter-title appears declaring: 'The rush of battle is often a potent and lethal addiction, for war is a drug.'[14] The screen goes blank: a man is shouting in a foreign language, wheels squeak and rattle. With a rush of motor sounds the screen bursts into light: a broadcast image appears, its scan lines and drop-outs momentarily obstructing our cognitive access to what the image depicts. 'Stranded' at the surface of the screen we try to fathom what we are looking at. Our eyes and minds adjust and the image resolves into depth, a judder-ing ground level forward tracking shot of a sun-drenched, dusty surface that lurches repeatedly into extreme close-up. It looks like a moonscape in mini-ature, the shadow of two metal 'claws' visible frame right and left. In place of a traditional establishing shot we have been pitched from the screen's surface up against a new, diegetic surface, but the arrangement of the wider environ-ment has yet to be clarified. The camera has adopted the 'optical' point of view of the machine which is whirring and juddering across the landscape. After a few more seconds there is a cut and we see the machine from the outside – a small robotic contraption with tracks for wheels and motorised claws which is making its way down a street while Iraqi and US soldiers shepherd people in the opposite direction. We follow the robot as it negotiates goats, people and street detritus as well as snatching more information about the situation in which it is participating: this is a lively street next to a busy road; there are women and children; a butcher is being marshalled away from his shop front; an Iraqi armed police truck arrives, sirens wailing, so too a US tank and an armoured 'humvee'; soldiers pile out and take up rifle positions around the area; Iraqis look on impassively from adjacent balconies and rooftops. The robot approaches a pile of sacks in the road, and as it does so the film cuts to the screen to which the robot images are being broadcast. Suddenly context is supplied: an EOD unit is clustered around the screen and controls for the 'Remotec Andros' robot, which has been sent in to investigate a suspected improvised explosive device (IED). The shots leading up to this moment are confusingly diverse, taking up a range of positions on the action, from high-angle long shots to extreme close-ups. They are also convulsively mobile, swiping pans and tilts alternating with crash zooms in and out, a disorienting effect exacerbated by jump cuts and editing strategies that refuse to illuminate the spatial co-ordinates of the scene. It is a full one and a half minutes before the narrative situation is clarified, a duration in which a more conventional film would already have established a substantial amount of information about characters, settings and dramatic situation. This thinness of narrative information is accompanied by a thickness of sensory stimuli, a cacophony of street sounds (goats, sirens, shouts, engines) accompanying a combination of camera angles and movements that refuse to orient us stably in relation to the fictional space, confuse our sense of direction, pitch us back and forth from distanced to extremely proximate positions, and bring the dust, debris and rubble of the street so close we feel we can almost touch it. The opening is an assault on the senses, confronting us with the difficulty of making sense of these early images and by implication the environment they depict. We experience the setting as overwhelming and unfathomable, the instability conveyed by the camera and the editing also communicating the volatility of the situation, which we will learn is based on the difficulty of 'making sense' of who is a threat and who is an innocent bystander. In this way aesthetic choices work through the body to allow the audience to experience first hand this environment's alienating inscrutability as well as its contingency.

The soldiers of the bomb disposal squad feel this inscrutability and instability keenly, each disposal job fraught with risk from accidental as well as purposeful detonations, every visible or hidden Iraqi on a rooftop, in a window or on the street potentially holding a remote detonator. The opening forces us to experience this risk-suffused environment as sensorially overwhelming before we watch the protagonists do the same, thus explaining in advance their constant paranoid glances, their unrelenting alertness, their checks through gun sights and over radios, attempts at optical mastery over this space that can only ever be partial. The taxing play with distance and proximity is revealed as a layered metaphor for the men's own circumstances, too close to the setting in which they find themselves, unable to adopt a critical distance on what is happening, a vantage point from which they could see the different unstable elements of the situation with clarity. This is thrown into relief by the first bomb deactivation attempt, in which bomb disposal expert Staff Sergeant Matt Thompson (Guy Pearce) dies. The men in the unit defuse the tension with jokes and try to impose order by following strict protocols, Thompson radioing in his position relative to the bomb at each milestone distance while the other two men scan the area for threats. But despite these measures a figure is able to slip under the men's radar by taking up position in the vacated butcher's shop, detonating the IED before Thompson can get out of the blast radius. This death intensifies the remaining men's perception of the environmental threat, as is clear from some of their language ('the bottom line is, if you're in Iraq you're dead' complains one) and their nervous responses at the next bomb disposal the unit attempts. The replacement bomb disposal expert is Sergeant First Class William James (Jeremy Renner), a man with a much more relaxed attitude to protocol and to the setting than his predecessor, much to his unit's dismay. On his first disposal job he fails to call in his position regularly, and his decision to detonate a smoke flare in order to obscure his whereabouts from potential bombers panics his team, who are responsible for his safety but cannot see his location. On his second job he takes off the bomb protection suit in order to work more freely on a car packed with explosives. In these situations he actively confuses established conventions of appropriate distance and rejects mediated modes of action (the robot and its screen, the unwieldy layers and isolating visor of the bomb protection suit) for more direct forms. As his unit members gasp and yell around him he remains calm, almost cavalier, metaphorically and sometimes literally rolling up his sleeves to get the job done. On one hand James interrupts the unrelenting tension of this environment (by remaining apparently relaxed) and on the other he completes it, playing by its rules of contingency, chance and proximity rather than trying to impose order from a distance (an approach that brings him into initial conflict with his team). The film's visual presentation depicts James embracing the risk of death in ways that distinguish him from his surroundings and mythologise his bravery: a long shot of James emerging out of smoke clouds in his bulky protection suit and helmet like an astronaut on an alien planet; a low-angle shot looking up at him as he marches towards a car bomb, his armoured humvee and unit mate Sergeant JT Sanborn (Anthony Mackie) following on behind; decisively walking through a static group of soldiers towards a man strapped with multiple explosives (the camera then adopts his point of view and his penetration of the area). His dark protection suit is often thrown into relief by the sun-scorched, flaxen landscape behind him, his direction of motion (towards the threat) highlighted by the movement of people in the other direction. Such shots construct him as the heroic 'figure in the landscape' who asserts his mastery over both the environment and the events unfolding within it despite the risks.[15] His possession of agency visually literalised, James thus strikes an imposing figure, marked out as the hero precisely because he penetrates the space of action in ways others are reluctant to. In the context of the sensory assault of continued swish pans, crash zooms and jump cuts, these moments at which we share his optical point of view or come into close proximity with his displays of purposeful action function to stabilise our relationship to the fictional world, even while we understand rationally that James is taking massive risks. Visual style thus underpins our alignment with and admiration for someone whose compulsion to embrace danger might have registered as alienating in another film. The film notably gives us no character history that could explain this compulsion, and the absence of this kind of psychologised explanation encourages us to conclude (prompted in part by the opening intertitle) that it is the experience of war itself that has precipitated James's attitude.

In its visual style and the performance of its main protagonists, the film is highly effective at evoking – and forcing the audience also to experience – the unrelenting intensity of the EOD unit's day-to-day lives. But this achievement is founded on a very specific characterisation of Iraq and Iraqi citizens, which can be illustrated once again in the detail of a moment from the film. As a suited-up James walks slowly down a deserted street towards a suspected IED, a taxi speeds through a loosely guarded makeshift checkpoint towards him, frenzied shouts from US soldiers marking the taxi's sudden unexpected arrival. James pulls a revolver from his suit and points it at the taxi, which screeches to a halt. While Sanborn frantically checks on James and shouts orders to approaching soldiers to stand down, James remains static, his gun pointing, his eyes fixed on the taxi in front of him. James gets closer to the vehicle, repeating the command for the taxi driver to get back, but the driver is unresponsive. James shoots the ground near the vehicle, to no effect, then shoots the windscreen out, to no avail. He presses his gun to the driver's head and repeats his instruction; finally this time the message appears to have been received, and the taxi driver slowly reverses the vehicle away from James. Once at a safe distance he is dragged out of the car and roughly pressed to the ground by hyped-up, swearing soldiers, at which James remarks wryly, 'Well if he wasn't an insurgent he sure as hell is now.' As in the rest of the film, the sequence is shot from a variety of angles with a twitching handheld camera, but all of the shots of the Iraqi taxi driver are marked by the same characteristic, regardless of the camera angle or distance: each in some way obscures his face. In a medium shot from behind James, towards the taxi, sunlight bouncing off the windscreen masks the taxi driver's head; in later shots of the taxi the same effect will be caused by the sun's glare or by the bodywork that frames the windscreen, whether the taxi is being framed in close-up or in a long shot from the street or from above. Even the rear view mirror inside the taxi cab has an obscuring effect, its partially cracked state distorting the reflection of the Iraqi's face into several pieces. At a key moment in the stand-off a close-up from the side of James peering out of his suit visor is followed by an extreme close-up of the Iraqi's eye. The potentially dehumanising effect of the suit helmet on our perception of James is mitigated by our access to his words and thoughts as he exclaims quietly (to himself but about the Iraqi), 'What the fuck are you doing?' The extreme close-up of the Iraqi gives us no such access, and prevents us from reading his expression by limiting our visual access to only his eye. The side view is also more limiting than a frontal shot, picking up reflections on the eye's surface that obscure the delineation of the iris so that it is impossible to establish what direction he is looking in or what he is focusing on. The effect is to lend him a bovine inexpressiveness, which is maintained through the actor's performance when the camera finally reveals his face to us near the end of the stand-off. As I have noted before in this study, these are all filmmaking decisions for which there were alternatives: the choices made construct the Iraqi's inscrutability in a strikingly overdetermined way. This is of course part of the director's declared project: to put the audience in the place of the bomb disposal expert, 'into those boots – that lonely walk towards what the rest of the world is running from' (Bigelow in Rose 2009: paragraph 8).

The film allows us to adopt a critical distance from the soldiers during only one episode, which makes explicit how much a sustained existence in a series of highly volatile situations has taken its toll on their ability to relate objectively to the Iraqis. The section of the narrative where James discovers and then searches for those responsible for a grisly body bomb, a dead Iraqi boy with his stomach packed full of explosives, is illustrative of the severe myopia that characterises the soldiers' state of mind. James mistakes the dead boy for a market stall youth working in the grounds of the US camp who calls himself 'Beckham'. Despite the fact that James has been trading teasing remarks with this boy for weeks, he cannot recall enough of Beckham's features to realise that 'Beckham' is not the same person as the corpse on the table in front of him, a stark illustration of his inability to individualise between Iraqis. James ends up going on a fool's mission into Baghdad at night trying to find out who has done this, dropped outside a random Iraqi house in the suburbs by the terrified market stall owner he has just questioned. Inside a professor (who, perhaps in self-preservation quickly expresses his support for the CIA) shows him hospitality ('You are a guest. Please sit down'). The sight of an Iraqi doing something so recognisably human seems utterly to throw James, and he backs out of the house taking no further action. While this episode takes us momentarily outside the soldiers' subjective experience it does so in a limited fashion, stopping short of putting us in the shoes of the Iraqi professor; we are quickly returned, through the film's style as well as its narrative focus, to experiencing events from the perspective of the US soldiers. For the most part across the narrative we share the same impressions of the Iraqis that the soldiers have: they are unknowable, mysterious, potentially dangerous. The problem is that the film's focus on individuals – while conforming to Bigelow's stated aims – excludes the Iraqis and any sense of them as people with ordinary lives, while its viscerally affective presentational style dehumanises them. Such strategies risk encouraging the same racialised myopia in Western audiences that plagues the soldiers; certainly they perpetuate still further the long established and racist cinematic stereotype of the Arab as 'different and threatening' (Shaheen 2009: 8). Putting the claims of apoliticality aside the film may well have been intended as a sharp reminder that troops were still in Iraq and Afghanistan, and that this needed to be interrogated, especially if we keep in mind the opening's quotation from Chris Hedges, an outspoken critic of the war. But in contrast to *The Kingdom*'s attempt to explore, albeit in a partial way, the feelings of both parties about the US presence in Riyadh, *The Hurt Locker* reinforces negative conceptions of Iraqis and offers the spectator the opportunity to forget the wider context and instead submerse themselves in the adrenaline-filled experiences of the individual. As Slavoj Žižek declares, 'we are there, with our boys, identifying with their fear and anguish instead of questioning what they are doing there' (Žižek 2010: paragraph 3).[16]

This chapter has illustrated the significant challenge in trying to use a mainstream narrative form of cinema to address a difficult real-world context. Alongside the cynical, modish references to 9/11, Iraq and Afghanistan, some quarters of Hollywood clearly have been interested in a more thoughtful approach and a more direct engagement with the issues arising from 9/11 and US political and military strategy since. However, the question remains whether the action film, with its reliance on simplifications of notions like heroism and justice, its often conservative representational hierarchies and its inexorable progress towards a thrilling, spectacular expression of the hero's mastery over clearly identifiable foes, will ever be able to accommodate adequately the complexities of the post-9/11 world. What is clear is that action cinema bears the traces of that world, whether through passing contextual references, direct engagement (accompanied by competing claims of political and apolitical stances – see the press responses and interviews with Bigelow that surrounded the release of *The Hurt Locker*), or the concomitant and persistent popularity of explicitly fantastical films across the same decade.

NOTES

1. See Geoff King for an insightful exploration of the ways in which the 9/11 WTC images were actually quite different from Hollywood movie sequences, despite the perceived similarities (King 2005).
2. Holloway's book *9/11 and the War on Terror* analyses 9/11 and its aftermath in terms of history and politics, and traces its ramifications across news media, television, cinema, literature, photography and visual art. It is tremendously illuminating for anyone interested in this period of US history.
3. For more details and analysis of these meetings see Bart 2001, Chambers 2002, Young 2006 and Hoberman 2006.
4. Public debate about the lack of a clear mandate for either Iraq or Afghanistan, and the huge numbers of civilian casualties put pressure on the notion of the soldier as hero, and on the notion of justified military aggression. The spectacle of military bombing campaigns, mobilised to gather support for the war effort, were tainted by news of civilian casualties, and the objectivity of journalists embedded with the troops, who circulated other images of violent action, was also in question. See Holloway 2008 for an account of these debates and how they circulated through public discourse and political and media culture.
5. Staffan de Mistura is currently the UN special representative of the secretary-general for Afghanistan and Georgette Gagnon is the director of UNAMA's Human Rights Unit.
6. Statistics obtained from the International Movie database. See in particular http://uk.imdb.com/year/2002 and http://uk.imdb.com/year/2003

7. These films are themselves worthy of study as responses to the post-9/11 world, but since they are not mainstream US action movies they remain outside the scope of this essay. Readers are encouraged to turn to Dixon 2004, Holloway 2008 and Prince 2009 for insightful work on these other films.

8. See Antonio Sánchez-Escalonilla 2010 for an account of Spielberg's allegorical exploration of 9/11's consequences in his first four films of the 2000s.

9. Cited in Maltby 2003: 269.

10. The general is unsympathetic partly because of an early scene in which he assumes a man is guilty without any compelling evidence, and beats the man to attempt to extract a confession. The projection of torture and incarceration without charge onto the Saudi National Guard could be seen as rather disingenuous given Guantànamo, the torture controversy and the US's alleged practice of rendition.

11. The other Academy Awards *The Hurt Locker* won were for Film Editing, Sound Editing and Sound Mixing.

12. Bigelow, at a question and answer session with the director following a preview screening of the film at the Institute of Contemporary Arts in London, 19 August 2009.

13. Wood takes as his example films like *Alice Doesn't Live Here Anymore* (1974) and *An Unmarried Woman* (1978), which reference women's liberation. He notes that they focus on the crises of an individual woman in a patriarchal society rather than on group issues or actions, and argues that this pays lip-service to the women's movement but in fact simultaneously depoliticises feminism (Wood 1986: 202).

14. This is a quotation from Chris Hedges' book, *War Is a Force that Gives Us Meaning*, which addresses the intoxicating nature of war. It is somewhat ironic that the filmmakers selected this particular sentence, since when restored to its original context it is accompanied by a critique of those who 'peddle' the drug: 'mythmakers – historians, war correspondents, *filmmakers*, novelists, and the state' (Hedges 2003: 3, italics mine).

15. In her seminal essay 'Visual Pleasure and Narrative Cinema', Laura Mulvey talks of a figure in the landscape who 'is free to command the stage, a stage of spatial illusion in which he articulates the look and creates the action' (Mulvey 1992: 753). While Mulvey's claims about the identificatory processes prompted by classical narrative cinema have been subject to challenge and debate, this observation about how mainstream cinema often seeks to construct its hero in relation to the space of action holds true, and particularly so in *The Hurt Locker*.

16. Žižek is highly critical of *The Hurt Locker*'s approach, and finds its choice of bomb disposal experts as the vehicle for its meditation on the psychological effects of the war disingenuous. He suggests that this decision 'is deeply symptomatic: although soldiers, they do not kill, but risk their lives dismantling terrorist bombs destined to kill civilians – can there be anything more sympathetic to our liberal eyes?' and continues, 'the focus on the perpetrator's traumatic experience enables us to obliterate the entire ethico-political background of the conflict' (Žižek 2010: paragraphs 2, 3).

CHAPTER 9

The 'European connection'

It is no secret that the Hollywood Studios dominate the world film industry. (Finney 2010: 4)

Measured in box office receipts, Europe is Hollywood's most valuable territory. (Miller et al. 2005: 17)

In this final chapter of *Contemporary Action Cinema* it is worth restating two of the key reasons for the book's focus on US action movies. The first is my conviction that the contemporary manifestation of this popular form of US filmmaking and its representational and aesthetic strategies, so often taken for granted or dismissed, demand a refreshed critical approach, one I have sought to propose in the preceding chapters. The second is the US form's global dominance, which flows from and helps to sustain (through its spectacle-driven aspects, as I noted in the Introduction) Hollywood's own dominance of world film markets. As the epigraph from Angus Finney above suggests this dominance is widely acknowledged and documented. In the main it is the result of Hollywood's aggressive attempts to control its market share domestically and in territories across the world, including emerging markets. Tino Balio notes the protectionist strategies adopted in the 1980s and 1990s to achieve this aim: an acceleration in corporate mergers creating entertainment conglomerates that could profit from multiple delivery routes (theatres, cable, satellite, network TV, video and later DVD, the Internet and pay-TV) and exploit synergies across ancillary markets (toys, books, music, computer games); the return to a form of vertical integration as well as the forging of domestic and international partnerships in attempts to control production, distribution and exhibition; and the reliance on ultra-high budget films, cross-media synergistic marketing and saturation release, with which smaller domestic and foreign companies did not have the means to compete (Balio 1998).[1]

These strategies continue today.[2] From the opening up of Eastern and Central European markets which began after the fall of the Berlin Wall, to Japan and growing markets in China and India, Hollywood's attempts to consolidate and increase market share continue to be forceful and impactful. Hollywood's international box office takings have increased year on year since 2005 in each non-US region (delineated by the MPAA as 'Europe, the Middle East and Africa', 'Asia Pacific' and 'Latin America'), and in 2009 its overall international box office returns increased 6.3 per cent to $19.3 billions (MPAA 2009: 3–4). Even in India, historically a market that has been fairly resistant to inroads by Hollywood films, in 2009 *Avatar* and *2012* earned more at the box office than most domestic productions (Datta 2010; see also Govil 2008). These box office takings from foreign markets are, when taken together, consistently larger year on year than those in the domestic territory (US/Canada): for example in 2009 domestic box office garnered $10.6 billions compared to international box office of $19.3 billions (MPAA 2009: 3). They are financially crucial to Hollywood: as Thomas Elsaesser points out, 'Hollywood's huge budgets have made it so dependent on its exports that for the first time in its history, it can no longer amortize its films on the home market' (Elsaesser 2005: 41). Some commentators suggest that Hollywood's reliance on foreign box office has led to an increased dependence on spectacle-heavy action blockbusters that have the capacity to travel well in non-English-speaking markets. In this chapter, I want to look at action films made outside the US that have aspirations to succeed in both English-speaking and non-English-speaking regions. How much do they draw on Hollywood action conventions and tropes and what are the consequences for the production of meaning? In answering these questions we bring with us the discussion of different areas of the contemporary US action film that has taken place in the preceding pages around issues of film style and representation. Thus this chapter offers the opportunity to 'step outside' of the Hollywood action cinema for a moment and, using what we have learned about the US form, to consider those non-US filmmakers trying to emulate its success. I say 'for a moment' because a comprehensive study of this topic is too large to fit into a single chapter. The intention here, therefore, is to point up a productive area for further investigation by making a case study of a particular region; that is, Europe and specifically recent French action films intended for the international market.

As the second epigraph from Toby Miller et al. suggests, when we drill down to the box office receipts for specific regions Europe remains Hollywood's most important market; in 2009 US films took 67.1 per cent of the total market share in Europe while US/European co-productions acquired a further 4.2 per cent share (EAO 2010: Table 3).[3] Europe is also a key partner in much mainstream US film production, as Hollywood – in the context of globalisation and the spiralling costs of feature film production – seeks to spread cost and risk by working with international partners. John Trumpbour has illustrated the increasing internationalisation of film production since the late 1990s, noting that in 2005 eight out of the top twenty films at the world box office had dual or multiple national origins (that is, US plus other countries), reflecting the multiple primary sources of investment on each project (Trumpbour 2008: 214–16). This is also the split in 2009: of the top twenty, all US-produced films, one was co-produced with Canada (*Night at the Museum: Battle of the Smithsonian*) but seven were produced with European involvement (*Avatar, Harry Potter and the Half-Blood Prince, Sherlock Holmes, The Hangover, Star Trek, Terminator Salvation* and *Inglourious Basterds*).[4] Apart from involvement with US co-producing partners, Europe is concerned to facilitate a strong pan-European film culture, to claw back some market share from the US. This has prompted a number of EU and member state government initiatives, including for example Eurimages, 'a pan-European fund for direct investment in European multilateral co-productions' which aims in particular 'to facilitate new co-production networks' between larger producer countries like France, Spain and Germany and smaller producer countries (Wayne 2002: 13; see also Miller et al. 2005: 17). Such co-productions work to spread risk and costs, and given that many of the European production companies are subsidiaries of television companies, can also help maximise marketing and distribution channels. They also provide one of the sites of ongoing debates – about the need to complicate the bald presumption of Hollywood's dominance of film production (rather than, for example, box office); about what constitutes a national or European cinema; and about how far (or if) European co-productions can (or should) protect a national or European cultural identity, however that might be delineated.

THE 'FRENCH CONNECTION'

In the context of wider debates about whether Hollywood's market domination constitutes a form of cultural imperialism, Elsaesser notes 'how persistently the different [European] national cinemas have positioned themselves in opposition to Hollywood, at least since the end of the first world war' (Elsaesser 2005: 16). This is particularly true of France, which has historically adopted the most protectionist stance of the European states in trade agreements pertaining to the culture industries, driven by a vigorous desire to preserve and fortify notions of French national identity and French national cinema, and a particular animosity towards what it sees as Hollywood's long record of 'cultural aggression' (Grantham 2009: 539; see also Jäckel 2007). France is a key player in European film production, its position shored up by many years of protectionist regulatory frameworks and a 'generous support system' of incentives which have made France a sought-after production partner (Jäckel 2007: 23). Indeed France now has 'co-production agreements with 44 countries on every continent' (ibid.: 26), and has been for many years the European leader in terms of the number of films produced (see Grantham 2009) until Germany's anomalous achievement in 2009, amassing 194 productions to France's 182 (EAO 2010: paragraph 6). More recently, with the aim of increasing its market share of worldwide audiences, France has adopted 'a more international approach to the business of film' by producing a series of films that are explicitly intended for international markets, and by deciding to shoot a proportion of those films in English (Jäckel 2007: 26). What Isabelle Vanderschelden has called the recent 'boom in French popular films with international ambitions' comprises movies such as *Taxi 2* (Fr 2000), *Les Rivières pourpres/The Crimson Rivers* (Fr 2001), *Le Baiser mortel du dragon/ Kiss of the Dragon* (Fr/US 2001), *Yamakasi – Les samouraïs des temps modernes/Yamakasi, Modern Samurais* (Fr 2001), *Blueberry/Renegade* (Fr/Mex/ UK 2004), *Taxi 3* (Fr 2003), *Immortel (Ad Vitam)* (Fr/It/UK 2004), *Un long Dimanche de fiançailles/A Very Long Engagement* (Fr/US 2004), *Les Rivières pourpes 2: les anges de l'apocalypse/Crimson Rivers 2: Angels of the Apocalypse* (Fr/It/UK 2004), *Banlieue 13/District 13* (Fr 2004) and *Danny the Dog/Unleashed* (Fr/US/UK 2005), and includes co-productions with other European countries and with the US, and French- and English-language films (Vanderschelden 2007: 48). Given its status as a 'pre-eminent commercial genre' (Tasker 2004: 1) it is not surprising that action cinema represents a significant proportion of this output (in France but also elsewhere – one thinks for example of the Russian-produced *Night Watch* franchise (2004, 2006) or the German-language *The Baader Meinhof Complex* (Ger/Fr/Cz 2008)). However, somewhat ironically given that they were conceived with the laudable aim to consolidate France's position as a leading producer of film, the contemporary French action film has become a key site of controversy in national debates about cultural imperialism, cultural identity and indigenous film style.

The most significant producer of French action movies with international ambitions is Luc Besson's France-based EuropaCorp production company, which adopts a model similar to that of a Hollywood studio (endeavouring to control both production and distribution), and has a track record of offerings that combine an 'an international cast and hybrid, if formulaic, mainstream genres and forms', such as the *Taxi* and *Transporter* franchises (Vanderschelden 2007: 43). EuropaCorp's films have come in for particularly vehement criticism from many French critics, accused of 'imitating American action films and recycling universal archetypes, rather than reaffirming a French cultural identity' (ibid.: 45). This anxiety is no doubt intensified by the fact that, aside from their achievements in worldwide markets, the more successful EuropaCorp productions seem increasingly to represent the kind of film many French filmgoers would prefer to see. In 2006, the year that the domestic 'market share represented by French productions exceeded that of American films for the first time since 1984', a significant proportion of this audience was buying tickets to only certain types of film, in what critics called the 'polarisation of the French film industry between the blockbuster and the *film d'auteur*' (Waldron and Vanderschelden 2007: 8, 9). Though it might be anathema to those who treasure France's tradition of auteur and art-house cinema, these purposely hybrid commercial products have their place in national film production, especially if they are able to reap the box office rewards they are designed to secure. Substantially successful films can help maintain the exhibition infrastructure necessary for smaller productions to receive a theatrical release: as O'Regan suggests, it is not just Hollywood but 'other dominant international cinemas' that play 'an important role in cinema capacity-building globally' (O'Regan 2009: 506). The phenomenal success of *Taxi* (EuropaCorp, Fr 1998), *Le fabuleux Destin d'Amelie Poulain/ Amélie* (Claudie Ossard and UGC, Fr/Ger 2001) and *Le Pacte des loups/ Brotherhood of the Wolf* (Canal+, Fr 2001) at the beginning of the 2000s – themselves cultural and stylistic hybrids (see Moine 2007 and Molia 2007) – helped consolidate the distribution and exhibition channels used for more traditionally 'French' genres and which EuropaCorp is now using to release a series of more modest action films targeted at an international audience, which include *Danny the Dog/Unleashed*, the *District/Banlieue 13* films, *From Paris with Love* (Fr 2010) and *L'Immortel/22 Bullets* (Fr 2010). The accusations of Americanisation levelled at such films are, at their core, driven by anxieties about the security, viability and visibility of national identity in the context of rampant globalisation and an expanding and diversifying European Union. As Thomas Elsaesser suggests, in these uncertain and ever-changing conditions, 'the adjective "national" functions both as a catch-all and a temporary place holder, showing its porous fabric in the very gesture of being invoked' (Elsaesser 2005: 25). The suggestion of Americanisation disavows 'how much of a two-way traffic European cinema has always entertained with Hollywood, however uneven and symbolic some of these exchanges may have been' (ibid.: 18), and is rejected for precisely these reasons by Christopher Gans, the director of another film accused of Americanisation, French blockbuster *Vidocq/Dark Portals* (Fr 2001). Gans was unapologetic about his filmmaking approach, on the basis that 'Hollywood's ownership of certain elements [. . .] must be challenged, in order to show that these elements have also long been present in European culture' (Molia 2007: 58). François-Xavier Molia uses Gans' position to propose an overturning of the term Americanisation, suggesting instead that films like *Vidocq* and *Le Pacte des loups/Brotherhood of the Wolf* undertake the 'gallicisation of the blockbuster form' (ibid.: 56). And yet this still constructs the US blockbuster aesthetic as a fixed, stable entity that is tied to US culture, something I would like to problematise in the following paragraphs.

The *Transporter* films (Fr/US 2002, 2005, 2008), which made British actor Jason Statham into a huge action star and led to his casting alongside Stallone, Schwarzenegger, Willis, Li and Lundgren in *The Expendables* at the end of the decade, are French co-productions, all completed with the involvement of EuropaCorp. The fact that we have discussed this particular action franchise in Chapter 5 under the rubric of contemporary Hollywood cinema reveals as much about the current status of the term 'Hollywood' in an era of co-productions and conglomeration as it does about the *Transporter* films' success, and is worth pausing to consider further. Aside from the mechanical problems of 'identifying the national origins of production' when films are 'created in firms owned by globalized media conglomerates' (Trumpbour 2008: 214),[5] Scott R. Olson suggests that,

> Hollywood has become an aesthetic, and is no longer just a place in California. That aesthetic has been increasingly adopted by other media production centers in other countries around the world. Contrary to what is commonly reported, Hollywood is not particularly an *American* aesthetic, at least not anymore. Hollywood is a global aesthetic, and that in a nutshell sums up its transnational appeal. (2009: 526)

There is a circularity to Olson's argument here – that Hollywood's transnational dominance has led to Hollywood's transnational appeal, which leads to Hollywood's transnational dominance. He also provocatively suggests in the wider essay that Hollywood has stumbled upon a 'golden mean of images' (ibid.: 527) that has a more universal magnetism than the aesthetic of other countries, which elides both the impact of Hollywood's market domination on audiences' choices and the long history of cultural exchange that has characterised cinema as a global phenomenon, a history which helped to shape Hollywood's creative approach. Rather than embracing these aspects of Olson's account, I would like to reframe (or rephrase) some of his assertions. There does seem to be a cluster of strategies that can precipitate a film's global appeal, which I would suggest includes action, visual spectacle, genre hybridity and cultural references that can work at both local and 'global' levels. We could call this cluster of strategies, following Olson, a 'global aesthetic', but that overstates the cluster's coherence and downplays the reality that different combinations of strategies may be possible or desirable. For the purposes of this chapter let's call it instead the 'internationalising formula', with the proviso that the formula is open to different permutations. Hollywood does not 'own' and did not invent the internationalising formula, it has simply demonstrated time and again how monetarily successful that formula can be in the right circumstances. In reality Hollywood is involved in the same endeavour as other film producers trying to compete in the global marketplace, albeit with more funds and better resourced infrastructures. Thus other film producing countries seeking to emulate US box office success are not appropriating a specifically American aesthetic, but adopting an internationalising formula that has emerged out of the cultural exchanges between different film producers over time. In both the French and the Hollywood case, critics often suggest that the end product sacrifices coherence for box office gains, but as Tom O'Regan points out this need not matter. At a pragmatic level,

> the 'conversation' between producers and audiences is designed to minimize obstacles to local and international participation alike on the part of potential audiences. But this strategy of incorporation is achieved through a communicative inefficiency . . . it does not particularly matter that wildly divergent or astonishingly convergent interpretations are routinely accomplished by audiences through Hollywood's global circulation so long as tickets are sold and videos rented. (O'Regan 2009: 506)

O'Regan is talking about Hollywood but one could say the same for those French films aimed at a global audience. The concept of an internationalising formula frees us to characterise cultural appropriation even more fluidly, as cyclical and constantly shifting rather a simple back and forth transaction, without losing a sense that some details of a particular film might have a cultural specificity of their own. Having suggested that Hollywood action films and their European competitors are reaching for the same 'Holy Grail' formula, I want to spend the rest of the chapter looking at specific EuropaCorp productions to map out the ways this endeavour shapes the films themselves. If the formula, like its US manifestation, includes action, spectacle, varied cultural references and generic hybridity, are the consequences of implementing it in the French context similar to those of its implementation in US films, in terms of representation and visual style?

VISUAL STYLE, PHYSICALITY AND THE INTERNATIONALISING FORMULA IN *BANLIEUE 13*

Banlieue 13 (or *District 13*) is directed by Pierre Morel, who has gone on to direct English-language 'transnational' formula action thrillers *Taken* (Fr/ US/UK 2008) and *From Paris with Love*, both co-productions involving EuropaCorp and the French television company and film producer Canal+. The film features a form of urban sport known as *parkour* in which practitioners find innovative ways to traverse the urban landscape by using its features in unconventional ways, and it builds on the surprise success of EuropaCorp-produced *Yamakasi – Les samouraïs des temps modernes*, the low budget action film based around *parkour* that had found a substantial audience in 2001. *Banlieue 13* is set in the near future in one of the low income housing projects (or *banlieues*)[6] of Paris that has been literally walled off from the rest of the city to prevent its gang- and drug-related violence spilling into wealthier areas. Leïto (David Belle) is a conscientious inhabitant of *banlieue 13*, raiding drugs from the local gang lord Taha Bemamud (Larbi Naceri) so that he can take them out of circulation (we first see him washing his latest haul down the bath plug hole). Taha retaliates by killing some of Leïto's crew and kidnapping his sister Lola (Dany Verissimo). In the process of a failed attempt to get Lola back, Leïto is double-crossed by the police: Lola is given to Taha and Leïto is jailed for his retaliatory attack on a police sergeant. Six months later police captain Damien Tomaso (Cyril Raffaelli) is recruited by the Secretary of State for Defence to infiltrate *banlieue 13* and defuse a nuclear bomb that has been stolen by Taha's gang and taken into the *banlieue*. Damien convinces Leïto to lead him to Taha's base and they work together to locate the bomb, in the process saving Lola and uncovering the fact that the bomb was planted by the Secretary of State for Defence in a plan to rid Paris of the *banlieue* problem.

The visual presentation of the film's introductory sequence immediately establishes its key narrative themes but also its aspirations. The traditional EuropaCorp logo is abruptly hidden from view as two grey walls slam together.

Leïto creatively traverses the urban landscape in *Banlieue 13*

After panning down the cracked barrier to catch a mouse emerging from a hole in its surface, the camera pulls back and cranes up and over the barbed-wire-topped wall and into the district. In a digitally constructed long take the camera travels through a burnt-out car, past a drug deal, through various concrete, rubbish-strewn spaces, through high-rise blocks populated with people nonchalantly sitting next to their guns, smoking drugs and drinking, and past a supermarket whose shop-front is completely obscured by graffiti. The camera continues past a makeshift shelter constructed in an abandoned car park and through a guarded high-rise to come to rest in Leïto's bathroom, where he is preparing to get rid of the drugs. While the soundtrack from Da Octopuss references a specifically French hip-hop culture, this opening's digitally enhanced look and effects work call to mind US films like *Fight Club* (1999) (the bomb in the van and gas explosion sequences in particular) and the films from the *Fast and Furious* franchise that appeared before *Banlieue 13*, claiming an aesthetic parity with those productions and signalling its aspiration to reach audiences beyond France. The highly stylised visuals also work to set up the narrative. The digital grading flattens and darkens the colour in the image giving a washed-out, industrial look to the *banlieue*'s dilapidated buildings. The camera's path through these spaces is convulsive, sometimes floating forward through the air, sometimes rapidly 'fast-forwarding', in a persistent repetition of the speed-ramping effect we discussed in Chapter 3. It is worth noting that the 'slow' sections of the camera's movement select very particular activities for our attention: a drug deal, armed gang members, marijuana, graffiti. At several moments – a street scene, a door, a corridor, passing a stairwell – the screen actually convulses: a digital manipulation 'pulls' the centre of the image towards us and then away from us, making it appear to bounce. It is an interesting stylistic flourish that reminds us of the presence of the screen and our separation from the fictional world. It also acts out a scrutinise-and-recoil response to the environment, as if imagining a spectator – or perhaps a character – who recoils momentarily from the world of poverty and casual crime unfolding before them. At the end of the sequence the effect is associated with the movement of the camera 'through' the glass spy-hole in Leïto's door (and the notional distortion of the image as the camera passes through the spy-hole lens), thus retrospectively assigning the effect as a motif of boundary crossing, or more accurately a motif for the momentary hesitation at the point of boundary crossing as an environment is assessed and a path decided upon. In a film in which boundary crossing is both a narrative concern and the *modus operandi* of its *parkour*-skilled protagonists, the screen-convulse effect combined with the camera's horizontal and vertical spatial penetration of the *banlieue* reads like the subjective perspective of a *parkour* practitioner on the move, leaping walls and traversing spaces with speed, and mentally pausing to assess each transition from space to space and surface to surface before executing it.

The concrete wall at the beginning of the sequence signals the isolation of the *banlieue* from the rest of Paris, a visual metaphor for the social alienation and claustrophobia felt by those characters who live inside, and arguably a literalisation of the real social divisions that characterise the relationship between the numbered Parisian districts and the rest of the city suburbs in the real world. Themes of boundary lines, social division and incarceration are returned to repeatedly as the film progresses, in the hero Leïto's imprisonment and escape, and his frustration at and subsequent action against the constraints imposed by government, police and the local gang lords. However the overt stylisation of the opening, which privileges an idealised flight through the environment over a pedestrian, restricted existence within it, and which elides other more banal realities of the *banlieue* in order to characterise it as a place where criminality and weapons are ever-present, suggests that the film is less interested in bringing to attention the socio-economic disenfranchisement experienced in the real *banlieues* than films like *La Haine/The Hate* (Fr 1995) and *L'Esquive/Games of Love and Chance* (Fr 2003). In fact, like many US films set in environments that are the site of real social or economic disenfranchisement or political tensions (such as the urban 'ghetto', or the Middle East settings discussed in Chapter 8), here the location is emptied of its controversial real-world sociopolitical resonances, so that the *banlieue* we are offered becomes a fictional, exoticised space, a depoliticised pretext for its violent narrative.

The *banlieue* existence in this fictional world is a vividly corporeal experience. Those characters not eating, drinking or smoking are being beaten up, shot or perpetrating the same physical acts on others. This is of course a facet of action cinema more generally and as we saw in Chapter 3, as in other action films, *Banlieue 13* ties certain types of physicality to particular constructions of masculinity and heroism. After the opening, which gives us a brief glimpse of Leïto, the first scene of the film cuts between two strands of action: the arrival of gang-lord Taha's right-hand man, K2 (Tony D'Amario) at Leïto's apartment block and his subsequent search for him; and Leïto's concurrent attempts to dispose of Taha's drugs. K2 is bulky and bullish, using his heft to break the neck of one guard outside Leïto's apartment block while he kicks the other bodily against the wall, fatally smashing his head into an external air vent unit. This is a criminal masculinity defined by brute force, and when we later gain access to the interior of Taha's camp, we see that Taha employs more of K2's type: the camp houses an entire dormitory full of large men (albeit more muscular than K2) whose default mode of violence is also brute force. K2's expansive body shape contrasts with that of Leïto, who possesses a slimmer, more contained physique. In motion the contrast is even more striking: K2 lumbers slowly through the apartment block, only able to send slimmer, fitter henchmen on the pursuit after Leïto initiates his escape and the scene develops into a chase, whereas Leïto is fast, nimble and creative in his decisions about the trajectory he plots across and through the *banlieue* tower blocks. When Leïto teams up with Damien, the police officer sent to infiltrate the *banlieue*, it is noticeable that Damien too is defined by a litheness and agility that matches Leïto's. Both men are flexible in the range and application of their skills: not just *parkour*, but marksmanship and martial arts combat skills. While K2's heft operates as a short-hand for his brutality and single-mindedness, Damien and Leïto's nuanced, creative responses to the landscape illustrate their refusal to be tethered by the criminalised milieu they are forced to move through (whether that is *banlieue* 13 or the potentially corrupt world of government and policing). As the film progresses the action sequences showcase the physical feats of these real-life *parkour* experts in a variety of situations. The similarity of their approaches reconfirms their shared morals and heroism, a point struck home rather unsubtly late in the film, when Damien reminds Leïto that even though they are on different sides of the law and live in different districts, they are both fighting for the same principles: *liberté, égalité* and *fraternité*.[7] The pairing of these apparent opposites (a convict and *banlieue* inhabitant versus an urbane police officer) can be read either as a version of the US buddy-film or as the mismatched pair trope familiar from French *policiers* and comedies. This way in which the film is readable at both local and 'global' levels arguably also applies to the film's racial politics, which finds its expression most directly in the contrast between the narrative's arch-villain, gangland boss Taha, and the other men in the film. Taha is a man of power, commanding scores of henchmen in the maintenance and protection of his drug-dealing operation, but the ways he uses his body do not visibly convey this power, marking him out from those around him (friends and foes). For example, in contrast to the musculature of Leïto, Damien and the majority of Taha's men, as well as K2's heft, Taha's physique is slim, and his spindly arms and flowing, baggy costume hint at a lack of muscle, while invoking an effeminacy that is also suggested by his oft-displayed petulance. He is persistently framed in passive poses, sitting behind his desk or – when he is held hostage by Leïto and Lola – rigid and moved around against his will. His authority is also reinforced using a physically distanced mode of violence – shooting people – that does not require the pitting of bodies against each other, and which contrasts with the physically stretching feats of his men and Leïto and Damien. This conflation of passivity, effeminacy and physical weakness is mapped onto a body that also registers as racially 'other' in the film. His men are a mix of black, Asian and Caucasian ethnicities, and Leïto (whose name indicates Galician or Portuguese ancestry) and Damien are Caucasian, but Taha is the only character (apart from, perhaps, his accountant, who goes by the Arabic name 'Jamal') marked as Algerian. This is not simply detectable because the actor playing him is of Algerian descent, but because of the character's Arabic name and his costume of loose tops and baggy trousers which references traditions of Algerian clothing. In the real world the difficult history of Franco-Algerian relations means that Algerians are often located as the racial 'other' in conservative French discourse, so the casting and characterisation of Taha is readable in problematic but culturally specific terms. Yet as we were reminded in Chapter 6 the convention of making the villain of the narrative the racial 'other' has a long history in US cinema too, as has the tendency to feature stereotyped Arabs as villains, so the conflation of Algerian ethnicity with villainy evident in *Banlieue 13* is readable beyond the boundaries of a specifically 'French' cultural perspective.

Rather than characterising *Banlieue 13* as simply appropriating 'Americanised' elements from Hollywood, I suggest that the film represents a much more dynamic attempt to achieve an internationalising formula by combining elements that are not straightforwardly easy to tie to particular film cultures. The generic conventions of the action film are fused with generalised references to the gangster movie, the buddy movie (or mismatched pair film) and the urban ghetto film, all three of which find forebears in both French and US cinematic traditions, as well as other national traditions, such as the Japanese *yakusa* film, the Chinese *triad* film and so on. The action sequences have multifaceted appeal because they blend French-invented *parkour*, Hong Kong-style martial arts and gunplay that is, once again, recognisable in a number of national cinema traditions. These combinations do result in a raced and gendered representational hierarchy that is familiar from Hollywood, but rather than suggesting therefore that *Banlieue 13* is 'Americanised', it is more accurate to say that the film's representational hierarchy is readable in the context of both French and other Western cultures. In the final section of the chapter I want to look at the results of another attempt at the internationalising formula, an English-language film that is more ambitious in its cultural and generic hybridity but less coherent in its results.

DANNY THE DOG AND THE DIVIDED TEXT

Danny the Dog/Unleashed (2005) is a French, US and UK co-production directed by Louis Leterrier, set in Glasgow and filmed in English. It stars an iconic figure of British gangster movies Bob Hoskins, African American Morgan Freeman and Chinese actor and martial arts expert Jet Li. Li has had a long career in action and martial arts films from China, Hong Kong and the US, and had previously starred in another English-language EuropaCorp co-production, *Le Baiser mortel du dragon/Kiss of the Dragon*. The narrative follows Danny (Li), brainwashed from childhood by Bart (Hoskins), the leader of a local protection racket in Glasgow, to be the human equivalent of an attack dog: kept in an underground cell, docile and non-communicative when his collar is on, and a brutally effective fighter when the collar is released. Danny is left to stand guard one day in an antiques warehouse filled with pianos while Bart collects money from the property owner in the room below. A blind piano tuner called Sam (Freeman) strikes up a conversation with him, and they bond over the tuning of a piano. It is a brief moment of intimacy before Danny returns to the familiar pattern of beatings and brawls. Bart subsequently puts Danny into an underground fight to the death for money, but when Bart and his crew are later attacked by a disgruntled customer and left for dead, an injured Danny escapes back to the antiques warehouse and is taken in by the piano tuner and his daughter Victoria (Kerry Condon). Withdrawn, scared and divided between his mindless fight mode and his inhibited 'collared' identity, during his convalescence Danny gradually comes out of his shell, learning to enjoy food, music and conversation, eventually reaching the point that he can trust himself to take his collar off without becoming violent. But Bart is alive and wants Danny back. After returning to his old life with reluctance Danny escapes again, precipitating a final confrontation with Bart and his men at Sam and Victoria's house, where Danny must choose between life as a 'dog' or as a human.

The opening of *Danny the Dog* introduces Danny's bleak, down-trodden life. Blurred, almost monochrome images gradually resolve to become slow-motion close-ups of Danny's averted eyes, downturned mouth and his clinking metal collar, before a brief two-shot shows him walking obediently beside Bart. Sounds are indistinct, muffled, resolving in and out to convey the subjective disconnect Danny is experiencing. In close-up Bart removes the bulky collar while snarling the words 'Get 'em.' Danny's pupils dilate, and in a wide shot of the goods depot in which they are both standing, Danny suddenly explodes into action, using martial arts to neutralise several attackers with speed and deadly efficiency. The camera is highly mobile, stressing the kineticism and force of Danny's movements as he fights the circling antagonists. Travelling shots push forward as Danny throws himself toward an opponent or dolly sideways to follow one of his lunges or kicks, while swish pans and tilts emphasise particularly forceful, bone-crunching impacts. Danny is highly effective, taking only seconds to incapacitate each opponent. But this physical effectiveness does not allow him to penetrate a wider landscape, as it does for Leïto and Damien in *Banlieue 13*. The depot Danny is fighting in is cramped and busy with various stacked goods, the field of combat a limited space closed in by crammed shelving units, the sense of containment underlined by the fact that his attackers are arranged in a circle: whenever Danny moves out to floor one opponent, he has to move back into the centre to take on the next. The claustrophobia is intensified by the dour colour palette and copious shadow, and by the fact that even wide shots are closer to the warring bodies than usual; the camera never moves beyond a certain distance away, making us feel the space's confined limits. In this and later fight scenes the staging and mise-en-scène thus reinforce what the dog collar has already led us to suspect: that unlike other action heroes, Danny's physical agility and strength cannot help him to achieve genuine agency. After each fight Danny is returned to a passive, virtually immobile state under the command of his 'owner' Bart. In the car on the way back from the depot and at Bart's dark, dingy, converted automobile repair shop, this sense of confinement continues in both metaphorical and literal ways. Danny is treated like a dog by both Bart (who feeds him treats by hand in the car) and his henchmen, who give simple commands before locking him back up in the makeshift 'kennel' or cell underneath the floor of the garage that is his home. For his part Danny is inexpressive and motionless, simply waiting to be directed. In the subsequent montage of time passing in Danny's cell, the objects that decorate it go some way to explain his almost catatonic state. Alongside a punchbag that serves to remind us of his violent 'day job', there is a worn teddy bear and a children's alphabet book that he can barely read, clear signals that he is suffering from a form of arrested development, having not been allowed to mature mentally or emotionally; his subsequent slurping of spaghetti out of a tin show his corollary lack of socialisation. In these still, quiet moments in Danny's cell what also emerges is his compulsion to explore texture. He touches the paws, nose and ears of the teddy bear in a way that suggests this is a regular ritual; he runs his fingertips over the surface of each page of the well-thumbed children's book; and when he accidentally splits the punchbag he cups his hands underneath the torn fabric to catch the sand granules now pouring out of it. The quietness of these moments provides a sharp contrast to the noise and freneticism of the depot fight, Danny's gentle finger-strokes very different from his earlier unsubtle punches, showing us another side to his character that is alive to the nuanced sensuality of touch. These images are far more haptic, and appeal to the spectator's senses much more richly, than those that characterise the fight sequences, a sign perhaps that the film is invested in moving Danny away from his life of combat to an existence in which he can explore his appreciation of simpler pleasures. Spectacular action is made available in the film, but it is framed by a more insistent focus on the simple pleasures of texture and quiet contemplation.

These two sides of Danny communicated in the first few minutes of the film are also indicative of the film's own divided nature. *Danny the Dog* is a generic hybrid whose hybridity is much more marked than that of *Banlieue 13*. The initial fight scene and the narrative set-up illustrate the two action traditions the film brings together: the protection racket storyline, Glasgow setting and presence of Bob Hoskins invoke a specifically British gangster film tradition, while the fight sequences featuring Jet Li directly reference Hong Kong martial arts films (the choreography is by Yuen Wo Ping, a key figure in Hong Kong action cinema who has also undertaken fight choreography in US productions like the *Matrix* and *Kill Bill* films). But, as the sequences following the fight reveal, *Danny the Dog* does not just combine two action-oriented modes, but brings these together with an emphatically non-action mode, a coming of age drama in which the physically adult but emotionally child-like protagonist must, with the help of Sam and Victoria, address his buried past and grow into his adult body. I suspect there is a rather crude analogy underlying the choice to make Sam a piano tuner; Danny is 'out of tune' because of his maltreatment at the hands of Bart, and must be 'tuned back up' by Sam. It is worth taking a moment to acknowledge the problematic racial overtones the film seems unwittingly to stumble towards here: Danny's radical disempowerment seems uncomfortably close to Western traditions of 'emasculating representations of Chinese men' (Hunt 2003: 54), while Sam – played as benevolent, patient, wise and nurturing – conforms to the reassuring archetype of the 'black angel' Krin Gabbard identifies in his book *Black Magic: White Hollywood and African American Culture* (2004: 143). Danny's first encounter with Sam, when the older man unexpectedly walks into the piano-filled space Danny is waiting in and starts to talk to him, inaugurates a revealing shift in shooting style that positions Sam's world – and Danny's experience of it – at odds with Bart's world of violence, coercion and criminality, and explains why Sam is able to reach Danny through the brainwashing Bart has imposed. Where the fighting sequences and scenes in Danny's cell are filmed and graded either in dark, sombre tones or harsh, overly bright tones, the antiques warehouse is suffused with a soft fill light that picks out warm, autumnal shades, while close-ups and medium close-ups have a haptic quality, a stronger key light picking out the texture and grain of different surfaces – the piano lid, the piano keys, the suede of the piano seat and later skin, hair and jacket fabric. Danny is drawn to the piano's surfaces, hesitantly pressing down a piano key in an exploratory fashion. In this instant Danny's impulse to touch (and brave decision to contravene Bart's instruction simply to wait) is doubly rewarded, by the feedback inherent in the sensation of touching something, as at the moment of contact its surface 'touches back', and by the aural response of the piano string. It is a two-way interaction in contrast to the one-way instruction and sensory deprivation to which Danny is routinely subjected, and the one-way assertions of mastery he directs at Bart's enemies; here instead there is '[t]ouching, not mastering' (Marks 2002: xii). There is a further 'reward', appearing seemingly out of nowhere as if called up by Danny's small act of defiance: as the piano responds by sounding out a discordant note, Sam, the person who will in due course help bring Danny into fuller contact with the outside world, appears in a doorway with the words, 'Aye-aye, sounds like someone in here could use my help,' his words resonating with both literal and metaphorical connotations. As they work on the piano together Danny is for the first time in the film an equal party in an interaction, both dramatically and visually: Sam respects his silences and makes clear his appreciation for Danny's help, while the sequence is primarily characterised by reverse field cutting that alternates two-shots framed from either side of the piano, intimacy and equality realised in the camerawork as well as the dialogue.

The subsequent scenes in the piano tuner's house emphasise that Danny is now existing in a space defined by sensory stimulation rather than deprivation, and by interaction rather than isolation. The autumnal hues of the antiques warehouse are replaced by warmer colours, and light, food, music and conversation are all in abundance. The inclusive, supportive and interactive nature of this new environment are underlined by compositions that bring Sam, Victoria and Danny together into the same frame but place them at different planes in the image, creating a sense of a deeper space in which freedom of movement is more possible. This is quite different from the shallow compositions and shallow focus that characterise Bart's milieu of denuded experience and coercive instruction. Inclusion and interaction bring learning: Danny learns to speak more freely, acquires table manners by copying the others, starts to play the piano, learns to laugh and take pleasure in things, learns to be the master of his own physical and emotional experiences. This is, then, a different kind of narrative of becoming that the film is pursuing: a becoming-human, perhaps, rather than a becoming-physically powerful. After a chance meeting with one of Bart's henchmen in a local supermarket Danny is forcibly returned to Bart but takes these lessons with him. Thrown back into the underground fight club he retains the impulse to touch rather than master, refusing to be the aggressor in the increasingly violent brawl and declining to finish off his opponents. Unlike the traditional action hero, Danny's journey of self-discovery is now being plotted not through tests of his physical stamina but his displays of physical restraint. He escapes back to Sam and Victoria who through music and some fortuitous connections help Danny to remember the traumatic event that disengaged him from the world as a child: his mother's murder at the hands of Bart. When Bart comes to Sam's apartment with a small army of fighters to reclaim his prize fighter, Danny's newly acquired sense of agency is confirmed by his ability to extend beyond the confined spaces he has been forced to fight in thus far. He is able to travel the length, breadth and height of the building in order to distract the attackers away from Sam's apartment block and take them on in manageable numbers. Moreover his recollection of his mother's murder and the identity of her murderer lends his fighting a renewed motivation, this time with a moral underpinning. Nevertheless it is physical restraint that will define his transition into 'adulthood'; Bart lies on the floor, bloodied but commanding Danny to give in to his 'animal' nature and finish him off, in final confirmation that he does not deserve to live alongside his new family; with help from Sam and Victoria, Danny holds back from delivering the fatal punch and finally resists his abusive father-figure's instruction. The epilogue shows Danny sitting in a smart tuxedo next to Sam, both in the audience for Victoria's piano recital. It is a somewhat overdetermined confirmation that Danny is back in the world of manners and civility, complete with an indication of his emotional recovery as he is able to cry at the sound of his mother's favourite music being played by Victoria, memories of happier times with his mother replacing the traumatic images he buried for so long. However, there is no sense of a wider world in which Danny will be able to find his place – he is still in a constrained milieu, having simply replaced one father figure with another, and a number of practical questions remain about the pragmatic realities of a continued existence with Sam (who plans to return to the US), including acquiring identification papers so that he can find a job, travel and so on. The scene also seems 'too good to be true' after the emphatic way in which Bart's world crashed into Sam's apartment block. *Danny the Dog* is not the first film to supply an ending that seems overly optimistic given what has preceded it, but the striking disparity between the generic tropes and tone of the climactic confrontation with Bart's men and this recital hall ending is indicative of the film's wider textual divisions.

Danny wants desperately to access and retain the domesticity that Sam and Victoria offer, and which represents the domestic life he lost when his mother was murdered. But this aspiration is repeatedly thwarted by Bart, the return of that which Danny seeks to repress, who on two occasions (the two car crashes, one caused by the disgruntled client, the other by Danny) comes back from apparently fatal accidents. The choice Danny is forced to confront between violence and non-violence also sums up the negotiations the film has had to undertake because of its generic hybridity, swinging between crowd-pleasing action sequences and quieter, slower, more intimate scenes, between different tonal registers and mise en scène, between competing worlds of violent criminality and civilised domesticity. The final showdown is an abrupt and excessive (in terms of numbers of opponents, different fight locations and methods of dispatching attackers) return to the mode of Hong Kong martial arts action with which the film began and then seemed to reject. Just as Danny has had to work through a choice between violence and non-violence, throughout the narrative progression the film itself swings between the generic tropes of action and gangster movies and those of muted melodrama, unable to bring them together into a coherent whole. The epilogue notably refuses to integrate these two worlds or resolve the tensions between them. Even the Glasgow location, which could have served to knit together the two milieus, is presented in fragments, the real-world connectedness of its geography elided in its fictionalised presentation. At a textual level the film's hybridity remains evident, prompting film critic Stephanie Zacharek to note that it is 'really two intersecting pictures, an action movie and a fable about the strength of family bonds' (Zacharek 2006: paragraph 1). And yet this did not put off audiences or critics, the overt, unresolved hybridity being read as a novel spin on the traditional action format, and box office comparing favourably to those US and US/European action film co-productions with roughly similar budgets released in the same year.[8]

In this example of the internationalising formula the hybridity obscures rather than providing a space for the cultural specificity of the creative forces behind the film – Frenchmen Luc Besson and Louis Leterrier – but this did not seem to deter the French audience, which helped the film to just under $5.4 million in domestic box office, a significant achievement in the context of French box office trends (Moine 2007: 38).[9] The reception of *Danny the Dog* proves O'Regan's point that, although a film must cluster its strategies to appeal widely (action, visual spectacle, genre hybridity, cultural references), these different cultural and generic elements do not have to cohere in order to achieve the 'local and international participation' of audiences (O'Regan 2009: 506). In this way *Danny the Dog* provides further rationale for the case the chapter as a whole has tried to make: that we may need to do away with notions of 'Americanisation', problematise notions of cultural identity and cultural dominance, and complicate our accounts of how non-US film productions attempt to, and achieve, the global appeal that is all too often assumed to be the preserve of Hollywood.

NOTES

1. See also Neale and Smith 1998: 45–90 and Wyatt 1998. Balio's essay contains an indicative example of Hollywood's propensity to expand market share in any particular territory: to combat the lack of good quality screens that was depressing box office receipts in Western Europe in the 1980s, 'the American majors and their European partners launched a campaign . . . to rebuild and renovate exhibition in Great Britain, Germany, Italy, Spain and other countries' (Balio 1998: 60).

2. See Miller et al. 2005, McDonald and Wasko 2008, Miller 2009, and for a pertinent and insightful account of current pressures Hollywood and international producer nations are having to deal with, see Finney 2010.

3. A film's official designation as a co-production can be complicated, since many arrangements are made under government initiatives (through which tax breaks and other incentives might be offered) with complex legislative 'small print' that can affect whether a co-production agreement is approved and on what basis.

4. Worldwide grosses for 2009 obtained from BoxOfficeMojo (accessed at http://boxofficemojo.com/yearly/chart/?view2=worldwide&yr=2009&p=.htm); film nationality details taken primarily from Film Indexes Online © British Film Institute (accessed at http://film.chadwyck.co.uk/fiaf/home), supplemented by the International Movie Database (accessed at www.imdb.com). All three Internet resources accessed 1 September 2010.

5. A recent news story provides an apt illustration: *The Guardian* reported that an Indian company was poised for a $2 billion buyout of the debt-ridden Metro-Goldwyn-Mayer studio (Wood 2010).

6. The word *banlieue* can simply mean suburb or district, but in the last fifteen years or so the phrase *les banlieues* has been used to refer to areas of rent-controlled housing (HLM or *habitation à loyer modéré*) where unemployment and crime is high.

7. This is the Republican motto of France, translated as 'liberty, equality and brotherhood', apt in its application to both the men's relationship to each other and the story in the near-future walled-up *banlieue* the film tells.

8. Positive reviews included those from Zacharek, Roger Ebert (2005) and from Manohla Dargis at the *New York Times* (2005). *Danny the Dog* had a budget of $45 million and took $50.8 million worldwide; the budget for *Elektra* (Canada/US) was $43 million and it took $56.6 million at movie theatres, while several similarly budgeted films suffered losses, for example: *Serenity* (US), budget $39 million, worldwide box office $38.8 million; *Domino* (Fr/US/UK), budget $50 million, worldwide box office $22.9 million; *Doom* (UK/Cz/Ger/US), budget $60 million, worldwide box office $55.9 million (figures from www.boxofficemojo.com).

9. Moine points out that there is a 'select circle of films whose ticket sales pass the 4 million mark. Only between five and seven films per year have achieved this over the last decade, with in general only one or two of them being French films' (Moine 2007: 38) (figures from www.boxofficemojo.com).

Afterword

The trailer for *The Other Guys* (Adam McKay, 2010) opens in a fairly conventional manner, mid-action sequence. It's a high-speed chase in which criminals are trading fire with two police detectives: Chris (Dwayne Johnson) is in a typical action pose, hanging onto the roof of a speeding humvee, and P.K. (Samuel L. Jackson) is following close behind in an unmarked police car. They trade quips before Chris leaps from the humvee onto the police car's bonnet and climbs into the passenger seat. The trailer voice over intones, 'in the toughest city in the world, nobody fights crime like these guys', and the action culminates in typically hyperbolic fashion with the police car being catapulted into the side of a parked double decker bus. All the traditional generic indicators seem to be present to indicate a straightforward action film: a physically agile and fearless hero, high-speed action and humorous quips. As the trailer develops, however, it becomes clear that this will be a spoof action film. We see that the focus will be on the 'other guys', the much less effective police detectives who work in the same office, and the scrapes they get into while aspiring to be like Chris and P.K., a narrative set-up that debunks some of the familiar tropes of the action film. *The Other Guys* is one of a number of mock or spoof action movies that have emerged towards the end of the 2000s, and which include *Tropic Thunder* (2008), *Black Dynamite* (2009), *Cop Out* (2010) and *Red* (2010). They show the same developed awareness of the conventions and tropes of action cinema as the nostalgic remakes or homages I mentioned in the Introduction, like *Predators*, *The A-Team* and *The Expendables*. Treating the framework of the action film as obvious, these films generate pleasure because they congratulate spectators on their own cultural and cult knowledge, but they also have a tendency to simplify the action film's form in the service of comedy or nostalgia. Publicity materials and press reviews often adopt a similarly simplifying approach, using a lively shorthand to summarise a particular action film's appeal, posters – and later, DVD covers – screaming press endorsements like 'the ultimate racing movie' (for *Speed Racer* (2008)), 'probably the most fantastically violent film ever' (*Rambo* (2008)), and of *Terminator Salvation*, 'the *Terminator* story recharges with a post-apocalyptic jolt of energy', while Warner Bros' description of an upcoming version of the tale of Odysseus (due 2013) as '*300* meets *Taken*' is typical of the high concept shorthand sales pitches in which studios engage.

Publicity, spoofs and homages have their place, but the appeal, pleasures and design of the contemporary action film are far from simple. This book has sought both to identify the complex operations of aesthetics, narrative and representation in action cinema, and to explore what is at stake in those operations. I have also argued that action cinema's pleasures rely in large part on a direct appeal to an embodied, sensing spectator, and that we must keep this address in mind when we attempt to articulate or interpret an action film's structural characteristics and the meanings it mobilises. I have deliberately not discussed in extensive detail recent advances in digital imaging technologies, not because the technologies are not important but because the questions with which the book has been engaged are primarily questions about meaning. Put another way, we have been focusing on the 'why' more than the 'how'. The presence of a particular technology should not in itself allow us to take our attention away from an action film's epistemological or indeed ideological operations. Context is important, however, and the contemporary action film, like other products of Hollywood and of popular culture is shaped by the historical, social, political, cultural and industrial moment in which it is produced. My hope is that *Contemporary Action Cinema* has succeeded in providing a nuanced account of the complexities of the form in its current manifestation, and a stronger sense of the contexts in which it is situated.

Bibliography

Aaron, Michele (2004), 'New Queer Cinema: An Introduction', in M. Aaron (ed.), *New Queer Cinema: A Critical Reader*, Edinburgh: Edinburgh University Press, pp. 3–14.

—(2006), 'New Queer Cinema', in L. R. Williams and M. Hammond (eds), *Contemporary American Cinema*, Maidenhead: Open University Press, pp. 398–409.

Altman, Rick [1989] (1992), 'Dickens, Griffith, and Film Theory Today', *South Atlantic Quarterly* 88.2 (Spring), pp. 321–59, reprinted in J. Gaines (ed.), *Classical Hollywood Narrative: The Paradigm Wars*, Durham, NC: Duke University Press, pp. 9–48.

Archer, Neil (2010), 'Virtual Poaching and Altered Space: Reading Parkour in French Visual Culture', *Modern & Contemporary France* 18.1, pp. 93–107.

Arroyo, José [1996] (2000), 'Mission: Sublime', *Sight and Sound* 6.7 (July), pp. 18–21, reprinted in J. Arroyo (ed.), *Action/Spectacle Cinema*, London: BFI Publishing, pp. 21–6.

—(ed.) (2000), 'Preface' and 'Introduction', in J. Arroyo (ed.), *Action/Spectacle Cinema*, London: BFI Publishing, pp. v–vi, vii–xiv.

Ashe, Arthur (1988), *A Hard Road to Glory. A History of the African American Athlete: Basketball*, New York: Amistad and Press Inc.

Balint, Michael (1959), *Thrills and Regressions (Philobatism vs Ocnophilia)*, New York: International Universities Press.

Balio, Tino (1998), '"A Major Presence in all of the World's Important Markets": The Globalization of Hollywood in the 1990s', in S. Neale and M. Smith (eds), *Contemporary Hollywood Cinema*, London and New York: Routledge, pp. 58–73.

Barker, Jennifer M. (2009), *The Tactile Eye: Touch and the Cinematic Experience*, Berkeley and Los Angeles: University of California Press.

Barnes, Steven (2008), 'Can a Brother Get some Love? Socio-Biology in Images of African American Sensuality in Contemporary Cinema: Or, why we'd Better the Hell Claim Vin Diesel as our Own', in M. S. Barr, *Afro-Future Females: Black Writers Chart Science Fiction's Newest New-Wave Trajectory*, Columbus: Ohio State University Press, pp. 182–90.

Barrios, Richard (2005), *Screened Out: Playing Gay in Hollywood from Edison to Stonewall*, London and New York: Routledge.

Bart, Peter (2001), 'Hollywood enlists in war: Nets, studios answer call to arms in fight against terrorism', *Variety* (Wednesday 17 October), accessed 15 July 2008 at http://www.variety.com/index.asp?layout=print_story&articleid=VR1117854476&categoryid=18

Baudrillard, Jean (1993), *Symbolic Exchange and Death*, trans. I. Hamilton Grant, London and Thousand Oaks: Sage Publications Ltd.

—[1981] (1994), *Simulacra and Simulation*, trans. S. Glaser, Ann Arbor: University of Michigan Press.

—[1992] (1994), *The Illusion of the End*, trans. C. Turner, Cambridge and Oxford: Polity Press and Blackwell Publishers.

Bellin, Joshua David (2005), *Framing Monsters: Fantasy Film and Social Alienation*, Carbondale: Southern Illinois University Press.

Bell-Metereau, Rebecca (2004), 'The How-To Manual, the Prequel, and the Sequel in Post-9/11 Cinema', in W. W. Dixon (ed.), *Film and Television after 9/11*, Carbondale: Southern Illinois University Press, pp. 142–62.

Belton, John [1985] (1992), 'Technology and Aesthetics of Film Sound', in G. Mast, M. Cohen and L. Braudy (eds), *Film Theory and Criticism: Introductory Readings*, 4th edn, Oxford: Oxford University Press, pp. 323–31. Originally appeared in E. Weis and J. Belton (eds), *Film Sound: Theory and Practice*, New York: Columbia University Press.

Beltrán, Mary (2004), 'Más Macha: The New Latina Action Hero', in Y. Tasker (ed.), *Action and Adventure Cinema*, London and New York: Routledge, pp. 186–200.

—(2005), 'The New Hollywood Racelessness: Only the Fast, Furious, (and Multiracial) Will Survive', *Cinema Journal* 44.2 (Winter), pp. 50–67.

—(2008), 'Mixed Race in Latinowood: Latino Stardom and Ethnic Ambiguity in the Era of *Dark Angels*', in M. Beltrán and C. Fojas (eds), *Mixed Race Hollywood*, New York: New York University Press, pp. 248–68.

Beltrán, Mary and Camilla Fojas (2008), 'Introduction: Mixed Race in Hollywood Film and Media Culture', in M. Beltrán and C. Fojas (eds), *Mixed Race Hollywood*, New York: New York University Press, pp. 1–22.

Benshoff, Harry M. (2009), '(Broke) Back to the Mainstream: Queer Theory and Queer Cinemas Today', in W. Buckland (ed.), *Film Theory and Contemporary Hollywood Movies*, London and New York: Routledge, pp. 192–213.

Benshoff, Harry M. and Sean Griffin (2006), *Queer Images: A History of Gay and Lesbian Film in America*, Oxford and Lanham, MD: Rowman and Littlefield Publishers, Inc.

—(2009), *America on Film: Representing Race, Class, Gender and Sexuality at the Movies*, 2nd edn, Oxford, Chichester and Malden, MA: Wiley-Blackwell.

Bignell, Jonathan (2000), *Postmodern Media Culture*, Edinburgh: Edinburgh University Press.

Blanchard, Tamsin (1997), 'A smack in the face for the gurus of heroin chic', *The Independent* (Friday 23 May), accessed on 2 June 2009 at http://www.independent.co.uk/news/a-smack-in-the-face-for-the-gurus-of-heroin-chic-1262928.htm

Bly, Robert (1990), *Iron John: A Book About Men*, Reading, MA: Addison-Wesley Publishing Company Inc.

Bogle, Donald (2000), *Toms, Coons, Mulattoes, Mammies, and Bucks: An Interpretive History of Blacks in American Films*, London and New York: Continuum International Publishing Group.

Bordwell, David (2000), *Planet Hong Kong: Popular Cinema and the Art of Entertainment*, Cambridge, MA and London: Harvard University Press.

—(2006), *The Way Hollywood Tells It: Story and Style in Modern Movies*, Berkeley and Los Angeles: University of California Press.

Britton, Andrew [1976] (2009), '*Mandingo*', in B. K. Grant (ed.), *Britton on Film: The Complete Criticism of Andrew Britton*, Detroit, MI: Wayne State University Press, pp. 241–61. Originally appeared in *Movie* 22 (Spring), pp. 1–22.

Buckland, Warren (1998), 'A Close Encounter with *Raiders of the Lost Ark*: Notes on Narrative Aspects of the New Hollywood Blockbuster', in S. Neale and M. Smith (eds), *Contemporary Hollywood Cinema*, London and New York: Routledge, pp. 166–77.

Bukatman, Scott [1994] (2003), 'X-Bodies: The Torment of the Mutant Superhero', in S. Bukatman, *Matters of Gravity: Special Effects and Supermen in the 20th Century*, Durham, NC and London: Duke University Press, pp. 48–78. Originally appeared in R. Sappington and T. Stallings (eds), *Uncontrollable Bodies: Testimonies of Identity and Culture*, Seattle: Bay Press.

—[1995] (2003), 'The Artificial Infinite: On Special Effects and the Sublime', in S. Bukatman, *Matters of Gravity: Special Effects and Supermen in the 20th Century*, Durham, NC and London: Duke University Press, pp. 81–110. Originally appeared in L. Cook and P. Wollen (eds), *Visual Displays: Culture beyond Appearances*, Seattle: Bay Press.

—[1998] (2003), 'The Ultimate Trip: Special Effects and the Visual Culture of Modernity', in S. Bukatman, *Matters of Gravity: Special Effects and Supermen in the 20th Century*, Durham, NC and London: Duke University Press, pp. 111–30. Originally published in IRIS (Spring), pp. 75–97.

—[2000] (2003), 'The Boys in the Hoods: A Song of the Urban Superhero", in S. Bukatman, *Matters of Gravity: Special Effects and Supermen in the 20th Century*, Durham, NC and London: Duke University Press, pp. 184–223.

Butler, Judith (1993), 'Critically Queer', *GLQ: A Journal of Gay and Lesbian Studies* 1.1, pp. 17–32.

Carroll, Lewis (1960), *Alice's Adventures in Wonderland*, London: Penguin.

Chambers, David (2002), 'Will Hollywood Go to War?' *Transnational Broadcasting Studies* 8 (Spring/Summer), accessed 18 June 2009 at http://www.tbsjournal.com/Archives/Spring02/chambers.html

Chapman, Rowena (1988), 'The Great Pretender: Variations on the New Man Theme', in R. Chapman and J. Rutherford (eds), *Male Order: Unwrapping Masculinity*, London: Lawrence and Wishart, pp. 225–48.

Charity, Tom (1997), '*G.I. Jane*' (film review), *Time Out Film Guide*, accessed on 25 August 2010 at http://www.timeout.com/film/reviews/70191/gi_jane.html

Child, Ben (2007), 'Should all CGI be banned?' *The Guardian* Film Blog (Wednesday 14 November), accessed 15 November 2007 at http://www.guardian.co.uk/film/filmblog/2007/nov/14/shouldallcgibebanned

Cisek, Paul and John F. Kalaska (2004), 'Neural Correlates of Mental Rehearsal in Dorsal Premotor Cortex' *Nature* 431, pp. 993–6.

Clover, Carol J. (1987), 'Her Body, Himself: Gender in the Slasher Film', *Representations* 20 (Fall), pp. 187–228.

—(1992), *Men, Women and Chain Saws*, London: BFI Publishing.

Cook, Pam (1976), 'Exploitation Films and Feminism', *Screen* 17.2 (Summer), pp. 112–27.

Corliss, Richard (2007), '*Live Free or Die Hard*' (film review), *rogerebert.com* (28 June), accessed 27 November 2009 at http://rogerebert.suntimes.com/apps/pbcs.dll/article?AID=/20070628/REVIEWS/70628002

Cox, David (2009), '*Avatar* Shows Cinema's Weakness, not its Strength', *The Guardian* Film Blog (Monday 21 December), accessed on 21 December at http://www.guardian.co.uk/film/filmblog/2009/dec/21/avatar-shows-cinemas-weakness

Cubitt, Sean (2004), *The Cinema Effect*, Cambridge and London: The MIT Press.

Dargis, Manohla (2005), 'Raised like a dog, crouching like a tiger' (film review), *New York Times* (13 May), accessed 7 July 2008 at http://movies.nytimes.com/2005/05/13/movies/13leas.html?_r=1

Darley, Andrew (2000), *Visual Digital Culture: Surface Play and Spectacle in New Media Genres*, London and New York: Routledge.

Datta, Sudipta (2010), 'Hollywood thrills India', in *The Financial Express* (India) (Wednesday,

6 January), accessed 1 September 2010 at http://www.financialexpress.com/news/
    hollywood-thrills-india/563725/0

Davies, Jude and Carol R. Smith (1997), *Gender, Ethnicity and Sexuality in Contemporary
    American Film*, Edinburgh: Keele University Press.

de Mistura, Staffan and Georgette Gagnon (2010), 'UNAMA releases mid-year civilian
    casualties report' (press conference transcript) (Kabul), *United Nations Assistance Mission
    in Afghanistan* (10 August), accessed 12 September 2010 at http://unama.unmissions.org/
    Default.aspx?tabid=1761&ctl=Details&mid=1892&Itemid=10050

Diawara, Manthia (1993), 'Black American Cinema: The New Realism', in M. Diawara (ed.),
    Black American Cinema, London and New York: Routledge, pp. 3–25.

Dixon, Wheeler Winston (2001), 'Twenty-Five Reasons Why It's All Over', in J. Lewis (ed.),
    The End of Cinema As We Know It: American Film in the Nineties, New York: New York
    University Press, pp. 356–66.

—(2004), 'Something Lost – Film after 9/11', in W. W. Dixon (ed.), *Film and Television after
    9/11*, Carbondale: Southern Illinois University Press, pp. 1–28.

Dyer, Richard (1982), 'Don't Look Now', *Screen* 32: 3–4, pp. 67–73.

—(1988), 'White', *Screen* 29.4: 44–65.

—(1993), 'Is *Car Wash* a Black Musical?', in M. Diawara (ed.), *Black American Cinema*,
    London and New York: Routledge, pp. 93–106.

—(1997), *White*, London and New York: Routledge.

— [1994] (2000), 'Action!' *Sight and Sound* 4.10 (October), pp. 7–10, reprinted in J. Arroyo
    (ed.), *Action/Spectacle Cinema*, London: BFI Publishing, pp. 17–21.

Ebert, Roger (2005), '*Unleashed*' (film review), *RogerEbert.com* (12 May), accessed 7 July
    2008 at http://rogerebert.suntimes.com/apps/pbcs.dll/article?AID=/20050512/
    REVIEWS/50504006

—(2010), '*Salt*' (film review), *RogerEbert.com* (21 July), accessed 10 August 2010 at http://
    rogerebert.suntimes.com/apps/pbcs.dll/article?AID=/20100721/REVIEWS/
    100729997

Elsaesser, Thomas [1975] (2004), 'The Pathos of Failure', *Monogram* 6, pp. 13–19, reprinted
    in T. Elsaesser, A. Horwath and N. King (eds), *The Last Great American Picture Show: New
    Hollywood Cinema in the 1970s*, Amsterdam: Amsterdam University Press, pp. 279–92.

—(2005), *European Cinema: Face to Face with Hollywood*, Amsterdam: Amsterdam University
    Press.

European Audiovisual Observatory (EAO) (2010), 'EU gross box office reached record high in
    2009 as European film production continues to grow' (press release) *European Audiovisual
    Observatory* (6 May), Strasbourg, accessed 1 September 2010 at http://www.obs.coe.int/
    about/oea/pr/mif2010_cinema.html

Everett, Anna (1995–6), 'The Other Pleasures: The Narrative Function of Race in the
    Cinema', *Film Criticism* 20.1–2: 26–38.

Faludi, Susan (1999), *Stiffed: The Betrayal of Modern Man*, London: Chatto and Windus.

Finney, Angus (2010), *The International Film Business: A Market Guide beyond Hollywood*,
    Abingdon and New York: Routledge.

Fischer, Hannah (2008), 'Iraqi Civilian Deaths Estimates', *Congressional Research Services
    [CRS] Report for Congress* (Order Code RS22537, updated 27 August 2008), accessed 1
    September 2010 at *www.fas.org/sgp/crs/mideast/RS22537.pdf*

Fradley, Martin (2004), 'Maximus Melodramaticus: Masculinity, Masochism and White Male
    Paranoia in Contemporary Hollywood Cinema', in Y. Tasker (ed.), *Action and Adventure
    Cinema*, London and New York: Routledge, pp. 235–51.

Fuchs, Cynthia (1993), 'The Buddy Politic', in S. Cohan and I. R. Clark (eds), *Screening the*

Male: Exploring Masculinities in Hollywood Cinema, London and New York: Routledge, pp. 194–210.

Fukuyama, Francis (1989), 'The End of History?', *The National Interest* 16 (Summer), pp. 3–18.

—(1992), *The End of History and the Last Man*, London and New York: Penguin Books.

Gabbard, Krin (2004), *Black Magic: White Hollywood and African American Culture*, New Brunswick, NJ and London: Rutgers University Press.

Gates, Philippa (2004), 'Always a Partner in Crime: Black Masculinity in the Hollywood Detective Film', *Journal of Popular Film and Television* 32.1 (Spring), pp. 20–9.

Gelder, Ken (1994), *Reading the Vampire*, London: Routledge.

Goldman, Robert, Deborah Heath and Sharon L. Smith (1991), 'Commodity Feminism', *Critical Studies in Mass Communication* 8, pp. 333–51.

Goll, Claire [1920] (2004), 'American Cinema', in R. W. McCormick and A. Guenther-Pal (eds), *German Essays on Film*, trans. Lance W. Garmer, New York: Continuum, pp. 50–2.

Govil, Nitin (2008), 'India: Hollywood's Domination, Extinction, and Re-Animation (with thanks to *Jurassic Park*)', in P. McDonald and J. Wasko (eds), *The Contemporary Hollywood Film Industry*, Malden, MA, Oxford, Carlton, Victoria: Blackwell Publishing, pp. 285–94.

Grantham, Bill [1998] (2009), 'America the Menace: France's Feud with Hollywood', in T. Miller (ed.), *The Contemporary Hollywood Reader*, Abingdon and New York: Routledge, pp. 536–43. Originally appeared in *World Policy Journal* 15.2, pp. 58–66.

Greven, David (2009), *Manhood in Hollywood from Bush to Bush*, Austin: University of Texas Press.

Gross, Larry [1995] (2000), 'Big and Loud', *Sight and Sound* 5.8 (August), p. 6–10, reprinted in J. Arroyo (ed.), *Action/Spectacle Cinema*, London: BFI Publishing, pp. 3–8.

Guerrero, Ed (1993), 'The Black Image in Protective Custody: Hollywood's Biracial Buddy Films of the Eighties', in M. Diawara (ed.), *Black American Cinema*, London and New York: Routledge, pp. 237–46.

Gunning, Tom (2000), 'The Cinema of Attraction: Early Film, its Spectator, and the Avant-Garde', in R. Stam and T. Miller (eds), *Film and Theory: An Anthology*, Oxford: Blackwell Publishers Ltd, pp. 229–35.

Hall, Sheldon (2002), 'Tall Revenue Features: The Genealogy of the Modern Blockbuster', in S. Neale (ed.), *Genre and Contemporary Hollywood*, London: BFI Publishing, pp. 11–26.

—(2006), 'Blockbusters in the 1970s', in L. R. Williams and M. Hammond (eds), *Contemporary American Cinema*, Maidenhead: Open University Press, pp. 164–83.

Haskell, Molly (1974), *From Reverence to Rape: The Treatment of Women in the Movies*, New York: Penguin.

Hedges, Chris [2002] (2003), *War Is a Force that Gives Us Meaning*, New York: Anchor Books.

Hillier, Jim (1993), *The New Hollywood*, London: Studio Vista.

Hills, Elizabeth (1999), 'From "Figurative Males" to Action Heroines: Further Thoughts on Active Women in the Cinema', *Screen* 40.1, pp. 38–50.

Hoberman, J. (2006), 'Unquiet Americans', *Sight and Sound* 16.10 (October): 20–3.

Holloway, David (2008), *9/11 and the War on Terror*, Edinburgh: Edinburgh University Press.

Holmlund, Chris (1994), 'A Decade of Deadly Dolls: Hollywood and the Woman Killer', In H. Birch (ed.), *Moving Targets: Women, Murder and Representations*, Berkeley: University of California Press, pp. 127–51.

—(2002), *Impossible Bodies: Femininity and Masculinity at the Movies*, London and New York: Routledge.

—(2004), 'Europeans in Action!', in Y. Tasker (ed.), *Action and Adventure Cinema*. London and New York: Routledge, 2004, pp. 284–96.

—(2005), 'Generation Q's ABC's: Queer Kids and 1990s' Independent Films', in C. Holmlund and J. Wyatt (eds), *Contemporary American Independent Film: From the Margins to the Mainstream*, London and New York: Routledge, pp. 153–66.

hooks, bell (1981), *Ain't I a Woman: Black Women and Feminism*, Boston: South End Press.

—(1991), 'Representing Whiteness: Seeing *Wings of Desire*', in b. hooks, *Yearning: Race, Gender and Cultural Politics*, London: Turnaround, pp. 165–72.

—(1992a), 'Madonna: Plantation Mistress or Soul Sister?', in b. hooks, *Black Looks: Race and Representation*, Boston: South End Press, pp. 157–64.

—(1992b), 'Representations of Whiteness in the Black Imagination', in b. hooks, *Black Looks: Race and Representation*, Boston: South End Press, pp. 165–78.

— [1992] (2000), 'The Oppositional Gaze: Black Female Spectators,' in R. Stam (ed.), *Film and Theory: An Anthology*, Malden, MA and Oxford: Blackwell Publishers Ltd, pp. 510–23.

Hunt, Leon (2003), *Kung Fu Cult Masters*, London: Wallflower Press.

Jäckel, Anne (2007), 'The Inter/Nationalism of French Film Policy', *Modern and Contemporary France* 15.1, pp. 21–36.

Jeffords, Susan (1993), 'The Big Switch: Hollywood Masculinity in the Nineties', in J. Collins, H. Radner and A. Preacher Collins (eds), *Film Theory Goes to the Movies*, London: Routledge, pp. 196–208.

—(1994), *Hard Bodies: Hollywood Masculinity in the Reagan Era*, New Brunswick, NJ: Rutgers University Press.

Jewell, Sue K. (1993), *From Mammy to Miss America and Beyond*, London: Routledge.

Kay, Jeremy (2010), '*The Expendables*: Sylvester Stallone's great comeback buoys Lionsgate', Hollywood Report Film Blog, *The Guardian* (Monday 16 August), accessed 16 August 2010 at http://www.guardian.co.uk/film/filmblog/2010/aug/16/sylvester-stallone-the-expendables1

Keathley, Christian (2004), 'Trapped in the Affection Image: Hollywood's Post-Traumatic Cycle (1970–1976)', in T. Elsaesser, A. Horwath and N. King (eds), *The Last Great American Picture Show: New Hollywood Cinema in the 1970s*, Amsterdam: Amsterdam University Press, pp. 293–308.

King, Geoff (2000), *Spectacular Narratives: Hollywood in the Age of the Blockbuster*, London and New York: I.B. Taurus.

—(2002), *New Hollywood Cinema: An Introduction*, London and New York: I.B. Taurus.

—(2003), 'Spectacle, Narrative, and the Spectacular Hollywood Blockbuster', in J. Stringer (ed.), *Movie Blockbusters*, London and New York: Routledge, pp. 114–27.

—(2005), ' "Just Like a Movie"?: 9/11 and Hollywood Spectacle', in G. King (ed.), *The Spectacle of the Real: From Hollywood to Reality TV and Beyond*, Bristol and Portland, OR: Intellect Books, pp. 47–57.

—(2006), 'Spectacle and Narrative in the Contemporary Blockbuster', in L. R. Williams and M. Hammond (eds), *Contemporary American Cinema*, Maidenhead and New York: Open University Press, pp. 334–55.

King, Geoff and Tanya Krzywinska (2000), *Science Fiction Cinema: From Outerspace to Cyberspace*, London and New York: Wallflower Press.

Langford, Barry (2010), *Post-Classical Hollywood: Film Industry, Style and Ideology since 1945*, Edinburgh: Edinburgh University Press.

Lehman, Peter (1993), *Running Scared: Masculinity and the Representation of the Male Body*, Philadelphia, PA: Temple University Press.

Leigh, Danny (2010), '*Inception*, effects-fests and the big budget unreality curse', on *The Guardian* Film Blog (Friday 23 July), accessed on 26 July 2010 at http://www.guardian.co.uk/film/filmblog/2010/jul/23/inception-effects-big-budget

Lewis, Jon (2008), *American Film: A History*, New York and London: W. W. Norton and Company.

Lichtenfeld, Eric (2007), *Action Speaks Louder: Violence, Spectacle, and the American Action Movie*, rev'd and expanded edn, Middletown, CT: Wesleyan University Press.

Lo, Kwai-Cheung (2007), 'Copies of Copies in Hollywood and Hong Kong Cinemas: Rethinking the Woman-Warrior Figures', in G. Marchetti and T. S. Kam (eds), *Hong Kong Film, Hollywood and the New Global Cinema: No Film is an Island*, London and New York: Routledge, pp. 126–36.

McAlister, Melani [2002] (2006), 'A Cultural History of War without End', in J. D. Slocum (ed.), *Hollywood and War: The Film Reader*, New York and London: Routledge, pp. 325–37. Originally appeared in *Journal of American History* 89.2 (September), pp. 439–56.

McCarthy, Todd (2010), '*Salt*' (film review), *Deep Focus* blog at the *IndieWire Blog Network*, accessed 10 August 2010 at http://blogs.indiewire.com/toddmccarthy/archives/2010/07/18/review_salt.

McDonald, Paul and Janet Wasko (2008), 'Introduction: The New Contours of the Hollywood Film Industry', in P. McDonald and J. Wasko (eds), *The Contemporary Hollywood Film Industry*, Malden, MA, Oxford, Carlton, Victoria: Blackwell Publishing, pp. 1–9.

MacDougall, David (2006), *The Corporeal Image: Film, Ethnography, and the Senses*, Princeton, NJ and Oxford: Princeton University Press.

McQuire, Scott (2000), 'Impact Aesthetics: Back to the Future in Digital Cinema?: Millennial Fantasies', *Convergence* 6.2 (2000), pp. 41–61.

Maltby, Richard (1998), ' "Nobody Knows Everything": Post-Classical Historiographies and Consolidated Entertainment', in S. Neale and M. Smith (eds), *Contemporary Hollywood Cinema*, London and New York: Routledge, pp. 21–44.

—(2003), *Hollywood Cinema*, 2nd edn, Oxford: Blackwell Publishing.

Manning, Erin (2007), *Politics of Touch: Sense, Movement, Sovereignty*, Minneapolis and London: University of Minnesota Press.

Marchetti, Gina (1991), 'Ethnicity, the Cinema and Cultural Studies', in L. D. Friedman (ed.), *Unspeakable Images: Ethnicity and the American Cinema*, Urbana and Chicago: University of Illinois Press, pp. 277–307.

Markovitz, Jonathan (2004), 'Reel Terror Post 9/11', in W. W. Dixon (ed.), *Film and Television after 9/11*, Carbondale: Southern Illinois University Press, pp. 201–25.

Marks, Laura U. (2000), *The Skin of the Film: Intercultural Cinema, Embodiment, and the Senses*, Durham and London: Duke University Press.

—(2002), *Touch: Sensuous Theory and Multisensory Media*, Minneapolis and London: University of Minnesota Press, 2002.

Martin, Adrian (2005), 'At the Edge of the Cut: An Encounter with the Hong Kong Style in Contemporary Action Cinema', in M. Morris, S. L. Li and S. C. Ching-kiu (eds), *Hong Kong Connections: Transnational Imagination in Action Cinema*, Durham and London: Duke University Press, pp. 175–88.

Martin, Sylvia (2006) *Futurism*, Cologne: Taschen GmbH.

Massood, Paula J. (2003), 'City Spaces and City Times: Bakhtin's Chronotope and Recent African American Film', in M. Shiel and T. Fitzmaurice (eds), *Screening the City*, London and New York: Verso, pp. 200–15.

Mellen, Joan (1977), *Big Bad Wolves: Masculinity in the American Film*, New York: Pantheon.

Mendible, Myra (2007), 'Introduction: Embodying Latinidad: An Overview', in M. Mendible (ed.), *From Bananas to Buttocks: The Latina Body in Popular Film and Culture*, Austin: University of Texas Press, pp. 1–28.

Mercer, Kobena (1994), *Welcome to the Jungle: New Positions in Black Cultural Studies*, London and New York: Routledge.

Merleau-Ponty, Maurice [1945] (2006), *Phenomenology of Perception*, trans. C. Smith, London and New York: Routledge.

Miller, P. Andrew (2003), 'Mutants, Metaphor, and Marginalism: What X-actly do the X-Men Stand for?', *Journal of the Fantastic in the Arts* 13.3, pp. 282–90.

Miller, Toby (2009), *The Contemporary Hollywood Reader*, London and New York: Routledge.

Miller, Toby, Nitin Govil, John McMurria, Richard Maxwell and Ting Wang (2005), *Global Hollywood 2*, London: British Film Institute.

Modleski, Tania (1991), *Feminism without Women: Culture and Criticism in a 'Postfeminist' Age*, London: Routledge.

Moine, Raphaëlle (2007), 'Generic Hybridity, National Culture, and Globalised Cinema', trans. J. Hensher, in D. Waldron and I. Vanderschelden (eds), *France at the Flicks: Trends in Contemporary French Popular Cinema*, Newcastle: Cambridge Scholars Publishing, pp. 36–50.

Molia, François-Xavier (2007), 'Peut-être à la Fois Hollywoodien et Français? French *Superproductions* and the American Model', trans. J. Hensher, in D. Waldron and I. Vanderschelden (eds), *France at the Flicks: Trends in Contemporary French Popular Cinema*, Newcastle: Cambridge Scholars Publishing, pp. 51–62.

Motion Picture Association of America (MPAA) (2009), *2009 Theatrical Market Statistics*, accessed 1 August 2010 at: http://www.mpaa.org/policy/industry

Mottram, Eric [1981] (2002), 'Blood on the Nash Ambassador: Cars in American Films', in P. Wollen and J. Kerr (eds), *Autopia: Cars and Culture*, London: Reaktion Books, pp. 95–114. (Excerpted from E. Mottram, *Blood on the Nash Ambassador: Investigations into American Culture*, London: Hutchinson.)

Mulvey, Laura [1975] (1992), 'Visual Pleasure and Narrative Cinema', in G. Mast, M. Cohen and L. Braudy (eds), *Film Theory and Criticism: Introductory Readings*, 4th edn, Oxford: Oxford University Press, 1992, pp. 746–55. Originally appeared in *Screen* 16.3 (Autumn), pp. 6–18.

—(2006), *Death 24x a Second*, London: Reaktion Books Ltd.

Naficy, Hamid and Teshome H. Gabriel (1993), 'Otherness – Consuming the Other', in H. Naficy and T. H. Gabriel (eds), *Otherness and the Media: The Ethnography of the Imagined and the Imaged*, Langhorne, PA and Reading: Harwood Academic Publishers, pp. ix-xi.

Neale, Steve (1983), 'Masculinity as Spectacle', *Screen* 24.6, pp. 2–16.

—(2000), *Genre and Hollywood*, London and New York: Routledge.

Neale, Steve and Murray Smith (eds) (1998), *Contemporary Hollywood Cinema*, London and New York: Routledge.

Negra, Diane (2009), *What a Girl Wants? Fantasizing the Reclamation of Self in Postfeminism*, London and New York: Routledge.

Newitz, Annalee (2009), 'When Will White People Stop Making Movies Like *Avatar*?' *io9.com* (18 December), accessed 20 December 2009 at http://io9.com/5422666/when-will-white-people-stop-making-movies-like-avatar

Newman, Kathleen (1992), 'Latino Sacrifice in the Discourse of Citizenship: Acting against the "Mainstream", 1985–1988', in C. A. Noriega (ed.), *Chicanos and Film: Representation and Resistance,* Minneapolis: University of Minnesota Press, pp. 59–73.

O'Day, Marc (2004), 'Beauty in Motion: Gender, Spectacle and Action Babe Cinema', in Y. Tasker (ed.), *Action and Adventure Cinema*, London and New York: Routledge, pp. 201–18.

Olson, Scott R. [2000] (2009), 'The Globalisation of Hollywood', in T. Miller (ed.), *The Contemporary Hollywood Reader*, Abingdon and New York: Routledge, pp. 526–35. Originally appeared in *International Journal on World Peace* 17.4, pp. 3–17.

O'Regan, Tom [2004] (2009), 'Cultural Exchange', in T. Miller (ed.), *The Contemporary Hollywood Reader*, Abingdon and New York: Routledge, pp. 500–25. Originally appeared in T. Miller and R. Stam (eds), *A Companion to Film Theory*, Oxford: Blackwell Publishing, pp. 262–94.

Palmer, Jerry (1987), *The Logic of the Absurd: On Film and Television Comedy*, London: BFI Publishing.

Pfeil, Fred (1995), *White Guys: Studies in Postmodern Domination and Difference*, London and New York: Verso.

Pidduck, Julianne (2003), 'After 1980: Margins and Mainstreams', in R. Dyer, *Now You See It: Studies in Lesbian and Gay Film*, 2nd edn, London and New York: Routledge, pp. 265–94.

Pomerance, Murray (2009), 'Baghdad Bad', *Film International* 7.5 (September/October), pp. 27–49.

Prince, Stephen (2002), 'True Lies: Perceptual Realism, Digital Images and Film Theory', in G. Turner (ed.), *The Film Cultures Reader*, London and New York: Routledge, pp. 115–28.

—(2009), *Firestorm: American Film in the Age of Terrorism*, New York: Columbia University Press.

Projansky, Sarah (2001), *Watching Rape: Film and Television in Postfeminist Culture*, New York: New York University Press.

Purse, Lisa (2009), 'Gestures and Postures of Mastery: CGI and Contemporary Action Cinema's Expressive Tendencies', in S. Balcerzak and J. Sperb (eds), *Cinephilia in the Age of Digital Reproduction: Film, Pleasure and Digital Culture, Vol. 1*, London: Wallflower Press, pp. 214–34.

Quigley, Adam (2010), 'Box office: why does *The Expendables* continue to thrive, while *Scott Pilgrim* continues to flounder?' at */Film: Blogging the Reel World* (Sunday, 22 August), accessed on 23 August 2010 at http://www.slashfilm.com/2010/08/22/box-office-the-expendables-stays-1–scott-pilgrim-drops-to-10/

Rehak, Bob (2007), 'The Migration of Forms: Bullet Time as Microgenre,' *Film Criticism* 32.1 (Fall), pp. 26–48.

Rehling, Nicola (2009), *Extra-Ordinary Men: White Heterosexual Masculinity in Contemporary Popular Cinema*, Lanham, MD and Plymouth: Lexington Books.

Rich, B. Ruby (1992), 'New Queer Cinema', *Sight and Sound* 2.5 (September), pp. 30–5, reprinted in M. Aaron (ed.) (2004), *New Queer Cinema: A Critical Reader*, Edinburgh: Edinburgh University Press, pp. 15–22.

—(2000), 'Queer and Present Danger', *Sight & Sound* 10.3 (March), pp. 22–5, reprinted in J. Hillier (ed.) (2001), *American Independent Cinema*, London: British Film Institute, pp. 114–22.

Rizzolatti, Giacomo, Luciano Fadiga, Vittorio Gallese and Leonardo Fogassi (1996), 'Mental Representations of Motor Acts', *Cognitive Brain Research* 3.2 (March), pp. 131–41.

Rose, Steve (2009), 'Kathryn Bigelow: back in the danger zone' (interview), *The Guardian* (19 August), accessed online 20 August 2009 at http://www.guardian.co.uk/film/2009/aug/19/kathryn-bigelow-iraq-hurt-locker

Rubidge, Sarah (2006), '*Sensuous Geographies* and Other Installations: Interfacing the Body and Technology', in S. Broadhurst and J. Machon (eds), *Performance and Technology: Practices of Virtual Embodiment and Interactivity*, Basingstoke and New York: Palgrave Macmillan, pp. 112–25.

Russo, Vito [1981] (1987), *The Celluloid Closet: Homosexuality in the Movies*, rev'd edn, New York: Harper and Row.

Sánchez-Escalonilla, Antonio (2010), 'Hollywood and the Rhetoric of Panic: The Popular Genres of Action and Fantasy in the Wake of the 9/11 Attacks', *Journal of Popular Film and Television* 38.1, pp. 10–20.

Schatz, Thomas (1993), 'The New Hollywood', in J. Collins, H. Radner and A. Preacher Collins (eds), *Film Theory Goes to the Movies*, London and New York: Routledge, pp. 8–36.

– (2009), 'New Hollywood, New Millennium', in W. Buckland (ed.), *Film Theory and Contemporary Hollywood Movies*, New York and London: Routledge, pp. 19–46.

Sconce, Jeffrey (2006), 'Smart Cinema', in L. R. Williams and M. Hammond (eds), *Contemporary American Cinema*, Maidenhead and New York: Open University Press, pp. 429–39.

Scott, Allen J. (2009), 'Hollywood and the World: The Geography of Motion-Picture Distribution and Marketing', in T. Miller (ed.), *The Contemporary Hollywood Reader*, London and New York: Routledge, pp. 162–84. Originally appeared in *Review of International Political Economy* 11.1 (February 2004).

Scott, A.O. (2009), '*The Hurt Locker*' (film review), *The New York Times* (26 June), accessed 18 September 2009 at http://movies.nytimes.com/2009/06/26/movies/26hurt.html

Sedgwick, Eve Kosofsky (1985), *Between Men: English Literature and Male Homosocial Desire*, New York: Columbia University Press.

—(1990), *Epistemology of the Closet*, Berkeley: University of California Press.

Shaheen, Jack G. [2001] (2009), *Reel Bad Arabs: How Hollywood Vilifies a People*, rev'd edn, Northampton, MA: Olive Branch Press.

Sheets-Johnstone, Maxine (1979), *The Phenomenology of Dance*, London: Dance Books.

—(2009), 'On the Challenge of Languaging Experience', in M. Sheets-Johnstone, *The Corporeal Turn: An Interdisciplinary Reader*, Exeter: Imprint Academic, pp. 363–81.

Shone, Tom (2004), *Blockbuster: How the Jaws and Jedi Generation Turned Hollywood into a Boom-Town*, London and Sydney: Simon and Schuster.

Simpson, Mark (1994), 'Here come the mirror men', *The Independent* newspaper (15 November), accessed 24 June 2009 at http://www.marksimpson.com/pages/journalism/mirror_men.html

—(2002), 'Meet the metrosexual', *Salon.com* (22 July), accessed 24 June 2009 at http://www.marksimpson.com/pages/journalism/metrosexual_beckham.html

Slotkin, Richard (1992), *Gunfighter Nation: The Myth of the Frontier in Twentieth-Century America*, New York: Athenaeum Press.

Smith, Kathy (2005), 'Reframing Fantasy: September 11 and the Global Audience', in G. King (ed.), *The Spectacle of the Real: From Hollywood to Reality TV and Beyond*, Bristol and Portland, OR: Intellect Books, pp. 59–70.

Smith, Murray (1998), 'Theses on the Philosophy of Hollywood History', in S. Neale and M. Smith (eds), *Contemporary Hollywood Cinema*, London and New York: Routledge, pp. 3–20.

Smith, Paul (1993), *Clint Eastwood: A Cultural Production*, Minneapolis: University of Minnesota Press.

Snead, James (1994), *White Screens, Black Images: Hollywood from the Dark Side*, London and New York: Routledge.

Sobchack, Thomas [1980] (1980), 'The Adventure Film', in W. D. Gehring (ed.), *Handbook of American Film Genres*, Westport, CT: Greenwood Press, pp. 9–24.

Sobchack, Vivian (1992), *The Address of the Eye: A Phenomenology of Film Experience*, Princeton, NJ and Oxford: Princeton University Press.

—(2004), 'What My Fingers Knew: The Cinesthetic Subject, or Vision in the Flesh', in V. Sobchack, *Carnal Thoughts: Embodiment and Moving Image Culture*, Berkeley, Los Angeles and London: University of California Press, pp. 53–84.

—(2006), ' "Cutting to the Quick": *Techne*, *Physis* and *Poiesis* and the Attractions of Slow Motion', in W. Strauven (ed.), *The Cinema of Attractions Reloaded*, Amsterdam: Amsterdam University Press, pp. 337–51.

Springer, Kimberly (2001), 'Waiting to Set It Off: African American Women and the Sapphire Fixation', in M. McCaughey and N. King (eds), *Reel Knockouts: Violent Women in the Movies*, Austin: University of Texas Press, pp. 72–199.

Street, Sarah (2001), *Costume and Cinema: Dress Codes in Popular Film*, London and New York: Wallflower Press.

Tasker, Yvonne (1993), *Spectacular Bodies: Gender, Genre and the Action Cinema*, London and New York: Routledge.

—(1998), *Working Girls: Gender and Sexuality in Popular Cinema*, New York and London: Routledge.

—(2004), 'Introduction: Action and Adventure Cinema,' in Y. Tasker (ed.), *Action and Adventure Cinema*, London and New York: Routledge, pp. 1–13.

—(2006), 'Fantasizing Gender and Race: Women in Contemporary US Action Cinema', in L. R. Williams and M. Hammond (eds), *Contemporary American Cinema*, Maidenhead and New York: Open University Press, pp. 410–28.

Taubin, Amy (2009), '*The Hurt Locker*: What Makes Kathryn Bigelow's Iraq War Procedural Tick?', *Film Comment* 45.3, pp. 30–6.

Teo, Stephen (1997), *Hong Kong Cinema: The Extra Dimensions*, London: BFI Publishing.

Tolchin, Karen R. (2007), ' "Hey, Killer": The Construction of a Macho Latina, or the Perils and Enticements of *Girlfight*', in M. Mendible (ed.), *From Bananas to Buttocks: The Latina Body in Popular Film and Culture*, Austin: University of Texas Press, pp. 183–98.

Trumpbour, John (2008), 'Hollywood and the World: Export or Die', in P. McDonald and J. Wasko (eds), *The Contemporary Hollywood Film Industry*, Malden, MA, Oxford, Carlton, Victoria: Blackwell Publishing, pp. 209–19.

Turan, Kenneth (2010), '*Salt*' film review, *Los Angeles Times* (23 July), accessed 10 August 2010 at http://www.latimes.com/entertainment/news/la-et-salt-review-20100723,0,1285496.story

Turner, Graeme [1999] (2001), *Film as Social Practice*, 3rd edn, London and New York: Routledge.

Tyler, Parker (1993), *Screening the Sexes: Homosexuality in the Movies*, New York: Da Capo Press.

UK Film Council (UKFC) Research and Statistics Unit (2010), *Statistical Yearbook 2010*, accessed 1 August 2010 at http://sy10.ukfilmcouncil.ry.com/Default.asp

Vanderschelden, Isabelle (2007), 'Strategies for a "Transnational"/French Popular Cinema', *Modern and Contemporary France* 15.1, pp. 37–50.

Virilio, Paul (1991), *The Vision Machine*, trans. D. Moshenberg, New York: Semiotext(e).

Waldron, Darren and Isabelle Vanderschelden (2007), 'Introduction', in D. Waldron and I. Vanderschelden (eds), *France at the Flicks: Trends in Contemporary French Popular Cinema*, Newcastle: Cambridge Scholars Publishing, pp. 1–15.

Waxman, Sharon (2004), 'Breaking Ground with a Gay Movie Hero', *New York Times* (20 November), accessed 25 July 2010 at http://www.nytimes.com/2004/11/20/movies/MoviesFeatures/20alex.html

Wayne, Mike (2002), *Politics of Contemporary European Cinema: Histories, Borders, Diasporas*, Bristol and Portland, OR: Intellect.

Weiss, Andrea (1992), *Vampires and Violets: Lesbians in Film*, London: Jonathan Cape.

White, Patricia (1999), *UnInvited: Classical Hollywood Cinema and Lesbian Representability*, Bloomington and Indianapolis: Indiana University Press.

Williams, G. Christopher (2003), 'Mastering the Real: Trinity as the "Real" Hero of the Matrix', in *Film Criticism* 27.3 (Spring), pp. 2–19.

Williams, Linda (1991), 'Film Bodies: Gender, Genre, and Excess', in *Film Quarterly* 44.4 (Summer), pp. 2–13.

— [1991] (1995), 'Film Bodies: Gender, Genre, and Excess', in B. K. Grant (ed.), *Film Genre Reader II*, Austin: University of Texas Press, pp. 140–58. Originally appeared in a slightly different form in *Film Quarterly* 44.4 (Summer), pp. 2–13.

Willis, Sharon (1997), *High Contrast: Race and Gender in Contemporary Hollywood Film*, Durham, NC and London: Duke University Press.

Wollen, Peter (2002), 'Speed and the Cinema', in *New Left Review* 16 (July–August), pp. 105–14.

—(2002), 'Introduction: Cars and Culture', in P. Wollen and J. Kerr (eds), *Autopia: Cars and Culture*, London: Reaktion Books, pp. 10–20.

Wood, Michael (1975), *America in the Movies*, New York: Basic Books.

Wood, Robin [1977] (1995), 'Ideology, Genre, Auteur', *Film Comment* 13.1 (January–February), pp. 46–51, reprinted in B. K. Grant (ed.), *Film Genre Reader II*, Austin: University of Texas Press, pp. 59–73.

—(1986), *Hollywood from Vietnam to Reagan*, New York and Chichester: Columbia University Press.

Wood, Zoe (2010), 'Indian firm joins producers behind James Bond films to buyout MGM', *The Guardian* online (Monday 20 September), accessed 20 September 2010 at http://www.guardian.co.uk/business/2010/sep/20/film-industry-mgm-takeover

Wyatt, Justin (1994), *High Concept: Movies and Marketing in Hollywood*, Austin: University of Texas Press.

—(1998), 'From Roadshowing to Saturation Release: Majors, Independent, and Marketing/Distribution Innovations', in J. Lewis (ed.), *The New American Cinema*, Durham: Duke University Press, pp. 64–86.

Young, Marilyn [2003] (2006), 'In the Combat Zone', *Radical History Review* 85, pp. 253–64, reprinted in J. D. Slocum (ed.), *Hollywood and War: The Film Reader*, New York and London: Routledge, pp. 315–24.

Zacharek, Stephanie (2006), '*Unleashed*' (film review), *Salon.com* (Friday 13 May), accessed 7 July 2008 at http://www.salon.com/entertainment/movies/review/2005/05/13/unleashed

Žižek, Slavoj (2010), 'Green Berets with a Human Face', *London Review of Books* Blog (23 March), accessed 1 June 2010 at http://www.lrb.co.uk/blog/2010/03/23/slavoj-zizek/green-berets-with-a-human-face/

Filmography

A Beautiful Mind (Ron Howard, 2001)
A Few Dollars More (Sergio Leone, 1965)
A Fistful of Dollars (Sergio Leone, 1964)
A Man Apart (F. Gary Gray, 2003)
Above the law (Andrew Davis, 1988)
Adam's Rib (George Cukor, 1949)
Aeon Flux (Karyn Kusama, 2005)
Air Force One (Wolfgang Petersen, 1997)
Alexander (Oliver Stone, 2004)
Alexander Revisited: The Final Cut (Oliver Stone, DVD 2007)
Alice Doesn't Live Here Anymore (Martin Scorsese, 1974)
Alien (Ridley Scott, 1979)
Alien 3 (David Fincher, 1992)
Alien: Resurrection (Jean-Pierre Jeunet, 1997)
Aliens (James Cameron, 1986)
Along Came a Spider (Lee Tamahori, 2001)
An Unmarried Woman (Paul Mazursky, 1978)
An Unseen Enemy (D.W. Griffith, 1912)
Armageddon (Michael Bay, 1998)
Assault on Precinct 13 (Jean-François Richet, 2005)
Avatar (James Cameron, 2009)
Bad Boys (Michael Bay, 1995)
Bad Boys II (Michael Bay, 2003)
Banlieue 13 / District 13 (Pierre Morel, Fr 2004)
Basic Instinct (Paul Verhoeven, 1992)
Batman Begins (Christopher Nolan, 2005)
Battle for Haditha (Nick Broomfield, 2007)
Behind Enemy Lines (John Moore, 2001)
Beowulf (Robert Zemeckis, 2007)
Big Bad Mama (Steve Carver, 1974)
Black Dynamite (Scott Sanders, 2009)
Black Hawk Down (Ridley Scott, 2001)
Black Rain (Ridley Scott, 1989)

Black Widow (Bob Rafelson, 1987)
Blade (Stephen Norrington, 1998)
Blade II (Guillermo del Toro, 2002)
Blade Runner (Ridley Scott, 1982)
Blade: Trinity (David S. Goyer, 2004)
Bloodsport (Newt Arnold, 1988)
Blueberry / Renegade (Jan Kounen, 2004)
Bonnie and Clyde (Arthur Penn, 1967)
Boys on the Side (Herbert Ross, 1995)
Bringing Up Baby (Howard Hawks, 1938)
Brokebank Mountain (Ang Lee, 2005)
Bruce Almighty (Tom Shadyac, 2003)
Bullitt (Peter Yates, 1968)
But I'm a Cheerleader (Jamie Babbit, 1999)
Caged Heat (Jonathan Demme, 1974)
Capote (Bennett Miller, 2005)
Casino Royale (Martin Campbell, 2006)
Charlie's Angels (McG, 2000)
Charlie's Angels: Full Throttle (McG, 2003)
Children of Men (Alfonso Cuarón, 2006)
China O'Brien (Robert Clouse, 1990)
Chloe (Atom Egoyan, 2009)
Clash of the Titans (Louis Leterrier, 2010)
Clear and Present Danger (Phillip Noyce, 1994)
Cloverfield (Matt Reeves, 2008)
Collateral Damage (Andrew Davis, 2002)
Commando (Mark L. Lester, 1985)
Cop Out (Kevin Smith, 2010)
Courage under Fire (Edward Zwick, 1996)
Crank (Mark Neveldine and Brian Taylor, 2006)
Crouching Tiger, Hidden Dragon (Ang Lee, 2000)
D.E.B.S. (Angela Robinson, 2004)
Danny the Dog / Unleashed (Louis Leterrier, Fr/US/UK 2005)
Daredevil (Mark Steven Johnson, 2003)
Dark City (Alex Proyas, 1998)
Death Race (Paul W.S. Anderson, 2008)
Death Race 2000 (Paul Bartel, 1975)
Death Warrant (Deran Sarafian, 1990)
Death Wish (Michael Winner, 1974)
Death Wish II (Michael Winner, 1982)
Death Wish 3 (Michael Winner, 1985)
Death Wish 4: The Crackdown (J. Lee Thompson, 1987)
Death Wish V: The Face of Death (Allan A. Goldstein, 1994)
Déjà Vu (Tony Scott, 2006)
De-Lovely (Irwin Winkler, 2004)
Die Hard (John McTiernan, 1988)
Die Hard: With a Vengeance (John McTiernan, 1995)
Domino (Tony Scott, 2005)
Doom (Andrzej Barkowiak, 2005)

Double Indemnity (Billy Wilder, 1944)
Dressed to Kill (Brian De Palma, 1980)
Duel (Steven Spielberg, 1971)
Eagle Eye (DJ Caruso, 2008)
Elektra (Rob Bowman, 2005)
Enemy of the State (Tony Scott, 1998)
Equilibrium (Kurt Wimmer, 2002)
eXistenZ (David Cronenberg, 1999)
Fahrenheit 9/11 (Michael Moore, 2004)
Falling Down (Joel Schumacher, 1993)
Fantastic Four (Tim Story, 2005)
Fast and Furious (Justin Lin, 2009)
Fight Club (David Fincher, 1999)
Finding Nemo (Andrew Stanton, Lee Unkrich, 2003)
Fist of Fury (Wei Lo, 1972)
Forced Vengeance (James Fargo, 1982)
48 Hrs (Walter Hill, 1982)
4: Rise of Silver Surfer (Tim Story, 2007)
Frida (Julie Taymor, 2002)
Fried Green Tomatoes (Jon Avnet, 1991)
From Paris with Love (Pierre Morel, 2010)
G.I. Jane (Ridley Scott, 1997)
G.I. Joe: The Rise of Cobra (Stephen Sommers, 2009)
Game of Death (Robert Clouse, 1978)
Gamer (Neveldine and Taylor, 2009)
Gladiator (Ridley Scott, 2000)
Go Fish (Rose Troche, 1994)
Gone with the Wind (Victor Fleming, 1939)
Green Zone (Paul Greengrass, 2010)
Guess Who's Coming to Dinner (Stanley Kramer, 1967)
Halloween (John Carpenter, 1978)
Hancock (Peter Berg, 2008)
Hard Candy (David Slade, 2005)
Harry Potter and the Chamber of Secrets (Chris Columbus, 2002)
Harry Potter and the Deathly Hallows: Part 1 (David Yates, 2010)
Harry Potter and the Deathly Hallows: Part 2 (David Yates, 2011)
Harry Potter and the Goblet of Fire (Mike Newell, 2005)
Harry Potter and the Half-Blood Prince (David Yates, 2009)
Harry Potter and the Order of the Phoenix (David Yates, 2007)
Harry Potter and the Philosopher's Stone (Chris Columbus, 2001)
Harry Potter and the Prisoner of Azkaban (Alfonso Cuarón, 2004)
Hero (Yimou Zhang, 2002)
High Art (Lisa Cholodenko, 1998)
Hostel (Eli Roth, 2005)
Hostel: Part II (Eli Roth, 2007)
Hulk (Ang Lee, 2003)
Humpday (Lynn Shelton, 2009)
I Am Legend (Francis Lawrence, 2007)
I Love You, Man (John Hamburg, 2009)

I Love You Phillip Morris (Glenn Ficarra and John Requa, 2009)
I Now Pronounce You Chuck and Larry (Dennis Dugan, 2007)
I, Robot (Alex Proyas, 2004)
I Spit On Your Grave (Meir Zarchi, 1978)
Imagine Me and You (Ol Parker, 2005)
Imitation of Life (Douglas Sirk, 1959)
Immortel (Ad Vitam) (Enki Bilal, Fr/It/UK, 2004)
In the Heat of the Night (Norman Jewison, 1967)
In the Line of Fire (Wolfgang Petersen, 1993)
Inception (Christopher Nolan, 2010)
Independence Day (Roland Emmerich, 1996)
Inglourious Basterds (Quentin Tarantino, 2009)
Internal Affairs (Mike Figgis, 1990)
Iron Man (Jon Favreau, 2008)
Iron Man 2 (Jon Favreau, 2010)
Jumper (Doug Liman, 2008)
Kickboxer (Mark DiSalle, David Worth, 1989)
Kill Bill: Vol. 1 (Quentin Tarantino, 2003)
Kill Bill: Vol. 2 (Quentin Tarantino, 2004)
Killers (Robert Luketic, 2010)
Kingdom of Heaven (Ridley Scott, 2005)
Kiss Kiss Bang Bang (Shane Black, 2005)
Kiss the Girls (Gary Fleder, 1997)
Kissing Jessica Stein (Charles Herman-Wurmfeld, 2001)
Knight and Day (James Mangold, 2010)
La Haine/The Hate (Mathieu Kassovitz, 1995)
Lara Croft: Tomb Raider (Simon West, 2001)
Lara Croft Tomb Raider: The Cradle of Life (Jan de Bont, 2003)
Law Abiding Citizen (F. Gary Gray, 2009)
Le Baiser mortel du dragon/Kiss of the Dragon (Chris Nahon, 2001)
L'Esquive/Games of Love and Chance (Abdellatif Kechiche, 2003)
Le fabuleux Destin d'Amélie Poulain/Amelie (Jean-Pierre Jeunet, 2001)
Le Pacte des loups / Brotherhood of the Wolf (Christophe Gans, 2001)
Les Rivières pourpres/The Crimson Rivers (Mathieu Kassovitz, 2001)
Les Rivières pourpres 2 – Les anges de l'apocalypse/The Crimson Rivers 2: Angels of the Apocalypse (Olivier Dahan, 2004)
Lethal Weapon (Richard Donner, 1987)
Lethal Weapon 2 (Richard Donner, 1989)
Lianna (John Sayles, 1983)
L'Immortel/22 Bullets (Richard Berry, 2010)
Lions for Lambs (Robert Redford, 2007)
Live Free or Die Hard (Len Wiseman, 2007)
Lock Up (John Flynn, 1989)
Mad Max 2: The Road Warrior (George Miller, 1981)
Magnolia (Paul Thomas Anderson, 1998)
Man on Fire (Tony Scott, 2004)
Max Payne (John Moore, 2008)
Men in Black (Barry Sonnenfeld, 1997)
Men in Black II (Barry Sonnenfeld, 2002)

Miami Vice (Michael Mann, 2006)
Milk (Gus Van Sant, 2008)
Mindhunters (Renny Harlin, 2004)
Minority Report (Steven Spielberg, 2002)
Mission: Impossible (Brian De Palma, 1996)
Mississippi Burning (Alan Parker, 1988)
Mr and Mrs Smith (Doug Liman, 2005)
Monster (Patty Jenkins, 2003)
Movie Crazy (Clyde Bruckman, 1932)
Ms 45 (Abel Ferrara, 1981)
Munich (Steven Spielberg, 2005)
My Big Fat Greek Wedding (Joel Zwick, 2002)
My Super Ex-Girlfriend (Ivan Reitman, 2006)
Night at the Museum: Battle of the Smithsonian (Shawn Levy, 2009)
Night Watch / Nochnoi Dozor (Timur Bekmambetov, 2004)
Off Limits (Christopher Crowe, 1988)
Once Upon a Time in China (Tsui Hark, 1991)
Once Upon a Time in China II (Tsui Hark, 1992)
Once Upon a Time in China III (Tsui Hark, 1993)
Once Upon a Tima in China IV (Bun Yuen, 1993)
Once Upon a Time in China V (Tsui Hark, 1994)
Once Upon a Time in China and America (Sammo Hung Kam-Bo, 1997)
Out of the Past (Jacques Tourneur, 1947)
Patriot Games (Phillip Noyce, 1992)
Personal Best (Robert Towne, 1982)
Pirates of the Caribbean: The Curse of the Black Pearl (Gore Verbinski, 2003)
Pirates of the Caribbean: Dead Man's Chest (Gore Verbinski, 2006)
Pirates of the Caribbean: At World's End (Gore Verbinski, 2007)
Pitch Black (David Twohy, 2000)
Predator (John McTiernan, 1987)
Predator 2 (Stephen Hopkins, 1990)
Predators (Nimród Antal, 2010)
Prince of Persia: The Sands of Time (Mike Newell, 2010)
Rambo (Sylvester Stallone, 2008)
Rambo: First Blood Part II (George P. Cosmatos, 1985)
Rebel without a Cause (Nicholas Ray, 1955)
Red (Robert Schwentke, 2010)
Red Sands (Alex Turner, 2009)
Red Sonja (Richard Fleischer, 1985)
Redacted (Brian De Palma, 2007)
Rendition (Gavin Hood, 2007)
Resident Evil (Paul W. S. Anderson, 2002)
Resident Evil: Apocalypse (Alexander Witt, 2004)
Resident Evil: Extinction (Russel Mulcahy, 2007)
Resident Evil: Afterlife (Paul W. S. Anderson, 2010)
Robin Hood (Ridley Scott, 2010)
Rocky Balboa (Sylvester Stallone, 2006)
Rollerball (John McTiernan, 2002)
Rope (Alfred Hitchcock, 1948)

S.W.A.T. (Clarke Johnson, 2003)
Safe (Todd Haynes, 1995)
Salt (Phillip Noyce, 2010)
Scott Pilgrim vs the World (Edgar Wright, 2010)
Serenity (Joss Whedon, 2005)
Set It Off (F. Gary Gray, 1996)
Shaft (Gordon Parks, 1971)
Sherlock Holmes (Guy Ritchie, 2009)
Shoot 'em Up (Michael Davis, 2007)
Shooter (Antoine Fuqua, 2007)
Silence of the Lambs (Jonathan Demme, 1991)
Silkwood (Mike Nichols, 1983)
Sin City (Frank Miller, Robert Rodriguez, Quentin Tarantino, 2005)
Single White Female (Barbet Schroeder, 1992)
16 Blocks (Richard Donner, 2006)
Souvenir Strip of the Edison Kinetoscope (William K.L. Dickson, 1894)
Speed Racer (Andy and Lana Wachowski, 2008)
Spider-Man (Sam Raimi, 2002)
Spider-Man 2 (Sam Raimi, 2004)
Spider-Man 3 (Sam Raimi, 2007)
Star Trek (J.J. Abrams, 2009)
Star Wars: Episode II – Attack of the Clones (George Lucas, 2002)
Stop-Loss (Kimberly Peirce, 2008)
Strange Days (Kathryn Bigelow, 1995)
Strangers on a Train (Alfred Hitchcock, 1951)
Street Kings (David Ayer, 2008)
Sunshine (Danny Boyle, 2007)
Superman Returns (Bryan Singer, 2006)
Surrogates (Jonathan Mostow, 2009)
Swordfish (Dominic Sena, 2001)
Swordsman (Siu-Tung Ching, King Hu, Raymond Lee, Tsui Hark, 1990)
Swordsman II (Siu-Tung Ching, Stanley Tong, 1992)
Taken (Pierre Morel, 2008)
Taxi (Gérard Pirès, 1998)
Taxi 2 (Jean-François Richet, 2000)
Taxi 3 (Gérard Krawczyk, 2003)
Team America: World Police (Trey Parker, 2004)
Tears of the Sun (Antoine Fuqua, 2003)
Terminator 2: Judgment Day (James Cameron, 1991)
Terminator 3: Rise of the Machines (Jonathan Mostow, 2003)
Terminator Salvation (McG, 2009)
The A-Team (Joe Carnaham, 2010)
The Awful Truth (Leo McCarey, 1937)
The Baader Meinhof Complex (Uli Edel, Ger/Fr/Cz 2008)
The Bone Collector (Phillip Noyce, 1999)
The Book of Eli (Albert and Allen Hughes, 2010)
The Bounty Hunter (Andy Tennant, 2010)
The Bourne Identity (Doug Liman, 2002)
The Bourne Supremacy (Paul Greengrass, 2004)

The Bourne Ultimatum (Paul Greengrass, 2007)
The Brave One (Neil Jordan, 2007)
The Cannonball Run (Hal Needham, 1981)
The Chronicles of Riddick (David Twohy, 2004)
The Color Purple (Steven Spielberg, 1985)
The Dark Knight (Christopher Nolan, 2008)
The Day After Tomorrow (Roland Emmerich, 2004)
The Departed (Martin Scorsese, 2006)
The Expendables (Sylvester Stallone, 2010)
The Fast and the Furious (Rob Cohen, 2001)
The Fast and the Furious: Tokyo Drift (Justin Lin, 2006)
The Flame and the Arrow (Jacques Tourneur, 1950)
The French Connection (William Friedkin, 1971)
The Gay Divorcee (Mark Sandrich, 1934)
The Good, the Bad and the Ugly (Sergio Leone, 1966)
The Great Train Robbery (Edwin S. Porter, 1903)
The Guardian (Andrew Davis, 2006)
The Hangover (Todd Phillips, 2009)
The Happening (M. Night Shyamalan, 2008)
The Hazards of Helen (Kalem Company, 1914–17)
The Hours (Stephen Daldry, 2002)
The Human Centipede (First Sequence) (Tom Six, 2009)
The Hurt Locker (Kathryn Bigelow, 2008)
The Incredible Hulk (Louis Leterrier, 2008)
The Kids Are All Right (Lisa Cholodenko, 2010)
The Kingdom (Peter Berg, 2007)
The Lady from Shanghai (Orson Welles, 1941)
The Last Airbender (M. Night Shyamalan, 2010)
The Last Samurai (Edward Zwick, 2003)
The Long Kiss Goodnight (Renny Harlin, 1996)
The Lord of the Rings: The Fellowship of the Ring (Peter Jackson, 2001)
The Lord of the Rings: The Return of the King (Peter Jackson, 2003)
The Lord of the Rings: The Two Towers (Peter Jackson, 2002)
The Maltese Falcon (John Huston, 1941)
The Mark of Zorro (Fred Niblo, 1920)
The Matrix (Andy and Larry Wachowski, 1999)
The Matrix Reloaded (Andy and Larry Wachowski, 2003)
The Matrix Revolutions (Andy and Larry Wachowski, 2003)
The Mummy (Stephen Sommers, 1999)
The Mummy Returns (Stephen Sommers, 2001)
The Mummy: Tomb of the Dragon Emperor (Rob Cohen, 2008)
The Next Best Thing (John Schlesinger, 2000)
The Other Guys (Adam McKay, 2010)
The Passion of the Christ (Mel Gibson, 2004)
The Perils of Pauline (Eclectic Film Co., 1914)
The River Wild (Curtis Hanson, 1994)
The Roommate (Christian E. Christiansen, 2011)
The Spirit (Frank Miller, 2008)
The Texas Chain Saw Massacre (Tobe Hooper, 1974)

The Texas Chainsaw Massacre 2 (Tobe Hooper, 1986)
The Transporter (Louis Leterrier and Corey Yuen, 2002)
The Truman Show (Peter Weir, 1998)
The Twilight Saga: Eclipse (David Slade, 2010)
The Wizard of Oz (Victor Fleming, 1939)
The X Files: I Want to Believe (Chris Carter, 2008)
3:10 to Yuma (James Mangold, 2007)
300 (Zack Snyder, 2006)
Top Gun (Tony Scott, 1986)
Transformers (Michael Bay, 2007)
Transformers: Dark of the Moon (Michael Bay, 2011)
Transformers: Revenge of the Fallen (Michael Bay, 2009)
Transporter 2 (Louis Leterrier, 2005)
Transporter 3 (Olivier Megaton, 2008)
Tropic Thunder (Ben Stiller, 2008)
Troy (Wolfgan Petersen, 2004)
Truck Turner (Jonathan Kaplan, 1974)
2012 (Roland Emmerich, 2009)
Twister (Jan de Bont, 1996)
2 Fast 2 Furious (John Singleton, 2003)
Ultraviolet (Kurt Wimmer, 2006)
Un long Dimanche de fiançailles/A Very Long Engagement (Jean-Pierre Jeunet, 2004)
Underworld (Len Wiseman, 2003)
Underworld: Evolution (Len Wiseman, 2006)
Underworld: Rise of the Lycans (Patrick Tatopoulos, 2009)
United 93 (Paul Greengrass, 2006)
Vanishing Point (Richard C. Sarafian, 1971)
Vantage Point (Pete Travis, 2008)
Vidocq (Pitof, 2001)
Volcano (Mick Jackson, 1997)
Waiting to Exhale (Forest Whitaker, 1995)
Wanted (Timur Bekmambetov, 2008)
War of the Worlds (Steven Spielberg, 2005)
Watchmen (Zack Snyder, 2009)
We Were Soldiers (Randall Wallace, 2002)
Welcome to the Dollhouse (Todd Solondz, 1995)
Windows (Gordon Willis, 1980)
Windtalkers (John Woo, 2002)
World Trade Center (Oliver Stone, 2006)
X-Men (Bryan Singer, 2000)
X-Men 2 (Bryan Singer, 2003)
X-Men Origins: Wolverine (Gavin Hood, 2009)
X-Men: The Last Stand (Brett Ratner, 2006)
xXx (Rob Cohen, 2002)
xXx 2: The Next Level (Lee Tamahori, 2005)
Yamakasi – Les samouraïs des temps modernes (Ariel Zeitoun, Julien Seri, Fr 2001)
Zombieland (Ruben Fleischer, 2009)

Television Series

Alias (Creator: J.J. Abrams, 2001–2006)
Buffy the Vampire Slayer (Creator: Joss Whedon, 1997–2003)
Charlie's Angels (Creators: Ivan Goff and Ben Roberts, 1976–1981)
Cleopatra 2525 (Creators: R.J. Stewart and Robert G. Tapert, 2000–2001)
Dark Angel (Creators: James Cameron and Charles H. Eglee, 2000–2002)
Hex (Creators: Shine, 2004–2005)
La Femme Nikita (Creators: Naomi Janzen and Larry Raskin, 1997–2001)
Seinfeld (Creators: Larry David and Jerry Seinfeld, 1990–1998)
The Avengers (Creator: Sydney Newman, 1961–1969)
The Simpsons (Creator: Matt Groening, 1989–present)
Witchblade (Creators: Marc Silvestri and J.D. Zeik, 2001–2002)
Wonder Woman (Creator: William M. Marston, 1976–1979)
Xena: Warrior Princess (Creators: John Schulian and Robert G. Tapert, 1995–2001)

Index